A SOCIAL-CONTRACT THEORY OF ORGANIZATIONS

SOUNDINGS

A Series of Books on Ethics, Economics, and Business

THOMAS DONALDSON, EDITOR

A Social-Contract
Theory of Organizations

MICHAEL KEELEY

University of Notre Dame Press
Notre Dame, Indiana

Portions of this book were drawn from the following previously
published articles:

Chapter 1 from "Values in Organizational Theory and Management Education," *Academy of Management Review* 8 (1983): 376–386. Used
with permission.

Chapter 2 reprinted from "Organizational Analogy: A Comparison of Organismic and Social Contract Models" by Michael Keeley published in *Administrative Science Quarterly* 25, no. 2 (June 1980): 337–362, by
permission of *Administrative Science Quarterly.* Copyright © 1980 Cornell
University. All rights reserved.

Chapter 5 from "Freedom in Organizations," *Journal of Business
Ethics* 6, no. 4 (1987): 249–263. Copyright © 1987 by D. Reidel Publishing Company. Reprinted by permission.

Chapter 6 reprinted from "Impartiality and Participant-Interest
Theories of Organizational Effectiveness" by Michael Keeley in *Administrative Science Quarterly* 29, no. 1 (March 1984): 1–25 by permission of *Administrative Science Quarterly.* Copyright ©1984 Cornell University. All
rights reserved.

Chapter 7 from "Realism in Organizational Theory: A Reassess-
ment," *Symbolic Interaction* 6 (1983): 279–290. Used with permission.

Library of Congress Cataloging-in-Publication Data

Keeley, Michael F.
    A social-contract theory of organizations.
    (Soundings: a series of books on ethics,
economics, and business; v. 2)
    Bibliography: p.
    Includes index.
    1. Organization.   2. Social contract.
3. Organizational behavior—Moral and ethical
aspects.   I. Title.   II. Series: Soundings (Notre
Dame, Ind.); v. 2.
    HM131.K377   1988   302.3'5   87-40621
    ISBN 0-268-01730-1

Contents

SOUNDINGS

A Series of Books on Ethics, Economics, and Business

A Social-Contract Theory of Organizations is the second book to appear in a new series of books by the University of Notre Dame Press on the topic of ethics, economics, and business. The series is designed to provide scholarly, graduate-level, book-length analyses of social and moral issues involving business or economics. SOUNDINGS was inspired by the lack of scholarly writings in an area well-supplied with textbooks and lower-level teaching materials. The scope of the series is interdisciplinary and embraces a variety of academic perspectives.

Thomas Donaldson
Editor: SOUNDINGS
Loyola University of Chicago

Preface

This book deals with theories of organization. It is addressed, first, to researchers and students trained in the social sciences, secondly to philosophers, managers, and others interested in the study of organizations. The concerns of social scientists, philosophers, and practitioners are somewhat different. I choose to emphasize the concerns of the first group because of my training in organizational behavior and because social scientists have been particularly influential in shaping our knowledge of organizations. This influence, I think, could be more constructive.

Two general orientations have characterized mainstream work on organizations. One is a preference for a positivist model of science: empirical data constitute the proper object of organizational theory and the only consideration in choosing between theories. The other is a preference for a teleological model of social systems: organizations are goal-directed entities, much like biological organisms (or purposive machines in some versions). It is not widely recognized that these *are* preferences, that there are alternatives deserving careful consideration. At least this is the thesis of the book.

I argue that the positivist model of science is simplistic. Organizational theories have normative as well as empirical implications; and ethical principles can complement empirical criteria (not replace them) in the evaluation of social theories. I also argue that traditional goal-based models of organization are simplistic. A rival social-contract view is offered and defended on both empirical and ethical grounds: it provides a more realistic picture of organizational life and directs attention to questions of wider relevance—for example, "Who *gets* what?" versus "Who *does* what?"

My intent is to identify some broad ideas historically associated with the social-contract perspective and apply these ideas to modern organizations. Accordingly, I will not dwell on details of recent quasi-contractual economic approaches (such as transaction-cost economics); instead, I will focus on more central social-contract themes, highlighting issues and concepts that are important in everyday affairs but neglected in popular theories of organization—for instance, issues of justice and concepts of rights. My basic aim is to explain why social scientists should take these things seriously. Philosophers may consider such explanations unnecessary, believing that justice, rights, and the like are already respectable topics of discussion. But I hope they will find my efforts to justify their beliefs informative, and I hope social scientists will find them convincing. Above all, I hope to encourage more interchange between philosophers and social scientists, more awareness of and respect for each others' work.

Roughly half of this book consists of published articles or parts thereof that were written with this eventual product in mind. For past assistance and for permission to incorporate this material in revised form, I wish to thank the editors of *The Academy of Management Review, Administrative Science Quarterly, Journal of Business Ethics,* and *Symbolic Interaction.* For their helpful advice at various stages, I would especially like to thank Bob Bies, Tom Donaldson, Ben Foo, Barry Graham, Jill Graham, Lawrence Mohr, and Pat Werhane. Finally, my gratitude to Don Meyer and Loyola University for supporting the project over several summers.

1. Introduction

Discussions of value issues in organizational theory and management education appear from time to time in the administrative science literature,[1] but many, if not most, students of organization still feel there is something improper about mixing value judgments with social science. This is the case even in areas that appear most value-laden—for instance, in work on organizational evaluation[2] or corporate "social responsibility."[3] According to received wisdom, to study what organizations *do* is serious research; to study what they *should* do falls somewhere between nonscience and nonsense.

A major theme of this book is that efforts to avoid value judgments in the study of organizations are misguided. Values are implicit, if not explicit, in "descriptive" theories of organization and the manager's role therein. Such values can be subjects of reasoned debate and relevant factors in theory assessment. This I will try to show at the outset. In this chapter, I will also summarize the book's main lines of analysis. These involve the importance of metaphor in social theory, the questionable empirical and ethical implications of popular organic metaphors, and the contrasting advantages of a social-contract model of organizations.

Fact and Value

Organizational and management theories impart both factual and normative information. This claim contradicts the widely held view that an administrative science can and should be value-free. Per-

---

[1] See Nord (1978), Scott (1979), Frost (1980).
[2] E.g., Steers (1977).
[3] E.g., Keim (1978).

1

haps the most influential proponent of the value-free view has been Herbert Simon, who states that "an administrative science, like any science, is concerned purely with factual statements. There is no place for ethical assertions in the body of a science."[4] Simon's ideal of non-normative science might be maintained if we just collected factual statements in a haphazard fashion. But, as a rule, we seek facts in an organized manner. And it is our *organization* of facts that entails a normative orientation.[5] To illustrate, consider the sort of "value-free" research that guides modern management education.

A highly regarded attempt at empirically grounded, nonnormative description is Mintzberg's study of *The Nature of Managerial Work*. Mintzberg (relying on Simon) contends that values reflect "someone's arbitrary belief of what 'ought' to be. A statement of values can be neither correct nor incorrect."[6] Therefore, he prefers factual information, which "can be tested as to its validity." Mintzberg assumes that the prescriptive function of a science of management is limited to showing managers how they can do *what they already do* more efficiently. And the main point of his research is that a precise, factual description of the manager's job is necessary before one can prescribe even in this limited sense. Mintzberg's own description "is based exclusively on the evidence from empirical studies of managerial work. . . . Hence, this book was written without preconceptions of the manager's job. The results of empirical research do the talking."[7]

The basis of Mintzberg's report is "intensive" and "comprehensive" observation of five chief executives, which yields an "inductive" theory of what managers do. This theory consists of ten working roles, or categories of activity, and six basic purposes of the manager. These purposes are particularly interesting. A few are:

1. The prime purpose of the manager is to ensure that his organization serves *its* basic purpose—the efficient production of specific goods and services. . .
2. The manager must design and maintain the stability of his organization's operations. . .

---

[4](1957: 253).
[5]Taylor (1967).
[6](1973: 72).
[7](1973: 4).

3. The manager must take charge of his organization's strategy-making system, and therein adapt his organization in a controlled way to its changing environment...

4. The manager must ensure that his organization serves the ends of those persons who control it.[8]

Mintzberg concludes by suggesting how a science of management should help to further these purposes—for example, by "reprogramming" managerial activities (after Frederick Taylor) and reeducating managers to perform them more efficiently.

Mintzberg wrings some surprisingly normative knowledge from his facts. One might ask how the results of empirical research can "do the talking" about what managers *must* do or what we *should* do to help them. The reason such normative things emerge is that this study is far from purely empirical. What Mintzberg recognizes but fails to solve is the problem of how to arrange facts—in this case, managerial activities—in a nonevaluative theoretical framework. He notes that descriptions must account for all managerial behavior:

> There has been a tendency in the literature to exclude certain work that managers do as inherently nonmanagerial.... Omissions such as these are arbitrary—they suggest a preconceived notion of the job which may not be in accord with the facts. If a manager engages in an activity, we must begin with the assumption that this is part of his job and seek to understand why he does it in the broadest sense of his responsibilities.[9]

However, some preconception of the manager's responsibilities is necessary to set even broad limits on the job; not everything a manager does can count as an *organizational* behavior. Mintzberg, in a methodological appendix, comments on his own problems in deciding whether his subjects' activities were relevant:

> Clearly it was inappropriate to include telephone calls from the manager's wife. The difficulty arose with certain other extra-organizational contacts. Where was the line to be drawn in such cases as lunch with a competitor to discuss trade gossip, a board meeting of the golf club? The manager may or may not have received important

---

[8](1973: 95).
[9](1973: 57–58).

> information related to the running of his organization at each of these
> meetings. A specific case was Manager A's testimony as a private indi-
> vidual at congressional hearings. He emphasized that all his activities
> were related to his work and he explicitly included those associated
> with the hearings. The difficulty with this view is that it meant I
> would have to study every verbal and written contact, social and oth-
> erwise. But clearly this could not be done. . . . The rule I used was sim-
> ply to include business-like work (for example, Chamber of
> Commerce board meeting) and exclude work that was ostensibly so-
> cial in nature (golf club board meeting). I also decided, perhaps arbi-
> trarily, to exclude the work associated with the hearings.[10]

Moreover, all contacts with the manager's secretary were excluded,
since "they were very numerous and different from the others."

It is obvious, now, that some prior idea of managerial responsibilities, some normative idea of "business-like work," is relied on in
deciding that lunch with competitors is "extra-organizational" gossip,
that contacts with secretaries or congressional committees are unimportant (in the latter case, despite the apparent claims of the manager
himself). Such an idea shows up in the normative purposes that
Mintzberg attributes to his subjects: managers are responsible primarily for organizational goal attainment. This inference has an ethical dimension that cannot be derived solely from facts about what a
manager does. Other observers, holding different values, might count
different activities in the managerial job, find diverse individual
(rather than organizational) purposes in the facts, or properly conclude that what managers actually do is not necessarily what they
should or must do.

Of course, most of us have been trained to interpret things much
as Mintzberg does. The value orientation implied in his study is not
readily noticed because it has so long pervaded organizational and
management theory. From classical through modern works, organizations have been commonly defined as systems *for* the attainment of
goals.[11] And organizational goal attainment continues to be a domi-

---

[10](1973: 271–272).

[11]Fayol (1949), Hall (1977), Scott (1981). Georgiou (1973) provides an extended discussion of the goal paradigm's dominance.

nant value in administrative science—in the measurement of system success or effectiveness,[12] in the selection of research questions and dependent variables,[13] and in prescriptions for organizational design.[14]

The need for *some* value to direct organizational inquiry is apparent, even to a positivist like Simon, since researchers must extract from rich and complex social realities a manageable set of items for analysis. Though one may exclude from analysis "unscientific" value assertions and investigate only factual statements, the number of facts that can be gathered about organizations is virtually infinite. A choice must be made regarding which facts are interesting and which are not; and values affect the choice. Simon admits this in noting that certain "ethical premises" must be adopted in order to focus inquiry. But he simply assumes, as "given," that these premises can only be the objectives of the organization under study, that an administrative science *should* consist of facts concerning how organizations attain or fail to attain their goals.

There are, however, alternative values one might adopt in studying organizations. One can define organizations as systems *for* something besides collective goal attainment and seek facts that bear on other, possibly more interesting problems. Alternative values deserve our attention for it is less scientific—not more—to simply accept, as given, an ethical premise for inquiry. The empiricist's fear that values are potential sources of bias in organizational analysis is well founded. But like other sources of bias (e.g., measuring instruments), values are integral to the process of inquiry, and we do not become purer scientists or educators by refusing to examine them.[15] We advance knowledge, instead, by carefully weighing our choices. The empiricist's belief that values are arbitrary, beyond the scope of rational choice, is *not* well founded. Some values are arguably better than others. Consider another study of managerial behavior.

---

[12]Steers (1977).
[13]Meyer (1977).
[14]Galbraith (1977).
[15]Hesse (1978).

Value Choice

Singer and Wooten[16] describe the administrative methods of an individual who was years ahead of his time as a manager and organization theorist. Though his career ended over forty years ago, he was "an exponent of some of the most advanced, participative, and 'humanistic' organization and management theories being endorsed today."[17] In response to the overly mechanistic management and resulting inefficiencies of a critical industry, he devised and implemented a theory he called "organized improvisation." This represented "an attempt to debureaucratize the...industry in order to make it 'results' oriented rather than authority oriented. The theory ...consists essentially of four major components: collegial decision making, fluidity of organizational structures, temporary organizational structures, and industrial self-responsibility [for local managers]."[18] Each component was put into practice, with impressive consequences.

With respect to the fourth, for example, he found that when he delegated authority for accomplishing objectives and linked rewards to individual initiative in problem solving, "his managers exhibited an enthusiasm for their work that was heretofore not characteristic of the ...work environment."[19] Thus, in line with current theory, "he recognized the importance of management principles that rest on the ability to reinforce positive commitment...to the goals of the organization." He anticipated other precepts of modern administrative science in developing strategies of enhancing organizational adaptiveness: he took steps to discourage "groupthink" among his subordinates, utilized project and matrix management structures, opened lines of communication, and built a climate supportive of contingency approaches to decision making. "The cumulative effect of all these strategies was to create a more flexible and 'results' oriented organization," and he thereby "molded one of the most productive and efficient industries known to man."[20]

---

[16](1976).
[17]Singer and Wooten (1976: 80).
[18]Singer and Wooten (1976: 82).
[19]Singer and Wooten (1976: 84).
[20]Singer and Wooten (1976: 85–88).

Yet, despite his considerable success in terms of organizational goal attainment,[21] his efforts were admitted failures in more important respects. His goal-focused system caused untold suffering. He was Albert Speer, Hitler's Minister for Armaments and War Production, and his error was to fashion an organization that devalued individual human beings.

What made Speer's achievement all the more remarkable, and all the more deplorable, was the fact that a large proportion of workers in his armaments industry were unwilling participants. In pursuing its objectives, the Speer Ministry relied on millions of forced laborers from occupied countries, concentration camp inmates, and prisoners of war. For many of these, "life in the Reich was one long, continual nightmare of hard work, insufficient food, inadequate quarters, personal discrimination, and cruelty."[22] Particularly severe treatment was experienced in Krupp armaments factories. Evidence produced at the Nuremberg trials illustrates the sort of "self-responsibility" exercised by Krupp management in order to achieve production goals, cut costs, and maintain discipline:

> Records found in the Krupp files plainly indicate that the practice of beating and torturing prisoners of war and foreign workers was deliberately prescribed by Krupp officials. Steel switches which were used to beat the workers were distributed pursuant to the instructions of Kupke, head of the Krupp camps for foreign workers. . . . The conditions under which the concentration camp workers existed at the Krupp camps and factories and the indignities and barbarities to which they were subjected are vividly described in affidavits by such workers. . . . In general, the affidavits disclose that these concentration camp laborers slept on bare floors of damp, windowless and lightless cellars; that they had no water for drinking or cleansing purposes; that they were compelled to do work far beyond their strength; that they were mercilessly beaten; that they were given one wretched meal a day, consisting of a dirty watery soup with a thin slice of black bread;

---

[21]Against heavy odds, "he increased . . . production from an average index figure of 98 for the year 1941 to a peak of 322 in July, 1944" (Singer and Wooten, 1976: 85).

[22]Homze (1967: 297).

and that many of them died from starvation, tuberculosis and overexertion.[23]

For their participation in such activities, Albert Speer, Alfried Krupp, and others were imprisoned by the Allies (and Fritz Sauckel, who supplied them with forced labor, was hanged).

The point of the tale is not that Speer was an active advocate of cruelty, or that his form of organization ensured brutality. In fact, Speer seemed concerned about working conditions, because his system might have been even more efficient were captive labor better treated.[24] But Speer was not concerned *enough*. Both he and his system were ultimately indifferent to the abuse of some human beings for the sake of achieving greater "organizational" goals. I assume that we are not so indifferent, that virtually all of us are outraged at the kind of treatment described at Nuremberg. This suggests that organizational goals and their attainment are not, in the final analysis, our most important private concerns.

If we believe, then, that there was something more basically problematic—wrong—about Speer's organization than whether or not its goals were accomplished, why should we accept system goals as primary values in our public science of organizations, as "ethical givens" for focusing research? Why should their attainment be the main dependent variables in our explanatory models, the main standards of worth in our effectiveness models, and the main emphasis in our approach to management education? Why, in short, should system-goal-directed activities define "business-like work" for administrators and business-like problems for administrative science to solve?

One cannot reply that organizations just *are* goal-directed systems, whose behavior our models simply describe. Even if organizations do seek goals, it does not logically follow that such behavior is their most noteworthy feature or their reason for being, as goal models imply. The latter is a debatable value judgment, not an obvious fact. To defend this judgment against the suspicions raised by Speer's ex-

---

[23]U.S. Chief of Counsel for Prosecution of Axis Criminality (1946, II: 800–804).

[24]Davidson (1966), Speer (1970).

cesses, one might say that his organization is a historical anomaly, that societies like ours put pressure on organizations to avoid extreme self-serving policies and, hence, that most organizations do more good than harm in pursuing their goals. All this is plausible. But in supposing these things, we suppose that fundamental problems of organizational control have already been solved (or are someone else's worry). Note that goal models rely heavily on extraneous, "environmental" factors (e.g., interest-group pressures, laws, customs, human recalcitrance) to set limits on the personal costs of producing organizational results. Furthermore, in goal-based theories such limiting factors appear chiefly as obstacles that organizations must "adapt to" or overcome, rather than things to be valued. It is taken for granted that these factors are already strong enough to prevent the sacrifice of individuals' interests for those of the organization. Yet, in Speer's case, they were not strong enough; and they may not be in all cases today, or tomorrow.

The real message of Speer's story is that it is possible to draw rather confident normative conclusions about the importance of organizational problems. When forced to examine the most troublesome social systems we can find, we also find grounds for agreement on the most serious problems social systems can present. I think most would agree that the primary problem with Speer's organization was its lack of *voluntariness;* and I propose that the preservation of voluntariness is a basic problem in any organization, more basic than, say, goal attainment, and too important to take for granted. The importance of voluntariness as a social concern and its priority over the value of collective goal attainment is affirmed in many everyday attitudes toward organizations—for instance, in our personal regard for academic freedom and rights of tenure, in our national labor and civil rights legislation, in our common law of torts, etc. By conveying the opposite priority, goal-based theories of organization and management become questionable on both ethical and practical counts.

Theory Choice

It may be helpful here to summarize a few points of the argument. Social (and physical) theories are problem specific. In the words of Karl Popper, every *rational* theory, no matter whether scientific or philosophical, is rational in so far as it tries to *solve certain problems*. A theory is comprehensible and reasonable only in its relation to a given *problem-situation*.[25]

Scientific theories are problem specific because we cannot explain, at once, everything about complex phenomena, such as organizations. We must select *some aspects* of these realities for analysis, choosing what we wish to explain in the process. Thus, our theories imply not only how a puzzling phenomenon *can* (in part) be explained—an empirical matter—but also what *needs* to be explained—a normative matter. It is in giving priority to particular needs for explanation, particular problems, that a theoretical framework emits its own notion of value and becomes subject to ethical as well as empirical criticism.

The problem-specific nature of our theoretical frameworks might not cause much ethical concern if we only set about solving "given" problems. We could, as Machlup suggests,[26] simply select a theory to fit the problem at hand. But, of course, problems are not always given. In management education, we typically teach the problems to be solved in addition to their solutions—all through ostensibly descriptive devices, such as general theories or models of organizations.

It is common, for instance, to model organizations after biological systems. In most texts aimed at present or prospective managers, organizations are depicted as social "actors" that possess the distinguishing features of living beings: goals, needs, welfares of their own, etc. Individual persons, in this model, are portrayed as functional "members," filling roles or serving as "human resources" to further the organization's ends. This sort of organismic model lends importance to certain problems by virtue of what it is able to explain; it is useful mainly for addressing questions of organizational well-being, that is, system survival and other forms of goal attainment. (Historically, organismic social models were devised—by Plato, Hegel, Comte, Fayol, and other theorists—specifically to address perceived problems of collective disorientation.) However, problems that are not prominent in living things, such as the emergence of voluntary cooperation among self-interested members or the allocation of individual

---

[25](1965: 199). See also Kuhn (1970).
[26](1967).

benefits and burdens of joint action, are not well explained nor given great importance when organizations are described as personified, goal-seeking entities. Organizations are not necessarily best described in this way.

Despite their long preeminence in organizational theory, models emphasizing shared goals and associated organismic properties have generated increasing criticism.[27] Some objections reveal empirical misgivings. It is difficult, for instance, to identify true *organizational* goals; goal models tend to confuse powerful individuals' goals *for* an organization with goals *of* the organization as a whole.[28] In underestimating conflict over ends, these models present an overly unified, rational, and rigid picture of social systems.[29] And they yield weakly supported propositions due to other operational difficulties.[30] Much of the objection to goal models, though, is normative in nature. Critics argue that these models idealize order, the functions of existing relations for system well-being, and, for the most part, the status quo.[31] They display a bias toward the interests of dominant participants, legitimating their purposes as goals of the organization.[32] And they divert attention from a number of interesting organizational questions, including questions of power and politics: Who gets what, when, and how?[33]

The latter kind of criticism may be the most telling. Even if a model has empirical content, it can be misleading in suggesting that facts about parochial problems are really of first importance in describing organizations. Social models used as *general* descriptive frameworks are especially liable to normative criticism on grounds of a misplaced problem priority (one inconsistent with considered ethical judgments); and ethical standards are appropriate complements to empirical ones in choosing between such models. Certainly, general models or theories must have reasonable empirical content to be taken seriously at all; but alternatives may stress facts about different prob-

---

[27]See, e.g., Zey-Ferrell and Aiken (1981), Lincoln (1985).

[28]Silverman (1970).

[29]Georgiou (1973).

[30]Freeman (1978).

[31]Krupp (1961).

[32]Albrow (1968).

[33]Allison (1971); Pfeffer (1981).

lems and thus be factually "incommensurable"—in which case ethical considerations of problem priority are relevant. I have argued that goal models of organization are questionable as general descriptive devices because they subordinate problems of voluntariness to problems of system goal attainment. Can an alternative model reverse this priority and still provide an empirically sound description of organizations?

The Contract Model

A traditional alternative to modeling social systems after goal-seeking biological entities has lately been revived by some philosophers, political scientists, and economists. The idea is to model social systems after *contracts*. From a contractual perspective, organizations are seen to be sets of agreements for satisfying diverse, individual interests. This model disputes popular claims that "[an] organization would not exist if it were not for some common purpose," which "is the basis for organizational activities."[34] The key insight of a contractual view is that organizations normally exist by virtue of agreement on the activities alone—which activities constitute joint means to *separate purposes* (possibly profits for some persons, wages for others, goods or services for another group, and so on).

Organization theorists employing a more or less contractual framework include Cyert and March,[35] who propose that organizations are coalitions of self-interested participants. "Participant" is a broader term than "member," designating anyone who takes part in a system of behavior: for example, "managers, workers, stockholders, suppliers, customers,...etc."[36] The authors explain the behavior of large firms as the result of serial agreements among these participants to cooperate for incentives generated by their joint action. Similar explanations are offered by theorists who portray organizations as "markets," which ultimately consist of "sets of contracting relations among

---

[34]Hall (1977: 83).
[35](1963).
[36]Cyert and March (1963: 27).

individuals."[37] Theories such as Strauss's[38] "negotiated-order" approach are even more specific in outlining how day-to-day working relations arise from processes of interpersonal bargaining. Strauss shows that many organizations that seem to be stable, functionally ordered systems are, in fact, fragile products of continual negotiation over the rights and duties (claims) of the participants. He suggests that it is tentative agreement on these rights and duties—not shared goals or instrumental role-taking—that explains how social order is possible. Social order, of course, may also result from coercion and, therefore, what contractualists like Strauss primarily explain is how a *voluntary* social order is possible.[39]

In emphasizing how voluntary cooperation can be achieved in organizations, a contractual model does not imply that most organizations have actually solved the problem of voluntariness (any more than organismic models imply that most organizations have actually solved problems of system goal attainment). The model simply stresses the common importance of the problem in contracts and organizations, and it draws attention to common features of these systems, agreements on individual rights, that might form the basis for solutions. Contractual theorists have not always appreciated the problematic nature of voluntary consent in contracts and other social systems. Some have relied too heavily on notions of "tacit" consent, inferring willing agreement from acts of mere participation. The issue requires a bit of clarification, for it has been a source of confusion ever since John Locke's famous theory of the social contract.[40]

One cannot assert that organizations just *are* voluntary contracts, or one might misidentify systems of enforced cooperation, as well as grant undeserved legitimacy to the social and economic inequalities they entail. Robert Hessen, for instance, does both in his book, *In Defense of the Corporation*,[41] which has been described in a respected management journal as "brilliant, concise, timely . . . [and perhaps] the

---

[37]Jensen and Meckling (1976: 311). See also Georgiou (1973); Pfeffer and Salancik (1978).

[38](1978).

[39]Day and Day (1977).

[40](1690).

[41](1979a).

most important book on corporations in the last 50 years."[42] I believe the merits of Hessen's analysis are somewhat overstated. His avowed aim is to defend modern corporations against their critics, and in so doing he claims that "at every stage throughout its growth, a corporation is a voluntary association based exclusively on contract."[43] In other words, "the contract model holds that a corporation is simply and literally a voluntary association of individuals, united by a network of contracts."[44] The term "voluntary" is problematic in this context, however, creating empirical and normative difficulties. Hessen does not substantiate the voluntariness of all, or even many, corporate arrangements. In the manner of classical contractual theorists, he only demonstrates that *some* existing arrangements *could have* resulted from contract-like acts. He goes on to propose that the presumed voluntariness of these hypothetical acts ought to immunize corporations against most forms of governmental regulation. All this is very controversial.[45]

Hessen's principal mistake, common in contractualist works,[46] is to read freely given consent into agreements whose voluntariness is unclear—for example, creditors' acceptance of the limited liability of shareholders for corporate debts. Hessen maintains that

> limited liability actually derives from an implied contract between the corporate owners and their creditors....Outsiders cannot be compelled to extend credit to a corporation on a limited liability basis. They can, and often do, insist that one or several of the shareholders become personal guarantors...for the debt....Because creditors have a choice in the matter, limited liability cannot be viewed as a state-created privilege that benefits the corporation at the expense of the creditor.[47]

Although certain creditors may have a choice, it is fair to question the voluntariness of some of these "implied contracts." Employees, because they lack either bargaining power or awareness of the risks they incur, are often not in a position to negotiate personal guarantees for

---

[42]Locke (1979: 477).
[43]Hessen (1979a: 43).
[44]Hessen (1979b: 1330).
[45]See, e.g., Hamilton (1979).
[46]See also Nozick (1974), Hayek (1976), Pilon (1979).
[47](1979b: 1332–1333).

unpaid wages. Several jurisdictions take account of this fact and impose liability on shareholders for such debts.

As Hessen admits, all kinds of organizational agreements are actually "contracts of adhesion," that is, agreements containing standardized terms set by dominant parties and only marginally negotiable (if understandable) by weaker parties to a transaction. Classic examples include insurance policies, form-leases, product warranties, and the like.[48] In these contracts, terms have often been skillfully designed to minimize the legal liabilities of their authors; and, although the "adhering" party is theoretically free to shop around for a better deal, one finds similar terms offered by competing organizations. Such agreements have been considered troublesome by legal scholars for quite some time. Over fifty years ago, Llewellyn stressed the importance as well as the problem of contract as an instrument of organizational control:

> Where bargaining power, and legal skill and experience as well are concentrated on one side of the type-transaction, . . . Law, under the drafting skill of counsel, now turns out a form of contract which resolves all questions in advance in favor of one party to the bargain. It is a form of contract which, in the measure of the importance of the particular deal in the other party's life, amounts to the exercise of unofficial government of some by others, via private law. . . . Factory employment, employment in a company town or on a sugar beet farm, or farm-lease in some share-cropping districts—these press to the point where contract may mean rather fierce control.[49]

No doubt, much has changed in the last half century to alter patterns of domination. Many contracts have been standardized by law with an eye toward equalizing the positions of the contracting parties; and the economic usefulness of standardized contracts, on the whole, is undeniable. But the voluntariness of adhesion contracts in organizations and their title to legal protection are still matters for debate with respect to consumer contracts,[50] employment-at-will contracts,[51] and

---

[48]Kessler (1943).
[49](1931: 731–732).
[50]Mueller (1969).
[51]Summers (1976).

others.[52] Thus, Llewellyn's point remains valid: "'Agreement' does not even today carry any necessary connotation of real willingness. Acquiescence in the lesser evil is all that need be understood" and the problem of contract remains "essentially one of determining what types of pressure or other stimuli are sufficiently out of line with our general presuppositions of dealing to open the expression of agreement to attack"[53]—in short, the problem of voluntariness.

Empirical Implications

I will argue throughout this book that it does make sense to describe organizations as series of contract-like agreements on social rules: rules of conduct specifying participants' rights and duties. These agreements, on the one hand, may be very unbalanced with regard to rights and duties assigned each party; they may be quite involuntary and unstable. On the other hand, they do signify a factual form of acquiescence. It is probably more accurate to describe even the most coercive organizations (like Speer's) as systems of temporary understandings about rules of behavior, versus organic systems pursuing common goals. Whether organizations are voluntary or not, we can draw an empirically valid picture of their operation from a contractual perspective. This picture is distinctive in bringing the concept of *rights* to the forefront of inquiry.

While other models focus attention on system "goals" or "roles," such concepts are secondary in a contractual view. In the latter, rights are recognized as the fundamental currency of social interaction. This emphasis contrasts sharply with the neglect of rights in mainstream organizational theory, but it is consistent with the importance placed on rights in daily affairs. Virtually all organizational participants *have* rights (if not always in equal measure). They *act* accordingly. And the general structure of an organization can be outlined entirely in terms of *who has what rights to which things*.

Empirically, rights can be defined as claims justified within a system of rules.[54] Entailed in organizational rules and the agreements

---

[52]Rakoff (1983).
[53](1931: 728).
[54]Feinberg (1973).

supporting them (articles of incorporation, employment contracts, warranties, informal customs, etc.) are various kinds of rights—for instance, "claim-rights," which entitle the holder to some benefit or performance by another; "privileges," which grant freedom to act in particular ways; "powers," which are capacities to alter the rights of others; and "immunities," or protections against having one's rights so altered.[55] Rights specify relations *between* persons, and each type of right typically involves correlative obligations or expectations on the part of another: "duties" to honor others' claim-rights; "no rights" to expect waiver of others' privileges; "liabilities" to have one's rights altered by powerholders; and "disabilities" to alter the rights of those with immunities.

For descriptive purposes, even such a simple taxonomy of rights is highly useful. It can help to clarify vague concepts (e.g., "ownership" or "authority") and poorly understood processes (e.g., organizational "governance" or "coupling") by breaking them down into the component rights held and exercised by different social participants. It can expose interesting contradictions in the application of organizational rules.[56] And, overall, it can add welcome detail to otherwise rough accounts of cooperative behavior. If researchers went to the trouble of identifying the claim-rights, privileges, powers, immunities, and the correlative obligations of organizational participants, we could have much richer descriptions of organizational life than the caricatures created from gross concepts like Mintzberg's managerial roles (which reflect only some rights and duties related to system goal attainment).

Descriptions could be enriched further by considering rights granted by different rule systems. Persons will usually have rights and obligations not only under organizational rules, but under sets of extraorganizational rules: say, *legal* codes or *cultural* practices. It would be instructive to catalog these; to document conflicts between organizational, legal, and cultural rights; to see how conflicts bring about social changes, and so on. There are other obvious empirical implications of a general contractual model. It suggests more deliberate inquiry into how rights originate in cycles of bargaining and

---

[55]Hohfeld (1923); Commons (1924).
[56]As Thomas Perry (1977) illustrates in the case of legal rules.

negotiation, how they are secured through systems of sanctions, how interpersonal contests over the ranking of rights are resolved; and it urges continuation of traditional research on how objects of rights are produced (goods, services, profits, wages, etc.). A number of such topics will be explored in subsequent chapters.

Normative Implications

Above all, however, the social-contract perspective draws our attention to a particular problem in organizations: the problem of voluntariness. Contracts, it is generally accepted, *should be* voluntary; Anglo-American common law, for instance, is designed to protect those that are volitional and discourage those that are not. The contract model extends this same judgment to organizations. It ultimately directs inquiry into the sorts of rights and obligations that characterize truly voluntary social systems. This has been the great contribution of the contract metaphor to political philosophy[57]—and is perhaps its greatest potential contribution to organizational theory as well.

Rights are really practical solutions to the problem of voluntariness. Organizational rights normally promise that the mutual expectations which cause people to voluntarily enter a relationship will be fulfilled. Legal and cultural rights normally set constraints on those expectations to inhibit coercive relationships. But, because these conventional rights sometimes fail to guarantee voluntariness, another category of rights has historically been recognized in contractual views. These are "moral" or "human" rights, which can be thought of as those rights individuals would possess in *ideally* voluntary systems. Such rights are often abstract and subjects of heated debate. They are not exactly the "self-evident truths" proclaimed by the American colonists in 1776. Yet, they are not hopelessly indeterminate or inseparable from narrow political ideologies.

Many human rights are widely acknowledged in ideal, international agreements, like the United Nations Universal Declaration of Human Rights (accepted without dissent, if not always observed, as "a common standard of achievement for all peoples and all nations").

---

[57]Gough (1957).

The least controversial of these rights include freedoms of religion, opinion, expression, and immunities from slavery, servitude, discrimination, and similar harms. Regardless of whether these rights are actually enjoyed by persons in given social systems, they serve as reasonable guides for governing and improving those systems—and they have just as much "reality" as collective goals, which serve the same function in goal-based social models. The contract model encourages us to ask what human rights might be specific to participants in complex organizations. The key theoretical question here is: "What concrete rights would self-interested participants agree to support *if* they were in a position to freely negotiate a set of rules for mutual benefit?"[58] Various employee rights, for example, might be derived from a hypothetical contract situation (analogous to an ideal collective-bargaining setting) in which each principal has veto power over the employment contract: possibly, rights to due process in termination decisions, to equal opportunity for promotions, to a hazard-free working environment, among others.[59] Human rights, too, will figure in later chapters.

As a rule, analysis of moral rights and obligations has not attracted much serious attention in organizational theory and management education. This type of analysis has been regarded as "too normative." But it is no more normative, and far less objectionable, than attempts to derive the responsibilities of managers and other participants from imperatives of organizational goal attainment. From a contractual perspective, the primary responsibility of those who manage organizations is to promote voluntary cooperation: to facilitate agreements on institutional rights and procedures that respect the human rights of *all* participants. This *is* a clearly normative inference, as

---

[58]Reference to "self-interested" persons in contractual theories has frequently been misinterpreted by critics. It does not imply that persons are egoists, concerned with no one except themselves, but simply that persons *care* about their own welfare (see, e.g., Rawls, 1971). They may also care about (a) the welfare of other natural persons, if not about (b) the well-being of some reified social entity (state, organization, etc.). Critics tend to confuse contractualists' disregard for (b) with insensitivity to (a) as a human motive.

[59]Note that reasoning from imaginary contracts is valid only insofar as conditions for an ideally voluntary agreement, such as an effective veto, are built into the theoretical setting for negotiation. Some contractual theorists are careful in specifying these conditions, e.g., Rawls (1971); others overlook them, e.g., Hessen (1979a).

is the inference that Simon and Mintzberg draw from a goal-based perspective: that is, managers are responsible primarily for furthering organizational goals. While neither inference can be directly checked against facts, the contractual claim is more credible when tested against common ethical judgments. It is very difficult to find fault with systems that display high degrees of voluntariness. The same cannot necessarily be said of systems that display high degrees of goal attainment, as illustrated in Albert Speer's case and in the routine findings of our courts, press, and other forums of public opinion.

In the next chapter, I will describe in more detail the normative and empirical advantages of the contract view, and I will try to demonstrate further how scientific and ethical tests can supplement one another—not *substitute* for one another—in the evaluation of social theories. The point of this introduction is that social science and ethics provide complementary criteria for theory choice. Social science can indicate whether a theory yields good (factual) solutions to specific problems. Ethics, on the other hand, can indicate whether a theory yields good (worthwhile) problems to begin with. Although neither scientific nor ethical tests are apt to be conclusive, only if both show reasonably acceptable results should we place much trust in the validity of a general theoretical model. The point of this book is that a social-contract model is trustworthy on each count.

2. Organizational Analogs

Analogy informs a great deal of organizational theory. At one time a machine analogy provided a popular orientation. From this perspective, organizations were seen as mechanisms for harnessing human energy, as in Frederick Taylor's view.[1] Mechanistic conceptions of organization still attract limited support—for instance, as structural models under certain conditions in contingency theories of design.[2] As a general picture of organization, however, the machine analogy had aroused much skepticism by the late 1950s. By this time, critiques of bureaucracy,[3] applications of functionalist thought to organizations,[4] and the promise of general system theory[5] had suggested a "new" analogy. In 1958, March and Simon described the nature of organizations in imagery that would become widespread over the next thirty years:

> A biological analogy is apt here if we do not take it literally or too seriously. Organizations are assemblages of interacting human beings and they are the largest assemblages in our society that have anything resembling a central coordinative system. Let us grant that these coordinative systems are not developed nearly to the extent of the central nervous system in high biological organisms—that organizations are more earthworm than ape. Nevertheless, the high specificity of structure and coordination within organizations—as contrasted with the diffuse and variable relations *among* organizations and among unorganized individuals—marks off the individual organization as a socio-

---

[1] (1911).
[2] Kast and Rosenzweig (1973); Mintzberg (1979).
[3] E.g., Gouldner (1954).
[4] E.g., Selznick (1949); Parsons (1956).
[5] E.g., Boulding (1956).

logical unit comparable in significance to the individual organism in biology.[6]

A premise of this book is that March and Simon's warning against serious application of the biological analogy has been largely ignored. An organismic model now represents a common point of departure for organizational theory. Organizations, we are told, act, grow, learn, pursue goals, satisfy their needs, couple, reproduce, foul their nests, go through life cycles, enjoy health or sickness, adapt, evolve, die, and so on. Some writers are explicit in their use of biological metaphor: Robbins states, "We are going to look at organizations ...as if they were living organisms, like plants, animals, or human beings."[7] Some writers are more subtle, avoiding overtly naturalistic jargon but taking for granted organic properties: Daft claims, "Organizations are social entities that are goal-directed, deliberately [functionally] structured activity systems with an identifiable boundary."[8] Whether explicit or implicit, the organismic analogy has major drawbacks. I will explain the drawbacks in this chapter, and I will contrast them with advantages of a rival, social-contract view.

Methodological Issues

At the outset, it is worth stressing that no perspective on organizations should be considered suspect simply *because* it is based on analogy. Although some theorists, particularly in the general system area, seem defensive about their extensive use of analogy,[9] this defensiveness is unwarranted. Analogies or metaphors are becoming recognized as respectable, even essential, tools of inquiry in diverse disciplines.[10]

---

[6](1958: 4).

[7](1987: 8).

[8](1986: 9).

[9]E.g., Rapoport (1968); von Bertalanffy (1968).

[10]See, e.g., Black (1962), Hesse (1966), Barbour (1974), Brown (1976), Ortony (1979). To clarify terminology, "analogy" and "metaphor" will be used as synonymous terms here, although I tend to prefer the former. "Analogy" evokes similarities in the *conceptualization* of different subject matters, which is my concern in this chapter. "Metaphor" evokes similarities in *language* used to describe those subject matters, a more superficial sort of comparison. Whatever the term, we will be dealing with more than mere figures of speech.

Analogical reasoning is a method of inquiry in which a problematic subject matter becomes better understood by exploring similarities with another subject matter, a model, that is more familiar or manipulable. Compared to an organization, a more familiar subject matter might be a machine; a more manipulable subject matter might be a laboratory game. In applying knowledge of games, say, to organizations, one hopes to discover significant game-like organizational properties and interesting game-like relations among those properties. Significant and interesting similarities may not be self-evident but may become evident as the analogy is explored—that is, as theories are suggested by the analogy and subsequently refined. Naturally, differences as well as similarities in subject matters will appear in the course of exploring an analogy, but this does not undermine the utility of analogical reasoning. Learning about some puzzling thing, event, or process by drawing parallels with a better-understood model is a very basic means of inquiry. It is probably unavoidable in everyday life, and it is certainly productive in the generation of scientific theory. In a sense, all description is metaphorical or analogical; Hesse notes, "I never reapply the commonest term, such as 'green', in *exactly* the same circumstances in which I learned it, but always by making a (perhaps unconscious) judgment that this new situation is sufficiently similar to the old to merit application of the same universal term."[11] So also in scientific description, "the difference between the literal and the metaphorical is, of course, a matter of social convention, of what is institutionalized and what is not."[12] Institutionalized or not, our analogies can and should be subjected to critical comparison; some are better than others.

Although various organizational analogs have been proposed by theorists, comparison of organizational perspectives at the level of analogy is rarely done in a serious way.[13] Assessment of perspectives at two other levels has been more common. One type of assessment involves comparing the predictive power of specific theories. Sometimes

---

[11](1976: 8).

[12]Barnes (1974: 53–54). Such points are overlooked by a few theorists who would try to replace metaphorical terms with "literal language" in scientific theories (e.g., Pinder and Bourgeois, 1982).

[13]Some recent efforts include Pondy et al. (1983) and Morgan (1986). In most such work, however, the emphasis is still on cataloging alternative metaphors rather than choosing between them.

this is fruitful; often, in the case of organizational theories, it is not. It is difficult, for instance, to compare the predictive value of exchange and functionalist theories. On the whole, they highlight different sets of facts, even if they refer to the same nominal object: an organization. In Kuhn's terminology,[14] these theories appear to be incommensurable; one seems to be "micro" in focus, the other "macro," and debate drifts away from the merits of particular theories toward the merits of macro and micro approaches.

Such drift has led to comparison of organizational perspectives at a second, more abstract level—namely, the level of paradigms or general disciplinary outlooks.[15] Since Kuhn's description of the paradigm concept in 1962, paradigm contrasts have multiplied in the social sciences and humanities.[16] Several of these studies are quite illuminating—for instance, Georgiou's comparison of goal and incentive-system paradigms,[17] which lays some of the groundwork for this book. But the value of analysis at the paradigm level has been questioned by philosophers of science,[18] as well as by social scientists.[19] The problem is that paradigms do not lend themselves to comparison at all. For one thing, the construct itself is too obscure to permit the ready identification of actual paradigms. More importantly, possible criteria for comparison, such as Kuhn's "puzzle-solving capacity," are too vague to permit reasoned choice among paradigms.[20] The result has been lack of an effective challenge to received views of organization. While there surely have been plenty of alternatives advanced in recent years, the challenge basically amounts to a proliferation of antirationalist paradigms, like Burrell and Morgan's "anti-organizational" perspective,[21] which are offered not as *better* in any way, but just as *different*. The hope, of course, is that different will lead to better in the long run. But novelty is not likely to threaten entrenched views if theorists can give no more reason for innovation

---

[14](1970).
[15]E.g., Lincoln (1985).
[16]Nick Perry (1977).
[17](1973).
[18]Lakatos and Musgrave (1970); Shapere (1971); Toulmin (1972).
[19]Stephens (1973); Nick Perry (1977); Mintzberg (1978).
[20]Shapere (1971).
[21](1979).

than the plea of Pondy and Mitroff that "it is time to change [paradigms] for change's sake."[22]

In short, comparisons of perspectives at the theory level may suppose overly positivistic evaluation criteria, while comparisons at the paradigm level may substitute overly relativistic, inconclusive ones. Comparison of views at the analogical level is a promising intermediate approach. The idea of analogy captures something of importance in Kuhn's paradigm construct—the suggestion that scientists draw on a more general conceptual framework, a dominant way of seeing, in developing theory. In fact, an analogical component may be the most significant aspect of the whole paradigm notion. Masterman[23] has identified analogy as a central *meaning* of the term "paradigm" (among the many offered by Kuhn), and Barnes[24] has stressed the primacy of analogy in a workable Kuhnian analysis. At the same time, the idea of analogy retains something of importance from the older deductivist view of a theory—the suggestion that the worth of a scientific model concerns its similarity to an obstinate external reality, not just its internal consistency or aesthetic appeal.[25] Indeed, it may be an analogical component that makes empirical assessment of theories feasible.

The importance of analogy or metaphor in theory assessment is summarized by McMullen:

> What counts, perhaps, most of all in favor of a theory is not just its success in prediction but what might be called its *resilience*, its ability to meet anomaly in a creative and fruitful way. This is *not* a matter of prediction, let it be stressed. It is rather a quality of metaphor in the theory which suggests to the scientist how its conceptual structures can be further developed to derive new results or to meet new challenges. Obviously, this is something which manifests itself only gradually over the course of time; one cannot attest to it until the theory has survived many tests and been extended in illuminating new ways. If one looks at the best established theories of science, the kinetic theory of gases for instance, or the nuclear theory of the atom, one immedi-

---

[22](1979: 21).
[23](1970).
[24](1974).
[25]Hesse (1976).

ately realizes that the confidence we place in them results not merely from their successful predictions of novel facts, but at least as much from their behavior as lead-metaphors in the process of conceptual and model change over a considerable period.[26]

Thus, rival theories may generate incommensurable predictions about different features of the same general phenomenon; but rival theory-generating analogies invite comparison of their ability, on the whole, to explain that phenomenon. As with paradigms, choice between analogies is apt to involve a judgment call by specialists in a scientific discipline. Still, the call need not be as subjective as a Kuhnian conversion experience.

Significant dimensions for analogical assessment correspond to the three aspects of analogy described by Hesse.[27] In applying an analogic model to some problematic subject matter, certain features are evidently shared by both: for example, both an organism-model and a problematic organization, like GM, have interrelated components. Such features comprise the *positive* analogy. There are other features evidently not shared: for example, an organism has one mind while GM includes many. Such features comprise the *negative* analogy. Still other features may or may not be shared; we are uncertain whether they belong to the positive or negative analogy: for example, an organism exhibits typical growth stages while GM may or may not. These features comprise the *neutral* analogy. Each aspect of an analogy suggests particular evaluative considerations. The positive aspect suggests *descriptive* considerations: How well does a model reflect what's going on? The neutral aspect suggests *heuristic* considerations: Is a model likely to be a constructive tool for inquiry? The negative aspect suggests *normative* considerations: Does a model have reasonable implications for social policy or change?

Assessment of theory-generating analogies requires that one identify them in operation over an extended period of time, as Mc-Mullen noted.[28] Consideration of the history of an analogy helps us sort out, for instance, its central features from loose, figurative talk. Within a community of specialists who have largely forgotten the his-

---

[26](1976: 597).
[27](1966).
[28](1976).

tory of a dominant analogy, these central features may not be obvious, for analogies lose their "as if" quality over time. Users come to treat analogic models as literal descriptions of gases, atoms, or organizations. It is worthwhile, therefore, to consult the historical record for the purpose of simply distinguishing rival analogies before we compare their descriptive, heuristic, and normative merits.

Contrasting Analogies

Two major analogs or models of social organization have contended in Western thought: an organismic model and a social-contract model. Since the former has long dominated sociology and organizational theory, a look back to classical Greek and neoclassical perspectives on large social systems may permit us to better distinguish typical features of organismic and contractual views.

Classical Contrasts

Ancient civilizations tended to accept social and political arrangements without question. However, a critical attitude toward social organization was spawned by the anthropological accounts of Greek explorers, who documented great diversity of custom and law in the Mediterranean world. To Athenians in the fifth century B.C., the facts of cultural diversity suggested that existing social arrangements were not natural developments but matters of convention or contract.[29]

Though a thoroughly contractual political philosophy was not worked out by the Greeks, elements of such a philosophy appear in the thought of the Sophists. Sophist writings are fragmentary, but it can be assumed[30] that a chief opponent, Plato, depicts a typical theory in his *Republic:*

> What they say is that it is according to nature a good thing to inflict wrong or injury [more probably: "it is a natural thing to pursue individual interests, which may result in injury to others"] and a bad

---

[29]Barker (1960).
[30]Gough (1957).

thing to suffer it, but that the disadvantages of suffering it exceed the advantages of inflicting it; after a taste of both, therefore, men decide that, as they can't evade the one and achieve the other, it will pay to make a compact with each other by which they forgo both. They accordingly proceed to make laws and mutual agreements, and what the law lays down they call lawful and right.[31]

A lawful social order, then, results from the voluntary acts of self-interested individuals; it is a working agreement among participants for the purpose of mutual satisfaction and it has only conditional validity.

While such thinking encouraged popular government in Athens, to Plato it only encouraged personal irresponsibility and social disorder. He therefore proposed, in the *Republic,* a holistic plan for an ideal state, built around an organismic analogy: just as the individual (soul) has three functional components—appetites, will, and intelligence—so Plato's preferred society has three corresponding classes—workers, auxiliaries (military, police, and executives), and rulers (philosopher-kings, who alone establish laws, educational policies, etc.). In this model, mobility among classes is limited for the good of the community as a whole. Like functionally differentiated organs, groups are seen to be naturally fit for the efficient service of particular community needs;[32] if one's nature is to be a worker, for instance, it is disfunctional, in fact unjust, to interfere with community governance. Justice means keeping one's place in the social organism, a unified entity whose welfare is distinct from and superior to individual welfares.

Neoclassical Contrasts

Political writings some two thousand years later provide a sharper contrast between contractual and organismic views. In the seventeenth and eighteenth centuries, the repressive nature of Western

---

[31]Pp. 358–359.

[32]Plato remarks: "Quantity and quality are . . . more easily produced when a man specializes appropriately on a single job for which he is naturally fitted" (p. 370) and which he is "to practice throughout his life to the exclusion of all others" (p. 374). Integration is achieved through inspired legislation that "uses persuasion or compulsion to unite all citizens and make them share together the benefits which each individually can confer on the community" (pp. 519–520).

European governments prompted intellectual developments along the lines of Athenian contractual thought.[33] The ideas of John Locke are most relevant. In his *Second Treatise of Government*,[34] Locke proposes that men originally exist in a state of nature where they are free and equal in right. Life in this state is not necessarily nasty, brutish, and short, but it involves a variety of "inconveniences." Consequently, to make their individual welfares more certain and secure, men *agree* to form a society entailing mutually satisfactory law—this is the social contract. They may further assign governmental functions to trustees, whose authority is valid so long as these agents fulfill their trust of promoting the public good (conceived in terms of individual well-being).

The idea that society originates in a single, explicit act of contract is, of course, historically unjustified. Yet Locke's political theory does not demand that we accept this idea literally. According to Locke, the social contract is continuously made as new participants expressly or tacitly assent to prevailing rules of order. Though individuals may sometimes have little choice but to tolerate established social and political arrangements, the requirement of assent to legitimate these arrangements is important. Locke can be interpreted as saying that unless social organization originates and continues *analogously to contract,* that is, through consent of the participants, it is morally indefensible and practically unstable. The basis of social cooperation, "the Rule betwixt Man and Man," is not coercion but *reason,*[35] which points to the intrinsic worth of individual persons, to the provisional value of associations for self-preservation, and to the right of persons to resist practices that harm life, health, liberty, or possessions.

Recognizing the limitations of human intelligence in matters of wholesale social redesign, Locke suggested prudent or cautious reform. This was distasteful to those who preferred quick implementation of an ideal social order, as well as to those preferring traditional institutions. Theorists tending in each direction ultimately found the organismic model useful; Rousseau, for example, combined both tendencies and freed himself from Lockean individualism with the help of Plato.[36] Underlying the terminology of Rousseau's major political

---

[33]Informative studies of this period are provided by Gough (1957), Riley (1982), and Lessnoff (1986).

[34](1690).

[35]*Second Treatise:* 172; see also section 6.

[36]Sabine (1961).

statement, the *Social Contract*,[37] is a basically organismic analogy. (Barker suggests that this work might have been more aptly titled the *Social Organism*.)[38] Rousseau proposes that the incorporation of people into a society involves not a mere compact but the creation of "a moral and collective body, . . . which body receives from this very act of constitution its unity, its dispersed *self,* and its will."[39] The resulting body politic is seen to have a life of its own and a *general will* that is distinct from an aggregate of individual wills. To this general will, individual rights are surrendered in the act of association. The general will aims, above all, at maintaining the well-being of the body politic; toward this end it enacts, through wise interpreters similar to Plato's rulers, laws that compel individuals to sacrifice personal interest and perform necessary duties for the sake of the whole.[40]

Many of Rousseau's themes were elaborated by later organicists, notably Hegel in his *Philosophy of Right*.[41] Following the French Revolution, organismic theory flourished. In the writings of de Maistre, de Bonald, Saint-Simon, Comte, and others, it promised a solution to social disorder, as it had in the *Republic*. Saint-Simon, for instance, revived the Platonic notion of natural classes, based on functional capabilities, and the idea that the most skilled should rule without interference.[42] He projected a science of organization that would describe the proper place of functional groups in the social organism (industrialists, scientists, and artists at the head) and would ultimately harmonize human interests in the pursuit of common goals (mainly industrial production). Saint-Simon's ideas have found their way to organizational theory through his disciple, Auguste Comte, and their

---

[37](1762).

[38](1960).

[39]*Social Contract:* I, vi.

[40]Although Rousseau believes that the general will cannot err, interpreters or guides are still required since "the blind multitude. . .often does not know what it wants, because only rarely does it know what is for its own good" (*Social Contract:* II, vi). Hence, inspired lawgivers, as in Plato's republic, inform people of what is to their collective benefit and shape desires along cooperative lines. The result is that individuals "freely" bear "the ceaseless privations which good laws will impose" (*Social Contract,* II, vii).

[41](1821).

[42]Manuel (1956).

sociological successors, Durkheim and the modern functionalists (e.g., Parsons and Selznick).[43]

Contemporary Contrasts

One distinction between organismic and contractual models is absolutely fundamental. It concerns whether or not social collectives have aims and interests of their own.[44] Organismic views suppose that social collectives, just like biological organisms, have a welfare over and above the welfares of participating individuals. Welfare, in this context, implies a "personal" preference for some states of affairs over others. Welfare-entailing properties commonly attributed to collectives include interests, needs, purposes, and goals (the attainment or satisfaction of which results in well-being of the whole). Properties of this sort—a general will, for example—have historically occupied a central place in organismic models, and it is the widespread attribution of such properties to organizations that underlies the earlier claim that organicism is a dominant contemporary perspective.

The prominence of collective goals in organizational theory has been well documented.[45] Interpreted broadly as "a state of affairs which the organization is attempting to realize,"[46] the goal idea is expressed in many ways: as a fairly specific operative end, such as profitability or the provision of some service;[47] as a functional requirement for system survival, such as integration;[48] as acquisition of a valued resource, such as human energy;[49] as general control over an environment;[50] and so on. Despite this diversity, it is commonly assumed that, as acting entities, organizations have some aims and that the behavior of functional members is directed toward them. Returns to members

---

[43]Wolin (1960) sheds much light on this line of development. Further accounts of social organicism since the French Revolution are provided by Coker (1910), Hayek (1955), Martindale (1960), Manuel (1962), Nisbet (1969), Mandelbaum (1971), and Phillips (1976).

[44]Agassi (1960).

[45]Georgiou (1973); Hall (1977); Mintzberg (1983).

[46]Etzioni (1975: 103).

[47]Price (1972).

[48]Lawrence and Lorsch (1969).

[49]Yuchtman and Seashore (1967).

[50]Katz and Kahn (1978).

for their cooperation are typically considered costs to the organization. Contractual views, in contrast, would consider such costs to be the very reasons for an organization's existence.

The social-contract model denies that social collectives have personal ends or welfares; only individuals are seen to be capable of preferring one state of affairs over another. Whatever properties collectives possess (and they may have many), welfare-entailing properties—goals, needs, interests, etc.—are not among them. The "purpose" as well as the binding element of social organization is the satisfaction of diverse individual interests; and "collective welfare," to the extent the term is meaningful at all, is a direct function of individual welfares (e.g., the level of satisfaction of particular persons).

Although there exists no developed social-contract model of organizations, some approximations were mentioned in the prior chapter. Cyert and March, for instance, propose that organizations are coalitions of self-interested participants.[51] Recall that "participant" is a broader term than "member," referring to anyone who interacts in a system of behavior. In a firm, participants would include "managers, workers, stockholders, suppliers, customers, lawyers, tax collectors, regulatory agencies, etc."[52] An organization is assumed to involve agreements among these participants to cooperate for benefits generated by their joint action. The negotiated order perspective of Strauss complements this view by suggesting that even everyday working relations are products of individual bargaining.[53] Organizations are seen as patterns of interaction worked out by participants through negotiation and tentative agreement on lines of behavior.[54] Incorporated in

---

[51](1963).

[52]Cyert and March (1963: 27).

[53]Strauss et al. (1963); Strauss (1978).

[54]Strauss et al. (1963: 148) explain:

Order is something at which members of any society, any organization, must work. For the shared agreements, the binding contracts—which constitute the grounds for an expectable, nonsurprising, taken-for-granted, even rule orderliness—are not binding and shared for all time. Contracts, understandings, agreements, rules—all have appended to them a temporal clause. That clause may or may not be explicitly discussed by the contracting parties, and the terminal date of the agreement may or may not be made specific; but none can be binding forever—even if the parties believe it so, unforeseen conthe negotiated order approach are many features of classical contractual philosophy—in particular, the idea that social arrangements are conventional, conditional, and open to debate.

Necessary details of both organismic and contractual analogies will emerge in the course of discussion. For comparative purposes, each analogy can be understood as a broad analytic framework. The contract analogy is more general than, for example, market[55] or game[56] analogies, which have certain contractual aspects. Similarly, the organismic analogy should not be narrowly construed. From a historical standpoint, both "mechanistic" and "organic" models of organization[57] are organismic variants. Mechanistic organizations are typically portrayed as hierarchically controlled systems of quite specific tasks, not unlike Plato's ideal state, while organic organizations are seen to entail less precisely defined roles and more diffuse authority relations. Still, both models share the same essential organismic feature; as Burns and Stalker observe, the aim of each type of organization is "to exploit the human resources of a concern in the most efficient manner feasible in the circumstances."[58] In sum, it is a general focus on organizational goals and well-being that distinguishes the organismic analogy, regardless of the language used to express the idea. A theory is contractual, on the other hand, to the extent that it *consistently* asserts something like the following: "People (i.e., individuals) have goals, collectivities of people do not."[59] A theory is *not* genuinely contractual if it employs contract terminology but supposes an overriding system goal, like organizational survival.[60] Given this distinction, let us compare the merits of organismic and contractual analogies.

---

sequences of acting on the agreements would force eventual confrontation. Review is called for, whether the outcome of review be rejection or renewal or revision, or what not. In short, the bases of concerted action (social order) must be reconstituted continually; or, as remarked above, "worked at."

[55]Georgiou (1973).

[56]Silverman (1970).

[57]Burns and Stalker (1961).

[58](1961: 119). The basic similarity of these models is illustrated in the organismic writings of early "mechanistic" theorists, like Fayol (1949). Georgiou's (1973) argument concerning the continuity of a goal paradigm is also relevant.

[59]Cyert and March (1963: 26).

[60]As in Pfeffer and Salancik (1978).

Descriptive Comparisons

Criticism of the organismic analogy on descriptive grounds has been occasionally expressed in the literature on organizations. Krupp has argued that the organismic model presents an overly harmonious picture of organizational life.[61] Its emphasis on functionally ordered relations obscures the obvious facts of individual interest-seeking and resulting conflict in organizations. And its emphasis on common interests obscures the fact that apparent organizational goals may simply reflect (or conceal) the personal goals of participants who have enough power to impose their preferences on others. Silverman has further developed the argument that organismic theories inhibit understanding by neglecting individual motives in favor of systemic purposes;[62] and Georgiou has extended this criticism to goal models in general.[63] These critiques are valuable and will be drawn on in subsequent discussion, but they provide objections to only a few of the possible conceptions of collective purpose (the central organismic property). I will try to show that difficulties follow from a wide range of collective goal notions, that truly organizational goals cannot be satisfactorily defined in principle, much less in operational terms. If this is so, organizations do not look much like organisms.

To develop a framework for analysis, it is useful to distinguish goals *of* an organization from goals *for* an organization.[64] Goals *for* an organization are preferences of people for organizational outcomes. Goals *of* an organization are future states preferred by the organization itself; they are properties of the collective, not of individuals. As suggested previously, contractual views do not recognize goals *of* an organization as theoretically legitimate concepts; participant goals *for* an organization are, however, acceptable. This position is somewhat messy since goals *for* an organization may vary greatly among participants and over time. The organismic alternative is to derive goals *of* an organization for the sake of theoretical or social order; the task, says Mohr, is to find a *"collective analog* of individual intent."[65]

---

[61](1961).
[62](1970).
[63](1973).
[64]Cartwright and Zander (1960).
[65](1973: 473).

Conceptions of organizational goals can be roughly categorized according to assumptions about (a) the degree to which goals *of* an organization are independent of participant goals *for* the organization, and (b) the extent to which all participants recognize the *same* goals of or for the organization. Figure 2–1 depicts these two dimensions. In this figure, line *a'd'* constitutes the contractual position: what are called organizational goals are only participant goals *for* the organization (which may or may not differ among participants). In other words, organizations have no goals at all. If representative positions to the contrary are demonstrated to be unsound, the organismic analogy is seriously damaged.

We can readily dispose of the position at point *a*—goals *of* an organization are goals *for* the organization that are shared by all participants. Few theorists have held this view without qualification, since participants frequently disagree over goals *for* an organization. Positions in quadrants A, B, C, and D are more interesting.

Goals *of* an organization are:

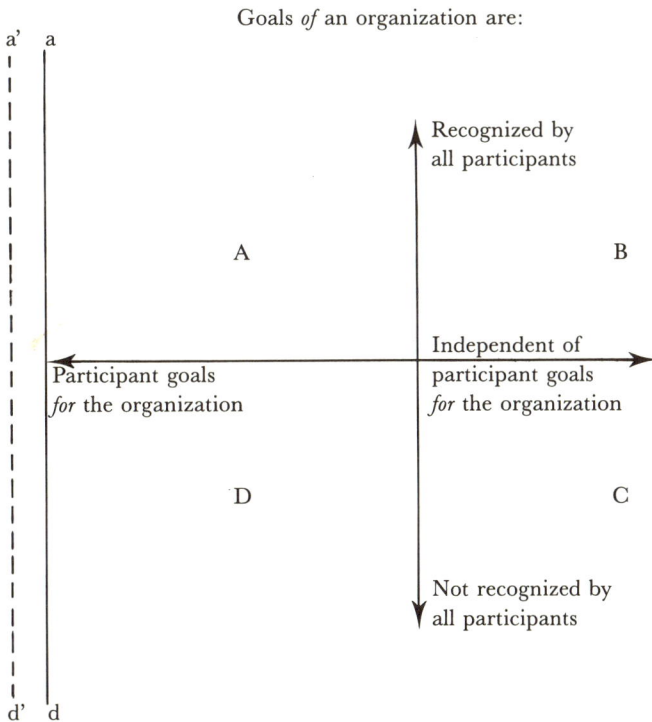

Figure 2-1. Alternative goal conceptions

Quadrant A

A representative position in quadrant A is described by Mohr.[66] For Mohr, goals *of* an organization are outcomes for which there exists a consensus of intent, rather than a sharing of desire. Consensus of intent on outcomes "connotes a certain unanimity, but it does not necessarily imply enthusiasm, spontaneous selection, top priority or exclusive preoccupation."[67] Mohr's organizational goals are not, he states, participant goals *for* the organization, yet they are similar in that his proposed goals have at least some value for participants (participants may assign them different but presumably still positive values). Compared to point *a,* this position permits goal definition under more circumstances. Nevertheless, it does not handle the stubborn fact that many organizations do not exhibit even consensus of intent. Participants in large governmental units or firms, for instance, may disagree not only about goal priorities, but about the very legitimacy of various goals. To deal with this problem, Mohr simply defines such systems as nonorganizations, saying that "many entities that are organizations in the legal sense are only barely organizations in the sociological sense: they are lacking in general commitment to outcomes that are truly organizational."[68] This conclusion severely limits the applicability of organizational theory.

Mohr accepts this limitation. Few theorists have been as willing to acknowledge the restrictive implications of choosing a definition of organizations to fit a preconceived goal idea. And Mohr is certainly not unique in saving a collective goal concept this way. Calling a social system that displays goal disagreement a nonorganization is only an extreme case of a more common practice. Organizations are often defined at an abstract level as patterns of interaction; this suggests that collective properties should be derived from those patterns. At a working level, however, it is usual to assume a defining collective property, such as a consensual goal, and then to discard as nonorganizational those interactions that do not fit the property. In this approach, one need not reject entire systems as nonorganizational if they fail to show

---

[66](1973).
[67](1973: 473).
[68](1973: 477).

goal consensus; one need only reject those parts of a system where consensus is lacking. The result is that organizations, instead of being sets of activities, become sets of certain people (members) who do, supposedly, share goals. Other participants (perhaps customers or suppliers) are seen as outsiders, and goal conflict is isolated among these residual or "environmental" elements. It has become apparent that this solution to the goal conflict problem carries a heavy price. It demands, for example, inside/outside distinctions between members and outsiders, between system and environment, that prove quite difficult to draw and defend, especially in cases of nonbureaucratic organizations.[69]

The snag, then, is that the consensual goal position requires a narrow definition of organizations. By definition, this narrows the scope of activity one can describe and it reduces the explanatory power of organizational theory. Thus, Mohr himself grants that "no doubt, a large proportion of what organizations and their members do is best explained with models that do *not* include the notion of organizational goals."[70]

Quadrant B

Alternatives in quadrant B attempt to widen the range of social systems that have goal-like properties by modifying the idea of participant intent. A representative position here is outlined by Gross.[71] Though Gross, like Mohr, sees goals of an organization as entailing consensus of intent, *intent* is now given a distinctly organizational meaning:

> By "intentions" we understand what, in the *participants' view*, the organization is trying to do. That is, what they believe the goals of the organization to be.... We are not speaking of personal goals nor of what the individual desires the goals of the organization to be. We are speaking of goals for the organization as a whole whether the participants desire those goals or not.[72]

---

[69]Freeman (1978).
[70](1973: 470).
[71](1969).
[72](1969: 284).

While Mohr implies that organizational goals must be desired or at least agreeable to participants, Gross does not. Intentions that have zero personal priority for some participants can still qualify as goals *of* an organization. Gross also adopts a narrow (member) definition of organizations, but his goal concept is broader than Mohr's, since agreement on perceived ends is more likely than agreement on desired ends.

Even so, a common perception of organizational ends may only exist at the level of mythical "official" goals—those vague aims offered for public consumption by organizational authorities.[73] Gross tries to rule out such fictions by stating that supporting activities are necessary to establish the existence of a goal. But the degree to which specific activities support one or another general goal is not easy to assess. Gross, in fact, makes little attempt at this sort of assessment in his own research on university goal structures;[74] and other reviewers have concluded that his idea of commonly perceived goals may admit only noncontroversial statements of purpose that hide disputes over actual ends and procedures.[75] (Compare, in this light, Gross's finding that universities are rather harmonious systems with the contrary observations of others, such as Cohen and March.[76]) A weak link between alleged organizational ends and participant behavior is characteristic of goal conceptions in quadrants B and C. This is a predictable result of proposing that goals *of* an organization are independent of goals *for* an organization.

In quadrant B, some historical problems of attributing independent, rational action to social collectives become evident. In the contractual view, social arrangements are rational if the participants (each, but in joint activities) act rationally with respect to their own ends. In the organismic view, social arrangements are rational if the collective (as though it were a single person) acts rationally with respect to collective ends; this position can be troublesome. To illustrate, in Plato's ideal state everyone contributes to the rational attainment of holistic goals by performing his or her function, come what may. If a carpenter is ill and a doctor prescribes a lengthy cure, Plato contends,

---

[73]Perrow (1961).
[74](1968).
[75]McConnell (1971); Baldridge et al. (1977).
[76](1974).

[the carpenter] will probably say that he's no time to be ill and that a life in which one must give all one's attention to one's ailments and none to one's proper job simply is not worth living. Then he will dismiss the doctor who has given the advice, go back to his normal routine, and either regain his health and get on with his job, or, if his constitution won't stand it, die and be rid of his troubles.[77]

Now, the carpenter's behavior may be considered rational within Plato's organismic framework, that is, with respect to collective ends. Yet, with respect to personal ends, the carpenter's behavior seems irrational in the absence of mitigating conditions. Individual and collective rationality may similarly diverge in any theory that proposes independent group goals, and one must explain why people will align their actions with goals other than their own. Gross's view calls for some such explanation.

Gross suggests that organizations offer inducements for participation. Ordinary inducements will hardly do, however, for people "must be motivated to the extent that they will give up their personal goals for the organization as a whole should these differ from organizational goals."[78] Gross employs a typical organismic strategy to account for this unusual level of motivation. Like Plato's carpenter, participants are portrayed as having organizational, rather than personally rational, mentalities. They acquire "bureaucratic personalities" that, for the sake of efficiency, support conformity with organizational procedures and discourage debate over goal preferences. In rivet manufacture, for instance,

it is absolutely essential that persons who are given the responsibility of making rivets should begin to believe that rivets *are* the most important thing in the world. It is essential that they give their full attention to making rivets rather than to the question of what rivets contribute to the overall organization whatever that may be.[79]

Gross leaves the question of who or what gives responsibility and ensures compliance unanswered. As Plato recognized, this is unsatisfactory. Some organizational participants may naturally behave like

---

[77] *Republic:* p. 406.
[78] Gross (1969: 279).
[79] Gross (1969: 283).

Plato's carpenter or Gross's rivet maker. They will trust that rivets are the most important things in the world, they will not question organizational ends, and they will subordinate their own interests. Nevertheless, a scheme that takes for granted this type of behavior (or relies on the emergence of shared goals to exact it) is incredible.[80] In short, problems of compliance, as well as consensus, are inadequately handled in quadrant B. These problems are dealt with more directly in quadrant C.

Quadrant C

In quadrant C, organizational goals become theoretical or normative in nature; that is, they are not necessarily recognized by many participants. This approach increases applicability of the goal concept, since lack of consensus is no longer an empirical barrier to goal specification, as in quadrants A and B.

A well-known representative of quadrant C positions is Philip Selznick.[81] His theoretical organizational goals are system *survival* and *integrity* (maintenance of values and a distinctive identity). Organizations, as living organisms, are seen to pursue these goals through the process of "institutionalization," by which they acquire human commitment and take on value as ends in themselves. Institutionalization requires that participants yield to organizational needs when these conflict with personal interest. But human participants can be a recalcitrant lot; moreover, they may fail to perceive where they are theoretically headed, and concrete objectives must be specified for them. Hence, Selznick proposes that *leader-statesmen* are necessary to shape organizational character and to "transform a neutral body of men into a committed polity."[82] Embodied in the leader-statesman is a truly classical resolution to questions raised by assuming that social entities have a welfare of their own—How is this welfare defined? How can it be achieved in principle? And how does it come about in fact? Selznick replies:

---

[80]Ellis (1971) discusses related issues at a more general level of analysis.
[81](1957).
[82](1957: 61).

> It is the function of the leader-statesman—whether of a nation or a private association—to define the ends of group existence, to design an enterprise distinctively adapted to those ends, and to see that the design becomes a living reality.[83]

As Selznick describes the leader-statesman role, it appears to demand no less vision, practical wisdom, tenacity, and selflessness than Plato requires of his philosopher-kings (who, of course, perform a similar theoretical function). The uncommon qualities bestowed on leaders in organismic models suggest a logical defect of independent organizational goals. If organizations are really oriented toward the goals theorists claim (e.g., survival, integrity), why are such extraordinary leaders needed to keep them on course? The reason is that goals like survival or integrity reflect preferences of theorists, not universal orientations of social systems. In fact, the natural direction of many organizations, according to Selznick, is toward drift and *dis*integration, and it is perhaps more accurate to say that leaders thwart tendencies of this sort. Why leaders *should* promote some theoretical goal is frequently unclear in organismic accounts.

One is certainly free to hypothesize numerous organizational goals, but the more removed they become from empirical tendencies and diverse participant goals *for* an organization, the more likely they are to reflect parochial value preferences. Selznick's preference for organizational integrity, for example, is a highly debatable value. Consider that a major threat to integrity is "excessive response to outside pressures":

> A...serious result is that outside elements may enter the organization and dominate parts of it. When this happens the organization is no longer truly independent, no longer making specific compromises as necessity dictates while retaining its unity and distinctive identity. Rather, it has given over a piece of itself to alien forces, making it possible for them to exercise broader influence on policy.[84]

As in previously discussed views, these "alien forces" turn out to be participants who lack organizational commitment—for instance, the

---

[83](1957: 37).
[84]Selznick (1957: 146).

public to be served by an adult education program.[85] The reasonableness of valuing program integrity over the preferences of such participants is far from obvious.

Value premises entailed in theoretical organizational goals will often seem unreasonable to people in organizations; many participants may not care very much about the integrity or survival of institutions whose welfare requires them to sacrifice personal interest. This is a problem that is not convincingly solved by the invention of figures like leader-statesmen. While some sacrifice of personal interest may occur in any system of cooperation, theorists such as Selznick do not take seriously enough the probability and intensity of disputes concerning whose interest gets sacrificed to what degree. Disputes over the performance of various functions, some of which are more rewarding than others, simply do not arise between the components of biological organisms; consequently, they are given inadequate attention by organismic theorists. Plato, Comte, Selznick, and others assume that the harmonizing of human interests is a mere technical task for scientific or administrative specialists, the intelligent among us who can specify the right ends. But, as Berlin notes,[86] the task may be ultimately impossible. At the very least, it is difficult; organismic views obscure this fact by depicting most organizational participants as exceptionally altruistic beings, if not (using Garfinkel's scientific term[87]) outright *dopes*. Like Gross, Selznick must eventually rely on participants who can be educated in holistic ways of thinking and acting. Education, a job for leader-statesmen, "does not shrink from indoctrination, [although] it also teaches men to think for themselves."[88] Thinking for one's self, however, seems to be sanctioned only when ingenuity contributes to system survival and integrity. Should participants be unconcerned about these goals, Selznick suggests that leaders propagate socially integrating *myths*. "These are efforts to state, in the language of uplift and idealism, what is distinctive about the aims and methods of the enterprise."[89] They "contribute to a unified sense of mission and thereby to the harmony of the whole."[90]

---

[85]Selznick (1957: 75).
[86](1958).
[87](1967).
[88]Selznick (1957: 150).
[89](1957: 157).
[90](1957: 152).

Indoctrination and myth are ancient devices for fashioning human materials into an integrated social organism. Plato's *Republic* is quite detailed in this regard; Rousseau's *Social Contract* is sketchier, but still to the point. Nevertheless, to base a system of cooperation on the susceptibility of participants to indoctrination and myth (and the selflessness of leaders to use these devices in good faith) is theoretically flimsy and historically nonconducive to the advance of knowledge or human well-being. Admittedly, myths of blood and soil and the like have been effective in mobilizing action for limited periods toward onerous ends. Yet, most of us find organizational myths, such as the claim of a hamburger chain to "do it all for you," too much to swallow. In the final analysis, independent organizational goals are not distinguishable from goals *for* organizations of theorists or leaders. Such goals, in the absence of selective incentives or coercion, may not be supported by other participants.[91] Quadrant D views, to some extent, incorporate these conclusions.

Quadrant D

An illustrative position in quadrant D is described by Thompson.[92] His general outlook is similar to Selznick's in that organizations are seen as natural systems, which seek survival and self-control through rational action. Thompson, though, tries to combine the natural-systems view with the coalitional view of Cyert and March.[93] Organizations are also seen as political systems, whose goals are goals *for* the organization of a dominant coalition—a group of powerful individuals who influence organizational direction by virtue of their control of critical resources. Thompson argues that his coalitional model avoids both the restrictive assumption that all participants agree on organizational direction (quadrants A and B) and the extreme reification involved in supposing that organizations have desires of their own (quadrant C). With respect to the latter, he states,

> This [coalitional] view also gives us a way of plausibly explaining the often noted tendency of organizations to seek survival and growth. So long as the organization presents favorable spheres of action to indi-

---

[91]See Olson (1965); Schelling (1971).
[92](1967).
[93](1963).

viduals in highly discretionary jobs [members of the dominant coalition], we have a strong motivation for them to avoid decisions which would end those spheres of action.[94]

Hence, even survival is a goal *for* the organization of dominant actors.[95]

This conceptualization of system goals emphasizes the obvious fact that those with power in an organization have a lot to say about what gets done. But Thompson makes a large logical leap in claiming that their intentions *for* an organization are goals *of* the organization as a whole. To logically make such a claim, one must assert either (1) that dominant actors have absolute power to impose their own goals on an organization, or (2) that dominant actors' goals represent goals *for* an organization of all participants with residual power. Thompson recognizes that the first assertion is unsatisfactory, since no individual or group has absolute power in most organizations. He, therefore, opts for an interpretation along the lines of the second assertion; this is a difficult position to defend in common cases. Diverse participant goals *for* an organization may not be represented in the goal set of dominant actors unless some special mechanisms (e.g., elections) encourage this. Thompson argues that organizational participants, powerful leaders included, will seek their own interests. He also argues that leaders will not retain power in the long run if they ignore the interests of others. So far, so good; but Thompson fails to deal with the possibility that leaders may overutilize power to promote personal ends in the short run. Thus, their goals at a particular time may underrepresent the interests of less powerful participants, and it is stretching matters to call such goals *organizational*. The point has more than logical significance; a power-based definition of goals may sanction expedient practices that contribute to the dissatisfaction of nondominant participants (a

---

[94](1967: 128).

[95]This conclusion is somewhat inconsistent with the natural system framework, in which organizational goals usually explain the motivation of people, rather than the reverse. A reasonable interpretation is that Thompson too casually mixes metaphors: a contractual, coalition model with an organismic, natural-system model. Such combinations have a history of inconsistent and confusing results, as illustrated in the works of Herbert Spencer (Simon, 1960; Francis, 1978) and a French contemporary, Alfred Fouilee (Gough, 1957).

primary contractual concern) and to system instability (a primary organismic concern).

To illustrate, consider the situation of customers or clients. Thompson assigns those participants to the *task environment*, though their position is similar to that of ordinary members. The organization needs their support and they must be induced to cooperate, so goods and services are offered for their participation. These goods and services must satisfy customer or client interests to the extent that they will continue to contribute resources to the organization. The power unsatisfied customers and clients have, Thompson assumes, is their ability to defect or resist and thereby to cause problems for the organization (like loss of resources). As such problems arise, members who can handle them by controlling customers or clients gain power themselves in the organization; they become part of the dominant coalition. To maintain their positions in the coalition, these members must continue to control their problematic clienteles. Because this control requires responsiveness to clientele preferences, customer and client interests get represented in policymaking through internal, political processes. The flaw is that even large and visible clienteles may at times be ineffective in forcing attention to their preferences.

Hirschman describes a relevant possibility.[96] In a manufacturing firm, policymakers can conceivably divert resources from product quality, without losing sales revenue, if other firms in the industry reduce quality as well (as, for instance, in the American automobile industry in the years before serious foreign competition). Disgruntled customers defect from a given firm, but this firm also acquires the disgruntled customers of competitors and no loss in sales may occur. Although accumulating dissatisfaction may eventually be relieved through legislative or economic reactions (such as invasions of foreign goods), customers have little effect on policy in the interim. Employees and other participants can, of course, experience the same sort of frustration.

In sum, one gains nothing in the way of descriptive insights by claiming that the goals of powerful individuals *for* organizations are anything more than just that. By calling them goals *of* an organiza-

---

[96](1970).

tion, one may underestimate conflict over ends and legitimate abusive practices.

Contractual Descriptions

As discussed above, there appears to be no satisfactory way of conceptualizing goals *of* an organization. This is important since attribution of a goal-like property to social systems is the central feature of the organismic analogy. If one cannot point out the collective analog of individual intent, the entire analogy looks contrived. All this does not imply that participants cannot share goals *for* an organization or that goals of leaders (or theorists) cannot represent those of all participants. The argument is simply that assumptions of common or representative goals are often invalid and that they are inadequate bases for a definition of organizational purpose. It seems more accurate to avoid talk of organizational goals and, instead, to rely only on participant goals *for* an organization, which may or may not be the same for everyone.

Contractual perspectives avoid the descriptive difficulties of organismic views by suggesting that systemic purposes are not only empirically suspect but theoretically unnecessary. Cooperative action, as in an organization, does not require participants to share collective goals in any sense. This is a fact, borne out by the existence of many organizations exhibiting goal conflict, that organismic views tend to ignore. It is a fact given prominence, on the other hand, in contractual models. What is seen to keep a system together is not necessarily agreement on the *results* of joint action but agreement to perform the *actions themselves,* because of what participants individually derive from association. What is derived, of course, might be a share of some common good, but it may also be the satisfaction of some unique purpose or even the avoidance of less desirable alternatives. Recognition of such possibilities allows for a more realistic view of organized behavior at several levels of analysis.[97]

By rejecting common ends as necessary bases of cooperation, a contractual approach not only escapes the severe problem of defining those ends but avoids the overly harmonious description of organiza-

---

[97]See Lindblom (1965); Blumer (1966).

tions that is characteristic of organismic accounts. Participants are allowed to behave in a self-interested manner, as they often seem to do. And conflicts among their purposes, rather than being wished away, are acknowledged as eventualities of organizational life, as they appear to be. A contractual approach does not, however, substitute an overly contentious picture for one of idyllic harmony; organizations are not made to look like jungles in place of barnyards. Despite possible dissimilarity of participant ends, reasoned accommodation is seen to be the norm and coordinated behavior is not considered exceptional. Lindblom gives examples of this sort of contractual coordination in various organizations.[98] He notes that Congressional action often results from agreement, by liberals and conservatives for different reasons and ends, on specific legislation. Also,

> Labor mediators report a similar phenomenon: the contestants cannot agree on criteria for settling their disputes but can agree on specific proposals. Similarly, when one administrator's objective turns out to be another's means, they can often agree on policy.... [F]or one administrator to seek to win the other over to agreement on ends as well would accomplish nothing and create quite unnecessary controversy.[99]

The primary descriptive advantage of contractual theory is, perhaps, its generality. Compared to organismic descriptions, fewer restrictive assumptions regarding the ends and motives of social actors are employed. While not precluded, common ends are not supposed, nor are altruistic or submissive participants. What an organismic model takes for granted, a contractual model incorporates as a special case. In this way, contractual theory can reflect more faithfully the diverse forms that organized action might take.

Typical objections to a social contract model rest on some historically persistent misunderstandings. Theorists with contractual leanings have been charged with a number of vague errors, such as denying the reality of social systems, overlooking their influence on individual behavior, and failing to grasp that "the whole is more than the sum of the parts." These accusations miss the point. Contractualists deny that social collectives are like organisms in any significant

---

[98](1959, 1965).
[99]Lindblom (1959: 83–84).

sense, but organisms are not the only realities imaginable or the only ones with regulative and synergistic properties.

The rejection of organismic properties (system goals) does not mean that organizations have no properties of their own or that they are simply aggregates of individuals. Certainly organizations, as systems of human interaction, produce *consequences* for participants that are properties *of* those organizations. Organizational consequences in the case of a firm might be profits, deficits, goods, services, salaries, growth, survival, industrial accidents, pollution, racial discrimination, and others. Such consequences are more than the summed effects of individual behavior; they occur because of the way people act *together.* They are true organizational properties, independent of individuals' reasons for acting. And they are real influences on system participants; people involved in organizations bargain, reach understandings, and, in general, adjust their actions to bring about personally desired consequences and avoid undesired ones. Organismic views go further, however, and attempt to establish a preferred subset of organizational consequences as ends of the system itself. It is this step that contractualists consider misguided; without a mind of its own, an organization cannot prefer one consequence over another, and participants will frequently prefer different consequences— shareholders, profits; employees, wages; customers, goods and services, etc. Hence, so-called organizational goals are relative to diverse individual or group interests; they are goals *for* a system, while organizational consequences are objective social facts that participants take into account in dealing with one another.

The proposition that participants *choose* activities to exploit the consequences of organized behavior raises another standard objection. This is that some features of social arrangements are not open to choice and are not, therefore, contractual.[100] The argument is ordinarily made by pointing out nonnegotiated terms that are taken for granted by interacting parties—for instance, laws prescribing allowable contracts, a common language that permits negotiation in the first place, or organizational norms that structure role relations. Such evidence is perhaps relevant to a claim that social conventions are arbitrary restraints, which are all thrown up for grabs whenever people

---

[100]Durkheim (1933).

decide to cooperate. But few if any contractualists have ever suggested this. Rather, it might be said that social rules are contractual in that they were agreed to by some persons, to some degree, at some time and they are subject to review at any time. The idea is not, of course, that existing institutions result from a single, explicit act of consent to governing principles, as in the signing of a political compact. Organizations entail a series of tacit understandings and expressed agreements on rules of behavior reached between a variety of persons at a variety of times. Rules settled upon in the past are not necessarily arbitrary guides to conduct, worth haggling over every time new bargains are struck; we build new agreements on old ones that prove beneficial.

Still, contractualists contend that old agreements concerning laws, language, organizational norms, and the like *can* be topics of negotiation if they turn out to be burdensome in present transactions. In fact, these things are commonly negotiated. Laws are circumvented and violations dismissed; linguistic conventions are suspended and modified; even an entire language may be a subject for bargaining between national or regional factions. In organizations, structural rules sometimes provide an unproblematic background for negotiation over specific, situational relations; other times, it is a situational relationship that provides the background for negotiation over general rules.[101] But no particular terms of interaction need be regarded as immutable commands of a superhuman social entity.

There remains a related objection that has more substance. While rules may be theoretically open to debate, they may not really be negotiable or contractual if some participants do not have enough power to influence the outcome of debate.[102] Contractualists since John Locke have tended to rely on the notion of tacit consent to indicate that participation in a social system is evidence of agreement to prevailing arrangements. Given this approach, however, even extreme arrangements, like indentured servitude, might be considered contractual; bound laborers agree to work and their masters agree to withhold punishment, maintain them, and so on. Although such practices *are* open to challenge, the risks of challenge are formidable,

---

[101]Strauss (1978).
[102]Day and Day (1977).

and it can be misleading to characterize this sort of interaction as contractual. In reply, contractualists would not want to claim that servitude or any other coercive system rests on a social contract, but what one might state is this: Even coercive arrangements have some contractual aspects; and, in describing these arrangements, a contractual model still has more utility than organismic alternatives. It is probably more accurate to say that coercive practices exist because of temporary understandings concerning behavior than because participants share holistic goals or because their interests are represented in the goal sets of authorities.

Nevertheless, as systems provide less opportunity for participants to effectively express dissatisfaction, they become less contract-*like*. Feelings of obligation to honor one's agreements may decrease, and direct efforts to subvert those agreements may increase, as relations become less voluntary. The concept of voluntariness and its place in a contractual theory will be discussed in detail in a later chapter. For now, it ought not be assumed that social transactions *are* voluntary. Some, no doubt, are coercive. And contractual views, despite their general descriptive advantages, entail a prominent negative analogy with respect to coercive social systems. This is not so bad.

Normative Comparisons

I have argued that the contractual analogy is superior to the organismic analogy on descriptive grounds. Any analogy will sometimes break down as a descriptive device, but in such cases the contractual analogy remains superior since its negative component is more instructive. A negative analogy—divergences between a model and an object of inquiry—proves to be rather uninteresting in the physical sciences.[103] This is not true in the social sciences. Both physical and social models serve to describe reality; however, social models usually do more. They tend to function as social ideals, implying how things *should* be. General organizational models, for example, inform practitioners how activities should be organized and managed, in addition to describing those activities. When an organizational model does not

---

[103]Harre (1972).

fit the facts, this is not necessarily seen as a failing of the model or a trivial result. Instead, this is often interpreted as a failure of one's subject matter, as an indication that the organization under study is "screwed up" and ought to change. Consequently, the negative analogy of an organizational model, its implications for transforming social reality, is an important concern.

The principal normative implication of the organismic analogy is that organizations should be (if they are not in fact) unified arrangements for the attainment of collective goals or welfare. The absence of organizational character or purpose might, for instance, be seen as a failure of leadership that ought to be remedied, as in Selznick's view.[104] In contrast, the principal normative implication of the contractual analogy is that organizations should be (if they are not in fact) like contracts: agreements on behavior that satisfy the separate interests of the participants. Coercive institutions, for instance, might be seen as undesirable systems that ought to be altered or abolished. To compare these implications, let us apply them to the business of preserving social harmony (which is valued in organismic theories for its own sake and in contractual theories to the extent that it furthers the well-being of all). Social harmony can be pursued from two directions, as noted by James Madison.[105] It can be sought by attempting to remove the causes of conflict or by controlling its consequences. Whereas Madison, a committed contractualist, prefers the latter strategy, the organismic analogy prescribes the former: just as functional organs have no independent interests, so the conflicting desires of social members should be transformed into common preferences for collective ends. This cure can be worse than the disease.

The central problem in prescribing focused interests concerns what to focus interests *on.* Even if we admit notions like a general will or goals *of* an organization, such things cannot be self-evident, or people would not disagree about them. Therefore, a choice must be made among the specific goals *for* a social system that might be proposed by various participants. The general organismic approach is to identify individuals with insight into "real" or worthy goals and grant them power to determine a course for the rest. Thus, philosopher-kings, leader-statesmen, dominant-coalition members, or other experts from

---

[104](1957).
[105]*Federalist* No. 10.

past and present generations provide the analog of a mind, combining both intelligence and control functions. Powers given to such authorities must ordinarily be considerable, for, as mentioned earlier, the focusing of interests is a difficult task. Unification is not likely to be accomplished simply through indoctrination, myth, animosity toward "outsiders," and other tricks sometimes advocated by organicists to dispel "intellectual anarchy" (as Comte called diversity of human aims). Power may be essential to preclude deviance. But power concentrations expose nondominant participants to obviously severe risks, since there is no sure way to tell in advance whether those given power will be wise guides, whose goals promote the welfare of all, or merely persuasive characters, whose goals benefit some participants (possibly themselves) at the expense of the rest.

To contractualists, the practical threat of oppressive or unwise leaders implies that authorities should be granted only limited powers and that goal diversity should be encouraged among others. While this may permit conflict, it allows for control of the consequences of conflict—as in Madison's plan of government, which involves independent bodies that compete for public support within a system of checks and balances (Madison's ideas will be analyzed further in Chapter 4). With respect to organizations, a contractual model suggests dispersal of power among participants through things like labor unions, multi-interest boards, complaint arbitration, etc. This does not mean that leaders should be dispensed with; in fact, they can be quite important in defending some participants from the excesses of others. Leaders, however, are seen primarily as interest mediators rather than interest focusers, ideally accountable to all organizational interest groups.[106] The intent of power dispersal is to ensure that no one's welfare is unduly sacrificed to achieve someone else's interest or someone else's conception of the common interest. This intent requires a bit of clarification.

Though not the ultimate element of social explanation, the individual person is the ultimate object of value in the social contract view, and one person has as much intrinsic value as another. Social systems are seen to exist for people, not the reverse. And organizations are well-ordered to the extent that they facilitate the attainment of person-

---

[106]Rhenman (1968).

ally desired consequences for *all* individuals, not to the extent that they facilitate attainment of "organizational" goals, which may only reflect the goals of *some* individuals. It follows that organizational change should aim at relieving the dissatisfaction of those participants whose interests and goals are being neglected, those who experience adverse outcomes such as injuries from hazardous products suffered by workers or consumers, harsh terms imposed on "captive" suppliers and distributors, default on obligations to creditors, destruction of a community's economy or environment, and so forth. In short, organizations become more contractual as their consequences become more agreeable to negatively affected participants.

The idea of minimizing the dissatisfaction of individuals, instead of maximizing the attainment of systemic ends, is a major normative theme in contractualist writings.[107] This emphasis on control of negative consequences does not imply contempt or unconcern for other organizational outcomes. Positive consequences, including many identified as organizational goals in other models, are accorded respect in a social-contract view; profits, for instance, though considered only goals *for* an organization of certain participants, are allowed since they benefit at least those participants and may encourage behavior that benefits all. Nevertheless, the production of positive outcomes for some individuals at serious cost to others is not approved. Such outcomes can occur because powerful participants deliberately satisfy themselves at the expense of others or simply because synergy in group behavior has more than a pleasant side. That is, seemingly innocent behaviors often generate negative consequences along with positive ones; employment discrimination, for example, may result from profit-related requirements for skills that deprived groups have little opportunity to develop. So, while agreeable consequences of organizations are the basic reasons for their existence (per the positive analogy), disagreeable consequences are overriding reasons for their modification (per the negative analogy).

Contractual implications for change have definite practical advantages over organismic alternatives. Controlling the disagreeable consequences of social systems generally seems more workable than focusing interests on collective ends. Compared to the exceptionally

---

[107]E.g., Locke, *Second Treatise;* Madison, *Federalist* No. 10; Lindblom (1965); Rawls (1971).

wise leaders and trusting followers needed for the latter task, participants with very ordinary intelligence and motives can handle contractual reforms. As argued by Lindblom[108] and Popper,[109] ordinary participants can usually identify painful consequences of interaction, if not mutually beneficial goals; and they can usually devise steps to minimize negative impact, if not plans for an ideal social order. More specifically, one can compensate individuals for unpleasant outcomes, even when one has no idea how to organize to avoid them; should unpleasant outcomes arise or remain for others, further corrections can be attempted and the process can be repeated in an experimental, incremental approach. Given participants with limited cognitive ability, such a strategy permits constructive action when a holistic solution is not apparent and when the risks of large-scale error are great. (Naturally, as experience accumulates or dissatisfaction intensifies, more sweeping changes become feasible; but even piecemeal change can be quite rapid and other strategies can be quite unpredictable.) Perhaps the most important aspect of a contractual approach is that consent-building steps need not involve the problematic job of imposing extraordinary sentiments, such as a high degree of altruism or commitment, on system participants. While altruistic sentiment or social commitment might be admirable, contractual reliance on the less lofty facility of *reason* appears more realistic and even more compassionate. One would seem to have a better chance of convincing people, through reasonable devices, that their actions should not bring harm to particular individuals than that they should dedicate themselves to some abstract social entity.

Efforts to elicit support for collective welfare raise moral as well as practical issues. Motivating participants to serve a social entity to the limits of their abilities has often been viewed as a clearly moral priority by organicists: dutiful service is central to Plato's notion of justice, Rousseau's notion of freedom, and Durkheim's notion of morality itself. In organismic views of organization, the rightness of maximizing the contributions of human resources to system welfare is typically taken for granted. Yet, the morality of emphasizing individual obligations and system well-being is hardly self-evident. A moral defect of the organismic analogy is that it does not sufficiently discour-

---

[108](1965).
[109](1966).

age the sacrifice of "noncritical" interests (say, those of renewable human resources) for the sake of others (say, the wishes of a dominant coalition). This defect stems from fixation on how alleged collective ends are attained and neglect of how cooperative benefits and burdens are distributed. Characteristic insensitivity to distributional questions is illustrated in Durkheim's sympathetic comments on Rousseau:

> It is quite unjustly that certain critics accused Rousseau of contradicting himself by condemning, on the one hand, the alienation of individual freedom for the benefit of a despot and, on the other, making such an abdication, provided it be in favor of the community, the basis of his system. If it is immoral in one case, they say, why not in the other? The reason is that the moral conditions under which it takes place are not at all the same. In the first case it is unjust because it subjects man to the power of a single individual—which is the very source of all immorality. In the latter, it places him under the authority of a general, impersonal force which governs him and, without reducing his freedom [to serve the community], transforms him into a moral being. The nature of the limits to which he is subject has merely changed from physical to moral. The objection springs solely from Rousseau's critics' failure to see the vast difference, from a moral point of view, between the general will and any individual will.[110]

This "vast difference," though, depends on the existence of a truly *general* will (or a truly *organizational* goal). As we have seen, such a thing defies definition. Moreover, the impersonality of a collective force has no necessary bearing on its morality. Due to organizational synergy, for example, carcinogens may be impersonally produced for workers along with consumer goods in a manufacturing process; but the fact that a system of interaction, and not an individual, imposes this burden on workers does not make it moral. It is not impersonality that lends moral status to the imposition of social goods and ills, but *impartiality* in their distribution.[111] At the very least, negative consequences must be fairly imposed if a system is to be judged moral, and such fairness is not assured by impersonal social forces. It is, of course, a quality like impartiality or fairness that is implied in the proposal that organizations should be similar to contracts. By encouraging this

---

[110](1960: 103–104).
[111]Rawls (1971).

quality—by suggesting, for instance, the minimization of harmful consequences like carcinogens (see Chapter 6)—the contractual analogy is less likely to permit practices offensive to moral opinions.

Heuristic Comparisons

On the basis of positive and negative analogies, the organismic model lacks both descriptive and normative credibility. It could yet have a promising neutral analogy, an unknown but significant application to organizations. By definition, a possibly interesting neutral analogy cannot be ruled out, and firm conclusions cannot be drawn regarding any analogy's heuristic potential. Still, after roughly twenty-five years of sustained effort on its organizational application (and after twenty-five centuries of general application), the organismic analogy's promise of fresh insights is questionable. The unfulfilled nature of this promise is reflected in disappointment with organismic systems models[112] and in emerging dissatisfaction with newer population-ecology models.[113] A few concluding comments on likely heuristic advantages of the social-contract analogy are worth consideration.

The primary heuristic advantage of the contractual analogy is its greater range: its ability to incorporate, with more consistency, perspectives on diverse social events at various levels of analysis. The contractual analogy has greater capacity for elaboration via specialized submetaphors, such as markets and bargaining games, which have meaning at levels from interpersonal to international. Furthermore, the contractual analogy can be applied on several levels of analysis simultaneously. One can readily conceive of organizations as coalitions of individuals or groups, and societies as coalitions of organizations, all interconnected through agreements of one sort or another; the image is that of contracts nested within contracts, which is logical and entails no necessary contradictions or discontinuities between levels of analysis. This type of consistency is not characteristic of the organismic analogy; the image of organisms nested within organisms is illogical.

---

[112]Thayer (1972); Phillips (1976); Lilienfeld (1978).
[113]Betton and Dess (1985); Perrow (1986).

To illustrate, Yuchtman and Seashore[114] note that their organismic approach to organizational effectiveness is inconsistent with an organismic outlook on society at large. The latter would consider organizations to be subordinate, functional organs for societal well-being. On the other hand,

> Taking the organization itself as the frame of reference, its contribution to the larger system must be regarded as an unavoidable and costly requirement rather than as a sign of success. . . . From the organizational point of view the question must be "How well is the organization doing for itself?"[115]

The point is that viewing societies as organisms denies the autonomy of components, like organizations. The same is true, of course, when one views the organization as an organism: people cannot then be regarded as autonomous organisms, as discussed above. Now, the problem posed by the organismic analogy is which level of events should be considered the organism? The common answer is whatever level a researcher is interested in. But, since all levels cannot be organisms at once, the result is incompatibility of theories that focus on societal, organizational, or individual entities.

In addition to its greater range, the social-contract analogy widens inquiry by offering a less simplistic criterion of organizational success—achievement of a just return to all participants, rather than attainment of one or a few goals.[116] In this respect, the analogy suggests broad investigations of organizational governance as it affects numerous stakeholders, instead of a narrow concentration on structural contingencies affecting sales, profits, and other limited criteria of effectiveness. I will deal with such themes in succeeding chapters. I have tried to show here that the social-contract analogy is superior to the worn, social-organism analogy on many grounds. To vary another worn metaphor, organization theorists have often been compared to sightless individuals who differ about what an elephant looks like because each touches a different part; perhaps, however, it is time we stopped theorizing with our hands on an animal and grabbed something more instructive.

---

[114](1967).

[115]Yuchtman and Seashore (1967: 896).

[116]Keeley (1978).

3. Rights

Alternative analogies suggest not only different general images of social organization, but they stress different concepts for analyzing social processes. While collective *goals* are given prominence in organismic models, individual *rights* are key concepts in a social-contract model. Further development of a contractual theory of organizations requires a better understanding of rights than most social scientists can claim.

If one tried to estimate the relative popularity of various concepts in organizational theory, rights would rank near the bottom of the list. A check of subject indexes in mainstream books on organizations will reveal few entries under "rights" (among the many under "norms," "roles," and other familiar elements of organizational structure). And rights receive little serious attention in studies of organizations appearing in leading journals. This situation is somewhat surprising, for rights are vital concepts in everyday life. If it is possible to ignore rights in theorizing about organizations, it is not possible to ignore them in actually dealing with organizations. Consider ordinary dealings in the process of research itself. In collecting data to verify theories, we must acknowledge rights: for example, in assuring confidentiality to respondents, in submitting proposals to review boards for the protection of human subjects, etc. In publishing research, we must acknowledge rights; social science journals often illustrate the relevance of rights in information for contributors, if not in regular articles, as in the following example from the *American Journal of Sociology:*

> Manuscripts are accepted for publication subject to nonsubstantive editing with the understanding that the *AJS* has the right of first publication. . . . Upon publication, all rights, including subsidiary rights, are owned by the University of Chicago Press. The author retains the

right to use his article without charge in any book of which he is the author or editor after it has appeared in the *Journal*.

This statement goes on to discuss copyright and more specific rights of both publisher and author. The personal rewards of publication, of course, include other rights granted by other organizations, such as rights of tenure, which are nontrivial incentives for conducting research in the first place.

Most participants in organizations believe they have rights, act in accord with these rights, and value them highly. Even in minor matters, employees, customers, shareholders, and others react quite negatively when they feel their rights are not respected (when a paycheck or dividend is late, when one's car is not properly repaired under terms of the warranty, when a fellow passenger lights a cigar in the nonsmoking section, and so on). In more serious matters, a great deal of litigation results from real or imagined violations of rights. As Lyons notes, rights are the principal currency in all sorts of social transactions and debates:

> The winner of a legal battle over property, contracts, or damages for injuries, for example, is understood to have a right thereby confirmed, while the opponent's contrary claim is thereby denied. Political constitutions acknowledge, establish, and secure rights.... Individuals also appeal to rights when public notice or intervention is not anticipated—as a consequence, for example, of promises made, debts unpaid, cooperative undertakings, or relationships of trust, consent, and dependence.[1]

In short, the concept of rights "is positively ubiquitous in political speeches, in the law, in the media, and indeed in the workplace and the marketplace."[2]

Because rights are ubiquitous, organization theorists have not been able to totally disregard them. Rights crop up in discussions of structural development;[3] they are implied in theories of exchange[4] and

---

[1](1979: 1).
[2]Flathman (1976: 33).
[3]Strauss (1978); Perrow (1986).
[4]Cook (1977).

power;[5] and they are explicitly considered in more specialized literature on organizations: e.g., in financial economics,[6] industrial relations,[7] personnel administration,[8] corporation law,[9] business ethics,[10] and other areas. Still, our *general* theories of organizations have reflected little awareness of rights and their historical significance in social thought.

Rights in Historical Perspective

As a first approximation, rights can be conceived of as personal claims justified within a system of rules[11]—rules such as laws in the case of legal rights, customs in the case of cultural rights, corporate policies in the case of organizational rights, ethical principles in the case of moral rights, and so forth. So conceived, the idea of rights is an ancient one.

Early societies or legal systems may not have had a specific term corresponding to our contemporary concept of a "right," but notions of justified claims are at least implicit in premodern social practices.[12] Hebrew society, for instance, recognized rightful claims to physical security, to basic necessities of life, to participation in community governance, among others.[13] Classical Greek city-states provided for rightful claims (of citizens) to private property, to freedom of association, and to equality before the law.[14] Roman law detailed rightful claims arising from private agreements (to performance of contracts, recovery for fraud, and the like) as well as liabilities arising from personal harms (delicts) which resemble modern torts.[15] Various tribal so-

---

[5]Pfeffer (1981).

[6]Jensen and Meckling (1976).

[7]Storey (1980).

[8]French (1982).

[9]Conard (1976).

[10]Donaldson (1982).

[11]Feinberg (1973). Rules need not be temporally *prior* to rights but may be devised after the fact to justify them. This situation occurs often with moral rights.

[12]Gewirth (1978).

[13]Konvitz (1972).

[14]Jones (1956).

[15]Buckland and McNair (1965).

cieties also developed complex systems of rights, for example, concerning ownership of fishing sites and damages for negligence among the Yurok Indians.[16]

As certain tribal law illustrates, right-entailing rules do not necessarily depend upon sanction or enforcement by a formal governmental unit or state (Hoebel cites the Ifugao of northern Luzon); nor do such rules necessarily grant rights that have much moral respectability. These are important points, especially applicable to rights in organizations and especially obvious in the history of criminal associations—say, groups engaged in piracy.

Bartholomew Roberts was one of the most successful pirate captains of record, taking almost 400 ships between 1719 and 1722.[17] Defoe has described a set of articles agreed to by Roberts and company "for the better Conservation of their Society, and doing Justice to one another."[18] These articles include the following rights:

> Every Man [except Irishmen] has a vote in Affairs of Moment; has equal Title to fresh Provisions, or strong Liquors, at any Time seized, and may use them at Pleasure.

> Every Man to be called fairly in Turn, by List, on board of Prizes... (over and above their proper Share) they were on these Occasions allowed a Shift of Cloaths.

---

[16]See Hoebel (1954). In analyzing tribal practices, Gluckman (1965: 36) cautions us not to confuse communal ownership with denial of personal rights:

> Widespread sharing of produce is the rule in tribal societies. Some early Western observers therefore concluded that they were "communistic," and that individual rights in lands and other goods did not exist. There is implicit in this judgment a false antithesis between "communistic" and "individualistic," arising from the way in which we say that a group "owns" a piece of land or some item of property. We are speaking loosely when we use this sort of phrasing: what is owned in fact is a claim to have power to do certain things with the land or property, to possess immunities against the encroachment of others on one's rights in them, and to exercise certain privileges in respect of them. But in addition other persons may have certain rights, claims, powers, privileges and immunities in respect of the same land or property. Hence, when we say that a particular group of kinsmen owns land, we are also saying that all the members of that group have claims to exercise certain rights over that land—maybe equally with one another, maybe varying with their status.

[17]Schonhorn (1972).
[18](1724: 210).

The Captain and Quarter-Master to receive two Shares of a Prize; the Master, Boatswain, and Gunner, one Share and a Half, and other Officers one and a Quarter.

No Man to talk of breaking up their Way of Living, till each had shared a 1000£. If in order to [do] this, any Man should lose a Limb, or become a Cripple in their Service, he was to have 800 Dollars, out of the publick Stock, and for lesser Hurts, proportionably.

The Musicians to have Rest on the Sabbath Day.[19]

In addition, trial by jury of one's peers was granted for violations of the agreement.

Despite its crudeness, and despite the ruthlessness of the venture it pertains to, Roberts' compact confers real, operative rights. And these rights exhibit a very modern feature. While generating corresponding duties that contribute to group stability, they acknowledge individual interests that do not derive their legitimacy from needs, goals, or welfare of the collective. That is, certain individual rights may take priority over functional requirements for a "tight ship" or unified association. Using a relevant—if mixed—metaphor, former Vice-President Spiro Agnew once complained (concerning the disfunctions of public protest) that "concern for individual rights was a headwind blowing in the face of the ship of state."[20] Toleration of individual rights certainly proved to be a formidable headwind for Roberts' ship. His crew's exercise of their right to liquor at pleasure, for example, ultimately spelled the end of their organization—most were drunk when attacked and captured by a British man-of-war. Yet, it is doubtful that Roberts could have held his band together as long as he did if such rights were denied. And it is doubtful that any association in Western Society could today persist for long without respecting *some* individual rights that override collective goals.

The modern notion of rights as claims giving individuals a sphere of autonomy vis-à-vis the collective (rather than for the sake of the collective) gained popular acceptance roughly around the time of Roberts' exploits: in the English Bill of Rights (1689), the American Declaration of Independence (1776), the French Declaration of the

---

[19]Defoe (1724: 211–212).
[20]Dworkin (1978: 204).

Rights of Man and Citizen (1789), through the writings of John Locke (1690), Tom Paine (1791–92), and others. Proclamations of individual rights, of course, were but the culmination of long intellectual and political struggles, particularly in the Middle Ages, during which the centrality of duty gave way to the priority of right.[21] The medieval period is interesting not only in accounting for the emergence of full-blown rights, but in demonstrating a contrast between social theory and practice, not unlike the contrast between organizational theory and practice in our own day.

Medieval Rights

Sociologists commonly depict society in the Middle Ages as an organismic system of functional relations: Coleman says that

> medieval society was composed of an articulated hierarchy of subordinate entities, each with its place and function. Medieval political theory conceived of that hierarchy as an organic unity, sometimes using direct analogies between the parts of society and the physical parts of an individual.... Historians of social theory...have ordinarily rejected, and sometimes scoffed at, the organismic conceptions. But they are wrong in doing so. The social theory of the Middle Ages *was* appropriately descriptive of the social structure.[22]

An organismic description of social structure in the Middle Ages, however, is at best a gross oversimplification. Gough argues that an opposing, contractual notion of government was implicit in medieval political structure—for example, in the relation between Teutonic kings and subjects, wherein "allegiance owed [to the king] by his subjects was dependent on his recognizing their rights,"[23] and especially in the relation between lord and vassal in feudalism, which was essentially a contractual system of governance involving mutual rights and obligations.

Ullmann provides an analysis that is quite helpful in clarifying the main issue.[24] He notes that *formal* theories of society and *official*

---

[21]Minogue (1978).
[22](1974: 25–26). See also Lukes (1973: 46–47).
[23](1957: 24–25).
[24](1966).

doctrines of government in the Middle Ages *were* thoroughly collectivist: "Society was pictured as a large organism in which each member had been allotted a special function which he pursued for the common good."[25] Individuals had no independent rights that they could assert against society as autonomous agents, but they were totally absorbed in society and subject to laws given to them, not made by them. Rights were attached to offices in a rigid hierarchy for the good of the whole; the higher the office (the more important its function), the more rights one possessed. Kings, who ruled by divine right, could grant certain rights to their subjects and they incurred certain duties to care for their subjects, but such rights and duties remained gifts from above; there was no theoretical basis for complaint from below. In what Ullmann calls this "descending theme" of government, the king's function was to make visible the rule of law (the invisible soul of the social organism), to reveal the demands of justice and interpret the interests of society. In formal law, "what mattered was the public weal, the public welfare, the public well-being, in brief, the good of society itself, even at the expense of the individual well-being if necessary."[26]

Yet, the formal doctrines and organismic theories of medieval society (like more recent theories of organization along the same lines) were not taken seriously by all social participants, nor were they truly descriptive of everyday working relations. Ullmann points out that

> the descending theme of government and law found its most notable manifestation in official expressions of governments and in the works of litterateurs, the latter especially in the writings of the Masters at the universities. . . . In actual fact the broad masses of medieval society were [little] affected by the somewhat rarefied speculative doctrines.[27]

As Ullmann explains, social structure in the Middle Ages rested on two kinds of law: first, the legislative enactments and associated ideology of rulers; second, the unwritten customary law by which lay people managed their daily affairs. The two were rather isolated from one another, inconsistent in many ways, and the second was far more important to the majority of the populace who occupied the "lower" ranks of society. In many cases, farmers, craftsmen, merchants, and

---

[25]Ullmann (1966: 40).
[26]Ullmann (1966: 36).
[27](1966: 53).

others were able to carry on their business without benefit of instruction, and without much regard for direction, from above. Regulations for the conduct of practical affairs were devised, as the need arose, by participants in the diverse associations, guilds, villages, and towns that typified medieval society. These regulations—for example, concerning agricultural practices, water rights, compensation for damage to property, working conditions in community industries, election of local officials, etc.—were often products of mutual agreement or tacit consent, and the basis of customary law was largely contractual. In *making* such law, in their ignorance of learned theories of natural or royally *given* law, common people "seemed in a most unsophisticated manner to take for granted that the individual had precisely those rights which the abstract descending thesis of government had denied him."[28]

Rights of self-determination in some political and economic matters, then, were not unusual facts of medieval life, but integral aspects of various customary practices that were beyond the power of kings to effectively abolish. Rulers, in tolerating customary law, were presumed to give their tacit consent as well, a legal fiction that squared theory and practice among the educated and allowed the rest to get on with their nontheoretical activities. What eventually forced more realistic provisions for individual rights in formal doctrines was the development of feudal practices, which were prevalent in Western Europe by the eleventh century.

Feudalism

"Feudalism" is a generic term for a variety of organizational arrangements designed to consolidate resources, such as land and military capabilities, for mutual benefit. The key elements were the lord, the vassal, and the fief.[29] In general, the head of the operation (the lord) granted a franchise or privileges of some sort (the fief, usually a leasehold on land and/or a license to conduct business in the lord's name) in return for goods or services and a pledge of subordination (from the vassal). Military power, for instance, was consolidated by granting to soldiers use of land controlled by the lord in return for

---

[28]Ullmann (1966: 55).
[29]Painter (1951).

service in the lord's army. Property was consolidated by granting to small landowners continued use of their land and protection by the lord in exchange for actual ownership of the land. Consolidation increased as local lords became the vassals of more powerful lords in a hierarchy of authority—although authority remained problematic and feudal structures were well integrated only in theory.

In some places, the king theoretically became the owner, as well as ruler, of all land in his kingdom; his vassals, the baronal lords, held parcels as fiefs; their vassals were lords over subparcels; and so on, down to the lowest vassals, the knights, who had fiefs consisting of just enough land and peasant labor to support themselves. In practice, this chain of command displayed many discontinuities. The strongest link was ordinarily the lowest vassal who had a defensible castle, which enabled him to defy his lord with impunity if the latter overstepped his bounds.[30] Most importantly, defiance of one's lord could be an exercise not only of might, but of right, because of the contractual nature of feudal arrangements. The bond between lord and vassal was a highly personal one, created by agreement, much like a modern private contract, entailing mutual rights and duties that carried over into the public sphere as legal obligations.[31] Violations by *either* party were legitimate cause for repudiating the contract and voiding one's duties to the other. Thus, "there was a perfectly legal means of resisting a feudal lord who had become a tyrant."[32]

The mutual rights and duties entailed in feudal agreements were not necessarily *equal* rights and duties; however, they provided a very real measure of autonomy to individuals who, under the descending theory of government, were considered unfit to exercise autonomy. The duties of vassals were often strictly limited, and their rights were often broad. According to Painter,[33] duties owed to the lord generally included well-defined economic obligations (e.g., toward the raising of ransom, should the lord be captured by enemies), military service of a circumscribed sort (e.g., forty days' participation in an offensive war), and court service at certain times for definite functions (of a judicial, advisory, or ceremonial nature). The rights of vassals included propri-

---

[30]Painter (1951).
[31]McIlwain (1932).
[32]Ullmann (1966: 64).
[33](1953).

etary (commonly hereditary) interests in the fief, defense against out-side threats to physical security, a voice in important policy matters, and justice in the lord's court—that is, resolution of disputes with the lord by an assembly of one's fellow vassals.

Over time, details of the feudal contract were worked out, through negotiation and personal initiative, to cover a wide range of contingencies, such as the degree of hospitality the vassal owed his lord. While the lord enjoyed the right to visit his tenants and to be en-tertained by them, vassals acquired rights against abuse: the maxi-mum number of visits in a year, their duration, the number of guests and horses allowed, and even their menus were sometimes fixed by mutual consent.[34] It is worth emphasizing that individual rights were not mere hypothetical constructs, but quite factual impediments to abuse; as suggested above, vassals had both legal and extralegal means of protecting their rights. Violations of feudal agreements were adju-dicated in the lord's court, wherein vassals tended to support one an-other in administering justice, and a decision for the lord might be disregarded in favor of war in any case. (To knights in the Middle Ages, war was great sport and often no more dangerous than football, given available armor and widely respected rules designed to mini-mize personal injury. As Painter notes, "In the great and decisive bat-tle of Lincoln in 1217, where some 600 knights on one side fought 800 on the other, only one knight was killed and everyone was horrified at the unfortunate accident.")[35]

As kings became feudal lords and parties to contracts with their vassals, they too became subject to very real constraints and demands of individual rights. Ullmann remarks that, despite the theocratic function of kings as divinely ordained lawgivers, "within the feudal function of kingship, law as the vehicle of government was arrived at by counsel and consent, . . . prompted, if not necessitated, by the indi-vidual and personal relationship between the king as feudal lord and his tenants-in-chief."[36] Of course, kings attempted to play up their the-ocratic role—with the help, again, of scholars and professional consultants—and minimize the contractual rights of their barons. But, in concrete situations, the latter tended to be vigilant in asserting

[34]Painter (1953).
[35](1953: 119).
[36](1966: 68–69).

their feudal rights and resisting their erosion by royal fiat. Magna
Carta (1215), forced on King John by his baronal vassals, is a classic
case, in which certain individual rights (e.g., due process) were finally
acknowledged in public law that even the king was bound to respect.
From this Great Charter sprang a growing body of English common
law, wider participation by common people in making such law, and
the idea of full-fledged individual rights, whereby persons gained a degree of autonomy for their own sakes and not for the sake of some alleged social organism.

Certainly, meaningful rights were denied to many persons of low
station in the Middle Ages. The direct beneficiaries of feudal agreements in general, and Magna Carta in particular, were a charmed circle of nobles. But the fact that some persons were able to achieve
considerable freedom and standing as individuals was of much future
significance in suggesting what all might achieve in civil society. Numerous privileges first won by medieval nobles were, centuries later,
claimed as universal "rights of man"—notably, rights and immunities
of the accused in criminal proceedings. Obviously, such rights did not
gain widespread legitimacy all at once; they necessarily began with
"recognition in *some* matters, to *some* extent, for *some* people, against
some organ of the State."[37] The original restriction of these rights to a
feudal aristocracy has nothing to do with their contemporary validity,
and it was not historically decisive.

Postmedieval events expanded the scope of individual rights and
the circle of beneficiaries. Public demands for extension of basic civil
and political rights intensified as a result of the practical campaigns
against royal absolutism waged by various groups in the sixteenth century (e.g., the French Huguenots), the seventeenth (e.g., the English
Levellers), and the eighteenth (e.g., the American colonists). Increasingly egalitarian conceptions of rights followed from theories of natural law (e.g., Locke's *Treatises of Government*) and manifestos of natural
rights (e.g., the influential Virginia Declaration of 1776 and the subsequent French Declaration of 1789).[38] The foundation for these developments, however, was laid in the distant past—in the fields and

---

[37]Lauterpacht (1950: 131).

[38]The Virginia Declaration of Rights was a model for many such documents.
It proclaimed that "all men are by nature equally free and independent, and have
certain inherent rights, of which, when they enter into a state of society, they cannot
by any compact, deprive or divest their posterity; namely, the enjoyment of life and

courts of medieval Europe, in the working agreements of "unenlightened" people. With due respect for the struggles to secure widely held rights before and after the Enlightenment, the famous declarations of this period essentially transformed into modern ideals traditional elements of feudal social structure. As Ullmann demonstrates,

> The Virginia Declaration of 1776 was no more and no less than a historically conditioned abstract manifesto epitomizing in succinct form the individual's rights, in the last resort deducible from thoroughly feudal documents and feudal practices. The pivotal point is that, through its becoming legalized, the feudal system fostered the idea of individual freedoms which were protected by the law.[39]

In sum, modern rights originated as pragmatic solutions to ordinary problems of social cooperation, far removed from theoretical speculation. They established areas of individual autonomy, carved out from below by contract and mutual understanding, not doled out from above by royal decree. And, from the private dealings of participants in feudal organizations, they came to pervade the political and economic life of Western society.

Rights and Social Theory

Because they built on the experiences and aspirations of practical people, the eighteenth-century proclamations of abstract natural rights had substantial impact on social policies (unlike the abstract

---

liberty, with the means of acquiring and possessing property, and pursuing and obtaining happiness and safety"; from these inalienable rights were derived specific obligations of government to guarantee fair representation, trial by jury, freedom of religion, immunities from arbitrary search and seizure, from excessive bails and fines, from cruel and unusual punishments, among other provisions. Claude (1976) provides a short, informative survey of related developments. For a more comprehensive discussion of theoretical and practical efforts to advance individual rights in the postmedieval era, see Gough (1957).

[39](1966: 96). Macfarlane adds:

> When Jefferson wrote, "We hold these truths to be sacred and undeniable; that all men are created equal and independent, that from that equal creation they derive rights inherent and inalienable," he was putting into words a view of the individual and society which has its roots in thirteenth-century England or earlier (1978: 202–203).

medieval doctrines of government). They directly inspired legislation for the protection of political liberties, such as the American Bill of Rights, and they prompted continued expansion of individual rights in the nineteenth and twentieth centuries (again, of course, not in all matters, for all people). Noteworthy examples of such expansion include the removal of institutional barriers to freedom, as in the abolition of slavery by various nations; the creation of new legal liberties, as in the legitimation of labor unions; the supplementing of simple liberties or "option rights" with "welfare rights" aimed at promoting personal well-being, as in the enactment of factory legislation; and the transfer of privilege from the few to the many, as in the establishment of public education.[40]

Social theorists, however, once more tended to lose sight of the significance of rights—either overlooking facts concerning rights expansion and redistribution or forcing them to fit supposed "collectivist" patterns of social development.[41] The source of reluctance to deal seriously with rights is important. It can be traced to a value judgment shared by prominent theorists (especially early sociologists) who provided the intellectual capital for sciences of society and organizations in the post-Enlightenment Age.

Intellectual Reservations

A critical event in deflecting scholarly interest away from rights was the French Revolution. Reactions to the excesses of the Revolution were swift and bitter, and it became fashionable to attribute these excesses to then prevalent notions of natural rights.[42] According to the French Declaration of the Rights of Man and Citizen (1789), "Men are born and remain free and equal in rights. . . . The aim of every po-

---

[40]See Perkin (1977); Friedman (1981).

[41]It has been assumed, for instance, that a shift from laissez-faire individualism to collectivism occurred in Britain during the nineteenth century. But Barker (1951: 268) makes a persuasive case that "generally the whole of the nineteenth century, far from being divided into two different parts, was a century of a single and homogeneous process; a process of the extension of personal rights, which may be called individualism, but a process entailing, at the same time, an extension of the service of government on behalf of those rights." Similar critiques of proposed collectivist patterns are offered by Goldthorpe (1964) and Perkin (1977).

[42]Sabine (1961).

litical association is the preservation of the natural and inalienable rights of man; these rights are liberty, property, security, and resistance to oppression." Leading the attack on claims of this sort were Edmund Burke and Jeremy Bentham, both of whom found it useful to talk of conventional rights (those embodied in positive law) but found the language of natural rights malicious nonsense, invitations to anarchy. Bentham's critique was particularly caustic and durable; charging that the object of the French Declaration was "to excite and keep up a spirit of resistance to all laws—a spirit of insurrection against all governments,"[43] he asserted:

> *Right*...is the child of law: from *real* laws come *real* rights; but from *imaginary* laws, from the laws of nature, fancied and invented by poets, rhetoricians, and dealers in moral and intellectual poisons, come imaginary rights, a bastard brood of monsters.[44]

> *Natural rights* is simple nonsense: natural and imprescriptible rights, rhetorical nonsense,—nonsense upon stilts....So much for terrorist language.[45]

Similar, if sometimes more subtle, criticisms were added in the nineteenth century by Saint-Simon,[46] Hegel,[47] Comte,[48] Marx,[49] Durkheim,[50] and others.

What this otherwise diverse group of thinkers had in common, and what they transmitted to twentieth-century social theory, was aversion to the fundamental point of natural rights: the priority of individual autonomy over a collective ideal (which priority is central to modern ideas of individual rights, "natural" or not). Although objections were frequently couched in terms of the dubious empirical reality of natural rights—and the contrasting true reality of social entities—the dispute was not over facts, but values. As Minogue explains,[51] the terminology of natural rights was not technically sophisti-

---

[43](1838–43: 501).
[44](1838–43: 523).
[45](1838–43: 501).
[46](1821).
[47](1821).
[48](1830–42).
[49](1843).
[50](1893).
[51](1978).

cated or neatly derived from natural law propositions. It was typically employed to advance an argument for personal freedom by pamphleteers (like Tom Paine), who were "using what they imagine[d] to be an impressive and classical vocabulary, . . . more or less unnecessarily, to state their case"; they wished "to put the desirability of certain liberties beyond the ups and downs of political deliberations and positive law. The currency of natural law made its vocabulary a convenient one for political use."[52] It was precisely the desirability of placing these liberties (regardless of their basis in natural rights) above the functional requirements of society, state, or community that critics sought to challenge.

Opponents of natural rights preferred communal values of various sorts, for various stated reasons. On the whole, however, their ideals were expressed in language no less rhetorical, and their arguments incorporated no more obviously correct moral assumptions, than the language and arguments of the revolutionary era pamphleteers. Burke, for instance, preferred to revere the state as a "true politic personality," whose ongoing institutions reflect collective wisdom and civilization, and whose continuity should take precedence over individual interests:

> The state ought not to be considered as nothing better than a partnership agreement in a trade of pepper and coffee, calico or tobacco, or some other such low concern, to be taken up for a little temporary interest, and to be dissolved by the fancy of the parties. It is to be looked on with other reverence; because it is. . . . a partnership in all science, a partnership in all art, a partnership in every virtue and in all perfection. . . .

> [God] who gave our nature to be perfected by our virtue, willed also the necessary means of its perfection—He willed therefore the state.[53]

In even stronger terms, Hegel glorified the state as "the march of God in the world,"[54] as a developing natural organism whose own will transcends and supersedes the separate interests of its members; it is in

---

[52]Minogue (1978: 16).
[53](1790: 93–95).
[54](1821: 279).

fulfilling one's duties to the state, not in pursuing capricious personal ends, that one achieves dignity, moral purpose, and true freedom:

> The rights and interests of individuals are established as a passing phase.... The individual's substantive duty [is]...to maintain...the independence and sovereignty of the state, at the risk and sacrifice of property and life, as well as of opinion and everything else naturally comprised in the compass of life.[55]

Saint-Simon substituted, for service to the state, duties to advance the cause of industrial organization and the goal of material production; such duties represent "the eminent role assigned to us by the march of civilization"[56] (as well as God), acceptance of which relieves personal anxiety about attaining individual freedom and the need for political mechanisms to maintain it:

> It cannot too often be repeated that society needs an active goal, for without this there would be no political system.... The maintenance of individual freedom cannot be the goal.... People do not band together to be free. Savages join together to hunt, to wage war, but certainly not to win liberty.... The vague and metaphysical idea of freedom, as it is held today...will tend to hinder the action of the mass on individuals. From this point of view, it would act against the development of civilization and the organization of a well-regulated system, which demands that the parts should be firmly linked to the whole and dependent on it.[57]

> [Lack of collective purpose] is the great gap in the Charter [the French constitution of 1814]. It begins, as do all the constitutions dreamed up since 1789, by putting forward the rights of Frenchmen, which can only be clearly determined when the purpose of society is established in a positive way, since the rights of every associate can only be based upon the abilities which he possesses and which contribute toward the common goal.[58]

---

[55](1821: 209).
[56](1821: 153).
[57](1821: 158).
[58](1821: 167).

Much the same point of view was expressed by Comte, who declared "the superiority of the social to the individual organism,"[59] elevated society to the status of "Supreme Being," and reduced the individual to a functional component:

> The workman must learn to look upon himself, morally, as a public servant, with functions of a special and also of a general kind.... The only danger lies in their insisting on the possession of what metaphysicians call political rights, and engaging in useless discussions about the distribution of power.[60]

The foregoing, conservative value orientation was aptly summarized by Durkheim, to whom society appeared as a divine-like organic entity, the "superior end of which [individuals] are the servants and instruments";[61] the individual's "nature is, in large part, to be an organ of society, and his proper duty, consequently, is to play his role as an organ."[62] Somewhat different (but still teleological) moral visions were supplied by more liberal theorists, like Bentham, and more radical ones, like Marx. Marx preferred the ideal of a classless society, in which individuals are developed and united in unfettered, productive association, not exploited and separated through division of labor, capitalist property relations, or egoistic rights of man; the abolition of such divisive elements is the presumed aim of the proletarian revolution and the immediate duty of the working class.[63] Bentham was perhaps the most specific of all in offering an overriding social goal, namely, the greatest happiness of the greatest number.[64] Though Bentham was skeptical of sociological abstractions, viewing society as a fictitious body composed of individual persons, his moral orientation remained basically collectivist. According to his utilitarian principle, it is the *aggregate* happiness of individuals, as a group, that represents the ultimate standard of right behavior and good government, not *personal* rights to happiness that individuals can claim for their own sakes (i.e., despite consequences for aggregate welfare).

---

[59](1830–42: 270).
[60](1851–54: 368).
[61](1924: 53).
[62](1893: 140).
[63]Marx (1875); Marx and Engels (1848).
[64](1789).

It is evident that critics of natural rights were concerned, above all, with advancing a normative alternative. They believed that the general well-being or goal attainment of some social unit should take precedence over the interests of participating individuals. Advocates of natural rights, of course, maintained the reverse, at least in some matters. By attacking the metaphysical character of natural rights, opponents obscured this central issue; they diverted attention from the questionable ethical status of their own normative beliefs and from the questionable metaphysical status of their own "empirical" concepts (such as anthropomorphic notions of state, society, or class, conceptions of a world spirit, national will, collective consciousness, etc.).

Ethically, the natural rights doctrine is not clearly inferior to holistic alternatives. While one might find disagreeable some of the particular rights claimed in eighteenth-century manifestos (e.g., unlimited property rights), others seem rather reasonable (e.g., immunities from cruel and unusual punishments); and a premise of twentieth-century declarations, that "disregard and contempt for human rights have resulted in barbarous acts which have outraged the conscience of mankind" is not without substance.[65] Empirically, the natural rights doctrine implies no more mysterious entities than rival doctrines of collective goals. To the present day, confusion exists on this point, and it is worth pursuing.

Individual Rights vs. Collective Goals

Dworkin observes that the term "natural rights" (or the more modern equivalent "human rights") still has "disqualifying metaphysical associations" for some scholars. As in the case of Bentham and the founding fathers of sociology,

> they think that natural rights are supposed to be spectral attributes worn by primitive men like amulets, which they carry into civilization to ward off tyranny. Mr. Justice Black, for example, thought it was a

---

[65]Quote from the United Nations Universal Declaration of Human Rights, 1948. The legalized atrocities of World War II prompted much new concern for natural (human) rights and new interest in international mechanisms to promote them. Robertson (1982) and Sieghart (1983) provide relevant details.

sufficient refutation of a judicial philosophy he disliked simply to point out that it seemed to rely on this preposterous notion.

> But...the assumption of natural rights is not a metaphysically ambitious one. It requires no more than the hypothesis that the best political program...is one that takes the protection of certain individual choices as fundamental, and not properly subordinated to any goal or duty or combination of these. This requires no ontology more dubious or controversial than any contrary choice of fundamental concepts would be and, in particular, no more than the hypothesis of a fundamental goal that underlies the various popular utilitarian theories would require.[66]

Dworkin's analysis suggests that, as in Tom Paine's day, the language of natural or human rights is not absolutely necessary to express the underlying normative idea—that is, the priority of individual choice in certain affairs—but it is useful for this purpose. And it is perfectly legitimate, given that theorists continue to employ comparable terminology expressing a reverse priority of *collective* choice: "public purposes," "organizational goals," "the general welfare," and so on. Such concepts have much in common with natural rights. First, they are *theoretical* constructs, having quite tenuous bases in reality: Collective goals and the like are not tangible, directly observable properties of social systems,[67] any more than natural rights are tangible properties of individuals. Second, both kinds of constructs are *formal* ones, entailing no specifically required content: Theorists often assume that social systems have goals, despite acknowledged difficulties of specifying exactly what those goals are;[68] it is just as logical to assume that individuals have natural rights, despite related difficulties of specifying their content. Finally and most importantly, both sorts of constructs have *normative* connotations, implying positive value: It is taken for granted that collective goals, welfare, etc., are generally good things, deserving of advancement, clarification, or at least serious attention (e.g., as dependent variables for inquiry);[69] natural rights are no different in this regard.

---

[66](1978: 176–177).
[67]Georgiou (1973).
[68]Hall (1977).
[69]Simon (1957).

In short, natural rights have roughly the same ontological standing as collective aims or welfare. Adopting Dworkin's metaphor,[70] natural (human) rights are hypothetical "trumps," held by individuals, over similarly hypothetical collective goals. Following Dworkin, let us call such rights simply "individual rights" in order to emphasize their theoretical parity with "collective goals" and their main difference— their individuated character. (Essential distinctions between types of rights will be drawn later.) Persons can be said to have individual rights, then, "when, for some reason, a collective goal is not a sufficient reason for denying them what they wish, as individuals, to have or to do, or not a sufficient justification for imposing some loss or injury upon them."[71]

For the conduct of practical affairs, the rationale for individual rights is fairly obvious: To deny their legitimacy is, ordinarily, to give overwhelming legitimacy and authority to collective goals (often the personal goals of leaders), which many people are unwilling to grant. Many social participants believe that there are *some* limits (some right-like restrictions) on the sacrifices one can be expected to make for the alleged "sake" of the collective. For the conduct of social inquiry, the rationale for individual rights is that these beliefs have factual, behavioral implications.

An important task of social science is to describe the normative context of everyday social life. People do orient their behavior, to a large extent, by reference to normative beliefs—ideas of good and bad, right and wrong, and so forth. These ideas might not form a well-integrated moral system. They may run the gamut from extremely altruistic or benign beliefs to extremely selfish or malicious ones. But some notion of what one *ought* to do or to have is normally a prerequisite for action; and it is helpful to take account of these notions in attempting to explain social action. Naturally, it can be quite difficult to describe all the particular normative beliefs that various actors might hold. However, it is possible to build into social theories very general normative frameworks, based on very generic types of orientations, such as goals, roles, rights, duties, and other structural elements whose particulars vary from case to case. The need to select,

---

[70](1978).

[71]Dworkin (1978: xi).

to attribute to social participants, some normative framework for action was well recognized by the nineteenth-century founders of sociology and organizational theory (as well as by their most eminent twentieth-century descendants, e.g., Parsons[72] and Simon[73]). What they failed to recognize was the arbitrariness of their choice of frameworks—a choice guided more by their own values than the values of their subjects. Such a choice bears reconsideration.

In choosing very general normative frameworks, our options are rather limited. Logical alternatives might be based on those normative elements that have figured prominently in major political and moral theories. Dworkin argues that historically significant theories have differed in stressing one of three concepts—goals, rights, or duties—as fundamental in orienting human action.[74] Goal-based theories take to be fundamental some collective goal, like increasing aggregate social welfare (as in Bentham's utilitarian theory); right-based theories take to be fundamental some individual right, like equality of liberty (as in Tom Paine's theory of revolution); and duty-based theories take to be fundamental some personal obligation, like acting as one would wish everyone to act (as in Kant's theory of categorical imperatives). Certainly, normative theories may employ all three concepts, and so might social theories that incorporate a normative framework. Similar to early sociological theories, for instance, popular goal-based theories of organization will typically specify duties that promote goal attainment and may even specify some participant rights.[75] The critical distinction, however, concerns which is the fundamental or "deep" concept that provides the basis for deriving or justifying the rest. According to Dworkin, "It seems reasonable to suppose that any particular theory will give ultimate pride of place to just one of these concepts; it will take some overriding goal, or set of fundamental rights, or some set of transcendent duties, as fundamental, and show other goals, rights, and duties as subordinate and derivative."[76]

Social theorists have tended to prefer goal-based frameworks, in which rights are derivative. But social behavior is often made more in-

---

[72](1949).
[73](1957).
[74](1978).
[75]See Thompson (1976).
[76](1978: 171).

telligible by a right-based framework, in which goals are the subordinate elements. To demonstrate, let us turn to what is arguably the high point in development of goal-based social theory—modern organizational theory.

Rights and Organizational Theory

There has, until very recently, existed widespread agreement that organizations are goal-oriented social systems.[77] This is true even among writers who might reject the claims of nineteenth-century theorists that classes, states, or societies at large are so oriented.[78] Mounting loss of faith in such teleological claims at the societal level is evidenced in frequent critiques of Hegelian organicism,[79] Comtean positivism,[80] Marxist historicism,[81] Durkheimian functionalism,[82] Benthamite utilitarianism,[83] and related collectivisms. Yet, the faith has been kept relatively secure that collective goals are essential to organizations at least. A key figure in preserving a secure niche for the faith was Max Weber, who expressed skepticism about holistic theories of *society* but stressed the purposive character of bureaucratic organizations *within* society.[84] In line with Weber's view, it has become common to set organizations apart from other social systems chiefly on the basis of their presumed goal-directed nature:

> Social scientists have found it useful to distinguish formal organizations from families, communities, and other forms of social organization precisely because formal organizations have explicit, specific, and limited goals. . . . Were we to drop goals from consideration, there would be no need for special theories or formal organizational structure and behavior.[85]

---

[77]Georgiou (1973).
[78]E.g., Ladd (1970).
[79]Phillips (1970).
[80]Giddens (1978).
[81]Popper (1961).
[82]Coser (1960).
[83]Rawls (1971).
[84](1925).
[85]Hannan and Freeman (1977: 111).

Organizations are distinguished from other types of groups because they have goals and operate in environments that are not always benign. The structure of relations among variables describing organizations is necessarily different from the structure of relations among variables describing other types of groups, hence the view of organizations as abstract entities isomorphic to social structures in general is inappropriate.[86]

Organizations exist for one or more purposes without which they would cease to exist.[87]

More influential than most modern theorists in perpetuating this view, and more thoughtful in defending it, has been Herbert Simon, whose work also illustrates its shortcomings.[88]

Boundaries of Administrative Science

Simon's general aim is to rid administrative science of the sort of moral language and metaphysical speculation that social scientists have historically found offensive. Thus, he points up the necessity of distinguishing objective facts from subjective value judgments and the need to exclude the latter from the scientific study of organizations: "An administrative science, like any science, is concerned purely with factual statements. There is no place for ethical assertions in the body of a science."[89] The number of brute facts that can be collected about complex phenomena like organizations is virtually infinite, however; and some means of identifying a set of "interesting" facts is required to focus inquiry. A focus is achieved by assuming a value, which is attributed to organizational participants as a fact concerning their own normative orientation, and which serves as a guide to the relevance of other facts. For Simon, this value is organizational goal attainment. He maintains that organizational participants, in making decisions, "must start with some ethical premise that is taken as 'given.' This ethical premise describes the objective of the organization in ques-

---

[86]Meyer (1977: 71).
[87]Daft (1986: 9).
[88](1957).
[89](1957: 253).

tion."[90] He infers, then, that in studying organizations we should begin with the same ethical premise, as given, in order to select interesting facts—that is, we should gather facts about how organizations attain or fail to attain their goals. This set of facts constitutes "the real substance of an administrative science."[91]

The credibility of Simon's position depends heavily on the extent to which organizational participants really do accept the value of collective goal attainment as an ultimate ethical premise for decision making. Simon goes to great lengths to argue for such acceptance, but his case is far from convincing:

> The values and objectives that guide individual decisions in organizations are largely the organizational objectives—the service and conservation goals of the organization itself. Initially, these are usually imposed on the individual by the exercise of authority over him; but to a large extent the values gradually become "internalized" and are incorporated into the psychology and attitudes of the individual participant. He acquires an attachment or loyalty to the organization that automatically—i.e., without the necessity for external stimuli—guarantees that his decisions will be consistent with the organization objectives. . . .
>
> In this way, through his subjection to organizationally determined goals, and through the gradual absorption of these goals into his own attitudes, the participant in organization acquires an "organizational personality" rather distinct from his personality as an individual. The organization assigns to him a role: it specifies the particular values, facts, and alternatives upon which his decisions in the organization are to be based.[92]

In the final analysis, Simon must rely on participants who are just as malleable (and at times just as fanciful) as those envisioned by Saint-Simon: workers, for example, who "sign a blank check" upon employment, pledging "not a specific service but . . . undifferentiated time and effort [placed] at the disposal of those directing the organization, to be used as they see fit."[93] In attempting to include other partic-

---

[90](1957: 50).
[91](1957: 249).
[92](1957: 198).
[93]Simon (1957: 115–116).

ipants, such as customers, among those who "become imbued with the organization aim," Simon's vision surpasses even Saint-Simon's.

Certainly, some organizational participants appear to subject their own personalities to goals of the organization, but many do not. The vast literature on problems of motivation, commitment, leadership, organizational design, and so on, is testimony to the fact that there are no "guarantees" that one's decisions will be consistent with organizational objectives. Like alchemists, Storey observes, students of organization have long been "in hot pursuit of the elixir which may turn the dissentient base metal of the troublesome employee into the rich gold of the compliant subordinate."[94] Even when employees do comply, organizational objectives must often be constantly "imposed on the individual by the exercise of authority." And the question then arises as to whether these objectives actually represent common purposes ("goals of the organization itself") or merely the purposes of some dominant people that derive from their assumed *right* to command—which right may have nothing to do with a common goal but derive from other rights, for instance, property rights of owners, statutory rights of trustees, or contractual rights of workers themselves.

The point is that it may be misleading to attribute collective goals to organizational participants, and it is simply not necessary to attribute them to organizations. Contrary to received doctrine, the existence of organizations does not require agreement or acquiescence to a "common *purpose* [which] is the basis for organizational activities,"[95] but only agreement or acquiescence to the *activities,* which serve the diverse and conflicting objectives of individual participants (profits for owners, wages for workers, goods and services for customers, etc.). As Storey suggests, what generally lends stability to patterns of organization is mutual acceptance of the rights of various participants in particular circumstances, and what lends a dynamic to organizations are disputes over these rights (and derivative duties).[96]

Important as contests among rights may be to actual organizational participants, they have little place in Simon's scheme of things. When participants begin to assert their personal motives and forget

---

[94](1980: 100).
[95]Hall (1977: 83), emphasis added.
[96](1980).

about organizational objectives, the organization for Simon literally "ceases to exist."[97] This myopic "unitary view" has been justly derided by Fox, who contends that

> conflict. . . is inherent in the very structure of industrial organization. Its overt expression is not in itself a sign of organizational ill-health, and to designate those who take an active part in this overt expression as "disloyal" is to fall victim to a terminology that in this context is as sentimental as it is analytically unsound. In other words, the idea that the industrial organization is or can be made a corporate unity pursuing one central set of over-riding objectives is a dangerously fallacious frame of reference for management to use in handling its personnel problems. Those brave slogans about team spirit embody as forlorn a quest as the search for the Holy Grail.[98]

Fox's argument goes beyond the standard "conflict is functional" approach, which emphasizes the value of conflict for the long-term well-being of the organization. Rather, Fox stresses that challenges to managerial authority can be legitimate means of advancing worker rights, "that 'loyalty' is not an appropriate measure of behavior in a contractual, impersonal employment relationship [and] that a man can be aggressive in defence of his or his fellows' rights and still be a valuable employee."[99] Though many managers and organization theorists might quarrel with Fox's normative stance, it is one shared by many workers; and his basic empirical claim has merit: An image of organization united by common purposes and unquestioned authority from above bears about as much relation to reality as the theories of the medieval university masters. Studies of British labor relations provide some of the best documented and most dramatic illustrations.

Boundaries of Administrative Control

In 1968, the Royal Commission on Trade Unions and Employers' Associations (Donovan Commission) acknowledged the presence of two systems of industrial relations in Britain, quite similar to the

---

[97](1957: 204).
[98](1966: 372).
[99](1966: 375).

two systems of law in the Middle Ages discussed earlier: "The one is the formal system embodied in the official institutions. The other is the informal system created by the actual behavior of trade unions and employers' associations, of managers, shop stewards and workers."[100] The first consists of general policies and procedures set forth in written union-employer agreements at the industry level. The second consists of unwritten customs and practices worked out through bargaining at the point of production. As in the Middle Ages, these two systems are often in conflict, and the second, unofficial system is much more significant in governing everyday working relations.

In describing this system, the Donovan Commission reported that

> commonly bargaining to supplement industry-wide agreements takes place between managers and representatives of particular groups of workers. In a company possessing two or more factories it is normal for managers in each factory to deal separately with representatives of groups of their own workers.... [S]pokesmen are representatives chosen from among themselves, usually called "shop stewards", and full-time officials are called in only where managers and shop stewards cannot reach agreement. Many of these agreements affect only one group of workers in a single shop, and may be settled between a shop steward and a foreman or departmental manager.... Workplace agreements may be written down, but are rarely collected together into a single coherent document. Many of them, especially shop floor agreements, are oral. These oral agreements are difficult to distinguish from "custom and practice". This is the body of customary forms of behaviour among groups of workers which managers have permitted to grow up and are therefore assumed to accept.[101]

Substitute "factory" (used by the commission to denote any workplace) for fields and towns, and Ullmann's[102] description of customary medieval law would fit almost as well. Workplace bargaining is highly autonomous, beyond the control of trade unions and employers' associations; it is fragmented, with different groups winning different con-

---

[100]Royal Commission on Trade Unions and Employers' Associations, cited hereafter as Donovan Commission (1968: 12).

[101](1968: 9).

[102](1966).

cessions at different times; and it is very pragmatic, creating rules as the need arises to resolve practical problems of cooperation.[103] Above all, it takes for granted that workers have individual rights of self-determination, rights not based in official decrees of the state, organization, or union.

Like the feudal kings, managers have preferred *tacit* acceptance of worker rights and informal agreements, so as to maintain the public fiction of hierarchically integrated institutions and to preserve what authority they do have. According to Donovan, managers fear that

> if agreements were formalized they would become established *de jure* rights which could not be withdrawn; even if existing stewards would not abuse formal confirmation the next generation might, and managers like to believe that they can vary privileges according to the response they get; once the process of formalizing began it would extend indefinitely; and, finally, "some *de facto* concessions could not be written down because management, particularly at board level, would not be prepared to admit publicly that they had been forced to accept such modifications in their managerial prerogatives and formal chains of command."[104]

For managers not to admit at least privately, however, that their authority is challenged, for them not to recognize that workers may value individual rights over loyalty to the organization, is simply unrealistic.[105] And for organization theorists to encourage such managerial aloofness by dwelling on institutional objectives, or by propagating the official mythology of formal institutional structure, is unhelpful at best.

More helpful are studies revealing the broad scope of informal workplace bargaining and how it actually works. Research sponsored by Donovan and subsequent investigations of the bargaining process confirm the key role of the "shop steward"[106] (again, a generic term, denoting any employee spokesman). The steward is somewhat analogous to the lowest feudal vassal with a defensible castle, which enables him to successfully defy his lord. Because of the sanctions available to

---

[103]Donovan Commission (1968).

[104]McCarthy (1966), quoted in Donovan Commission (1968: 28).

[105]Storey (1980).

[106]E.g., Batstone et al. (1977; 1978).

the steward (ultimately, work stoppages, in place of war), his counsel and consent are often required before management can implement policies, and he may initiate changes on behalf of his constituents. As the representative of a group of workers, the steward derives power primarily from below rather than from above, although he may be responsible to the union in some matters (e.g., for communications to members) or have supervisory responsibility (e.g., where there are no unions or where unions refuse official recognition of stewards). Depending on the power of the work group itself to disrupt operations, the steward may negotiate with management over a wide range of issues: pay (in excess of industry-wide agreements), hours, level of overtime, discipline, work pace, manning of equipment, introduction of new machinery or workers, transfers of assignment, etc. Moreover, "there are many shop floor decisions on these issues in which managers take no part at all. 'Ceilings' on piecework earnings and limits imposed by road haulage drivers on the scheduling of their vehicles are examples of the regulation of work by the workers themselves. The distribution of overtime is another matter which may be left to the stewards."[107]

Despite the countervailing authority of stewards, the Donovan Commission noted that managers do not generally find them obstructive and that stewards are normally more concerned with maintaining order than provoking disorder: "For the most part, the steward is viewed by others, and views himself, as an accepted, reasonable and even moderating influence; more of a lubricant than an irritant."[108] In fact, the Commission found widespread satisfaction, among direct participants, with the bargaining process as a whole, because of its adaptability to local conditions and its day-to-day practicality. (It frees managers, for instance, from dealing with union officials, union officials from dealing with workers, and workers from dealing with either.) Of course, the British system of informal workplace bargaining has had less agreeable effects on indirect participants, for example, consumers who suffer the inflationary impact of "wage drift." These effects have prompted attempts to formalize the process through greater intervention of government and unions—as in the Employ-

---

[107]Donovan Commission (1968: 27).

[108]McCarthy (1966), quoted in Donovan Commmission (1968: 29).

ment Protection Act of 1975, part of an explicit "Social Contract" between the Labour Government and the Trades Union Congress entailing an exchange of statutory worker rights for union support of pay restraint.[109] Managers have also tried to gain more control of the process by institutionalizing the shop steward role. Such efforts have met with limited success in curtailing workplace bargaining and curbing assertion of unofficial worker rights.

In a rare longitudinal study, Storey compared the extent of bargaining in five industries (96 establishments) between 1971 and 1978.[110] In spite of a depressed economy and high unemployment during this period, Storey found an increase in shop floor challenges to managerial prerogatives on many nonwage issues central to job determination. The most frequently bargained issues involved shifts, manning, overtime, job content, discipline/dismissal, and speed of work, all of which were negotiated at a majority of establishments surveyed in 1978. Among these "task control" issues, the largest increases in bargaining occurred over manning, job content, and discipline (about 10% above 1971 levels). Between one fourth and one third of establishments also reported bargaining over operational issues at "the edge of accepted negotiability": production techniques and methods, subcontracting, scheduling of operations, level of output/services, and new hires (all but production techniques increasing). Even some strategic issues traditionally left to managerial discretion showed increases in negotiation (e.g., investment policy); and others evidenced heightened interest among stewards, if not serious bargaining in many establishments (e.g., pricing of products or services).

In surveying managers and stewards, Storey was more concerned with what issues were being pressed than with who won or lost on an issue; however, in-depth study of several sites revealed frequent episodes "where the theoretical managerial right to 'direct and control' as designated in managerial literature is subject, in practice, to 'rules'

---

[109]See Storey (1980); Palmer (1983).

[110]Storey (1980). A fairly broad spectrum of industries was represented. The five studied were fiber manufacturing, a capital-intensive process dominated by a few large chemical firms; textile spinning and weaving, more traditional types of work carried out in many small mills; brewing, another traditional (but more economically stable) industry; mechanical engineering, the largest British manufacturing sector; and bus transport, a major service industry.

imposed by workgroups."[111] In many cases, even written agreements reaffirming managerial authority had little relation to the actual balance of rights:

> For example, at [a brewery] one clause stated: "there shall be complete flexibility in the deployment of labour to suit operational requirements..." Yet the draymen had imposed a wide spectrum of restrictions on this. Transfers of personnel were subject to a number of safeguards; the draymen refused to pre-load vehicles; they refused to carry in excess of certain customary loads; they imposed a ban on carrying certain "mixed loads," such as wines and spirits, on a beer run; they required specific crew levels for different kinds of work; and also there were "rules" concerning the use of particular sizes and types of vehicles for certain runs.[112]

Obviously, not all workers have actual rights as extensive as those exercised by Storey's draymen. Both critics of British practices[113] and more sympathetic observers[114] concur that workplace bargaining is prevalent; but it is hard to say exactly how representative Storey's examples are. On the one hand, it is probable that negotiated work rules and *de facto* worker rights are underreported, due to the elusiveness of localized, unwritten agreements. On the other hand, it is probable that there are major differences in the extent of bargaining and resultant rights between work groups, establishments, and industries.[115] With respect to the degree of worker power in organizations, it is unwise to generalize from some English firms in the 1970s to any other time or place (contrasting American conditions of declining worker power in the 1980s will be discussed in the next chapter). The point of British labor studies, then, is *not* that workers always win significant rights of self-determination; like their feudal predecessors, some have and some have not. But, as Storey shows, neither do managers always win exclusive control over the workplace. Theorists have tended to assume such managerial control—sometimes because of commitment to

---

[111]Storey (1980: 141).
[112]Storey (1980: 141).
[113]E.g., Maitland (1983).
[114]E.g., Aldridge (1976).
[115]Batstone et al. (1977); Storey (1980).

alleged organizational goals, as in Simon's case,[116] sometimes because of opposition to alleged capitalist domination, as in Braverman's case.[117] The result has been neglect of how managers struggle to defend their rights and how workers use rights of their own to resist formal authority.

The main lesson of British labor research is the importance of paying attention to rights. The same thing is suggested by some classic studies of American organizations: by Chamberlain,[118] Dalton,[119] Strauss,[120] Kanter[121] and others. More recently, insights very similar to the Donovan Commission's have been reported by Finlay in a study of informal bargaining among West Coast longshore workers.[122] In all sorts of settings, rights provide a framework for describing organizational structures-in-use and for discovering the real balance of power in a given organization at a given time. With a little development, this framework may be much more revealing than anything conjured out of impersonal collective purposes. Let me sketch a few likely lines of development.

Types of Rights

Rights were defined earlier as personal claims based in some system of rules. To get more specific, we must distinguish between different types of claims and different types of rules. As a medium of social exchange, rights are not all the same currency. A rights typology is useful both for clarifying the concept of rights and for identifying basic building blocks of social structures. One of the most durable and practical approaches is Hohfeld's typology of legal rights.[123] While Hohfeld focused on legal rules, his scheme of classifying claims is applicable to other rule systems, especially organizations, which consist of working

---

[116](1957).
[117](1974).
[118](1948).
[119](1959).
[120]Strauss et al. (1964).
[121](1977).
[122](1987).
[123](1923).

rules governing what participants must, may, can, and cannot do.[124] In explaining this typology, I will use examples of organizational rights, which may or may not be legal rights as well.[125]

Because rights are grounded in social rules, they specify relations *between* persons. Hence, one person's claim is associated with a correlative obligation or expectation on the part of someone else. According to Hohfeld, the term "right" is used indiscriminately to cover any one of four distinct kinds of claims (legal advantages), entailing one of four distinct correlatives. One type of right, a "claim-right," entitles the holder to some benefit or performance (action or forbearance) by another. The correlative obligation to perform or to render a benefit is a "duty" of the other party, something he or she *must* do with regard to the rightholder. Employees, for instance, have claim-rights to compensation, which is a duty of employers. In return for compensation, employers have claim-rights to the performance of certain jobs, and employees have corresponding duties to perform.

The absence of a duty is a "privilege," a second type of right that specifies what one *may* do without penalty under the rules. One who holds a privilege is free to act in ways that are not (wholly) restricted for the benefit of others. Others, however, have no corresponding duty not to interfere, but only a correlative "no right" to expect the privilegeholder to refrain from acting. For example, employees usually have the privilege to seek promotions through hard work. Others have no right to expect them not to try. But others also have no duty not to interfere—coworkers may compete for the same promotion and employers may ultimately award promotions on the basis of personal reasons, like family ties.

The third sort of right is a "power," which specifies what one *can* do to modify the existing relationship with another. Whereas privileges tend to be weak rights, powers are strong rights in that they enable the holder to alter the rights of others. The correlative expectation is a "liability" on the part of another to have his or her rights so altered. In many organizations, employers have the power to terminate employees, who are liable to dismissal at any time. Unlike a mere privilege, the employer's power has the effect of voiding at least some

---

[124]Commons (1924); Leblebici (1985).

[125]I will also rely heavily on Corbin's (1919) presentation of Hohfeld's categories.

organizational rights of the employee. The employee's liability to dismissal is also stronger than a simple "no right" to expect continued employment. It implies an incapacity to interfere with the act of termination (though not necessarily a duty to cooperate).

If the employee does have deterrent capacities, these are "immunities," the final type of right. An immunity is a protection against having one's rights altered by another. Its correlative is a "disability" or lack of power to change the relationship (something another *cannot* do). Perhaps due to a labor agreement, an employee may have certain immunities against dismissal. The employer, in turn, has disabilities, no power, to terminate employment except for causes outlined in the contract. In practice, a right may involve more than one of these four types of relations, but typically one tends to dominate.[126]

Such a classification system has numerous advantages. It can help to avoid confusion and errors concerning the application of social rules. To illustrate, a frequent mistake in judicial cases cited by Hohfeld was the careless assumption that a legal privilege or liberty (e.g., to operate a business) was infringed by any actions that interfered (e.g., labor strikes). Judges today are much clearer on the matter and less prone to infer a general duty of noninterference from a mere privilege. Just as Hohfeld's typology has increased precision in legal analysis, it can do the same in other areas of social inquiry.[127] It can sharpen useful but vague concepts, like "property," by breaking these down into specific claim-rights, privileges, liabilities, disabilities, etc. And it can permit the replacement of other outworn concepts that are too crude to capture the richness of social affairs. Prime examples are "role" conceptions in studies of formal organizations.

It is common to read statements to the effect that "role concepts are critical for the understanding of human behavior in organizations,"[128] or that "the network of standardized role behaviors constitutes the formal structure of an organization,"[129] or even that "human organizations can be *defined* as role systems."[130] Yet there has long been suspicion among some sociologists that the idea of social role has little

---

[126]Wellman (1985).

[127]Thomas Perry (1977) provides additional illustrations.

[128]Naylor et al. (1980: 115).

[129]Katz and Kahn (1978: 45).

[130]Kast and Rosenzweig (1985: 317), emphasis added.

cash value. Dewey has remarked that "one has but to omit the word 'role,' or the phrase 'the role of,' from passages selected at random from social science literature to discover that this often changes the meaning not at all, and on occasion clarifies it."[131] (In organizational literature, contemporary authors sometimes confirm this inadvertently: After faithfully mentioning how important roles are as fundamental components of organizational structure, text writers are apt to forget about them until the obligatory chapter on stress, where we find a couple of paragraphs about role conflict and an old figure from Kahn et al.[132])

Critics complain that role concepts are simplistic,[133] redundant,[134] and ideologically conservative.[135] Originally conceived by Linton,[136] among others, as a collection of rights and duties, "role" now is normally used in a narrower sense to designate a bundle of expectations. Daft and Steers describe it as "an expected behavior pattern assigned or attributed to a particular position that defines individuals' responsibilities on behalf of the group."[137] Katz and Kahn add that roles stem from "task requirements" incumbent on anyone "in a given functional relationship, regardless of personal wishes or interpersonal obligations irrelevant to the functional relationship."[138] In short, roles consist of just *duties*—and not *any* duties at that, but only ones functional for collective aims. The question is why we need another term for a bundle of duties when, as Coulson notes, "to develop, or to apply the concept, we at once have . . . to untie the bundle, and to trace back the relationships between positions and expectations which have been lumped together within it."[139] "Bundling" concepts can of course be convenient at times, but why are functional duties so important that they deserve to be singled out and dressed up with all the analytically sounding terminology of role theory?

It may well be that role concepts do not really bring to light any-

---

[131](1969: 309).
[132](1964).
[133]Dewey (1969).
[134]Coulson (1972).
[135]Gerhardt (1980).
[136](1936).
[137](1986: 192).
[138](1978: 43).
[139](1972: 118).

thing new but, rather, conceal a value choice: once again, the preference of theorists for the value of collective goal attainment. By confining roles to goal-related duties, and by depicting organizational structure as composed of such roles, one makes anything else (such as expressions of individual rights or moral duties) seem like inappropriate organizational behavior. That organizational participants do not necessarily see it this way, that they therefore persist in engaging in a great deal of inappropriate behavior, is not seen as theoretically troublesome but as a technical problem of securing compliance in organizations.

I think the critics who *do* consider role notions troublesome have an easier view to defend. In the interest of scientific accuracy and impartiality, it does appear cleaner to say "duties" when we mean duties and to drop role jargon altogether.[140] Individual researchers, if they wished, could still focus on selective duties derived from collective goals. But the selectivity involved would become more evident, the scope of social science might become broader, and social theorists might become more aware of what their subjects already know: that not only duties, but rights, no-rights, privileges, powers, immunities, liabilities, and disabilities are raw materials of social structure. Recent attention to powers has certainly improved our understanding of organizations;[141] further gains could result from explicit recognition of the other half dozen of Hohfeld's elements.

As a case in point, Brown shows how some of these elements interact in the development of British industrial "custom and practice" alluded to earlier.[142] Beyond the formally agreed-upon *duties* of managers and workers, managers generally retain traditional rights to direct operations. Brown calls these "prerogatives"; in Hohfeld's terms, they are *privileges* since they do not entail correlative duties of noninterference acknowledged by workers. For their part, workers use what-

---

[140]Avoiding role jargon might be more straightforward even if roles are not restricted to duties. Some social scientists, for instance, try to derive rights from roles: "A right is anything to which an actor (individual or otherwise) is entitled by virtue of occupying a recognized role" (Young, 1982: 20). But this position leads to absurdities like invoking (in Young's words) "the role of human being," which can be "regarded as carrying with it a right to life." It is unclear what role terminology contributes here.

[141]See, e.g., Pfeffer (1981); Allen and Porter (1983).

[142](1972).

ever *powers* they have to press for advantageous deviations from organizational rules. (Drivers, say, balk at loading their own trucks, as observed by Storey.) Should management not prohibit these deviations by insisting on *immunities* from unilateral rule changes, they soon acquire the legitimacy of established custom, and workers acquire privileges of their own to continue the custom. Managerial acquiescence over a longer period of time eventually creates worker *claim-rights* to engage in the practice. (Thus, drivers come to stand around while their trucks are being loaded; nobody remembers why; but management must now negotiate with the workers if they wish to modify the practice.) Brown's study yields a number of testable propositions—e.g., the higher the rank of managers who acquiesce, the shorter the time to establish precedent—and it suggests how Hohfeldian categories of rights can enrich our accounts of organizations.

Accounts can be enriched even more by distinguishing the rights that individuals have under different types of rules. Usually, persons will have rights not only by virtue of organizational rules, such as custom and practice, but by virtue of extraorganizational rules, such as legal codes. In the United States, for instance, workers have legal claim-rights to minimum wage levels, legal privileges to express religious beliefs, legal powers to win promotions from employers who award these on the basis of race or sex, and legal immunities against retaliation for the filing of discrimination complaints. Workers can have still other rights under other rule systems: cultural norms may provide for claim-rights to basic fringe benefits; moral principles may provide for privileges to refuse unethical orders; and so forth. Although these latter rights might have no state or organizational protection, they sometimes elicit social sanctions for violations (adverse publicity, corporate campaigns, etc.), and they have at least some normative authority. Consideration of extraorganizational rights not only adds another dimension to our typology but introduces interesting dynamics.

If we catalog the rights and correlatives of organizational participants under various rule systems, inconsistencies will often show up. Some organizational rights may conflict with legal or cultural conventions: for example, rights of lenders to collect usurious finance charges. Some legal or cultural rights might be denied in organizations: for example, claim-rights to a minimum wage. A right may differ in type under cultural, legal, and organizational rules: for example, the legal claim-right of customers to prompt repair of warranted products may in fact be only an organizational privilege. And the same type of right may vary in strength under different rules: for example, under cultural rules, the right of employers to fire workers at will may be a weak power (subject to many exceptions or immunities); under legal rules, a stronger power (subject to a few exceptions); and, under organizational rules, a nearly absolute power (subject to almost no exceptions). Such inconsistencies represent tensions that produce changes over time in one or another rule system. Further research may be able to specify when organizational rights cause legal changes (as in the history of labor legislation), when legal rights cause organizational changes (as in most civil rights legislation), when institutional changes are prompted by cultural or moral rights, what kinds of inconsistencies cause violent change, what factors facilitate or delay change, among other things.

Besides implying a full agenda for empirical research, the rights typology outlined here provides a robust theoretical framework for describing social structures. There is not a lot more to be said about the configuration of any organization after one has itemized

   (1) the rights, privileges, powers, immunities, duties, no-rights, liabilities, and disabilities
   (2) under organizational, legal, cultural, and moral rules
   (3) of managers, workers, investors, customers, suppliers, and other participants.

While these might be tedious to inventory, they are not difficult to locate—in sources such as legal statues, common law cases, company policies, and contracts of all sorts. And the resulting picture, even if fuzzy in places, might be much truer to organizational life than images fashioned from gross elements like roles and goals. (The picture can be sharpened by drawing finer distinctions between types of rules. There are a great many potential *subsets* of organizational, legal, cultural, and moral rules, giving rise to a great many potential rights.)[143]

Keeping in mind the many different forms that rights can take, let's return now to some of the larger issues and pull together the main arguments of this chapter.

---

[143]See Wellman (1985), especially his chapter on "institutional rights."

Conclusions: Toward a Right-Based Theory

William Blackstone, in his famed *Commentaries on the Laws of England,* observed that "there is nothing which so generally strikes the imagination and engages the affections of mankind" as do rights.[144] This is no less true of men and women in modern organizations. The findings of Brown,[145] Storey,[146] and others indicate that at least some workers act as though they had broad individual rights. Many more workers probably believe they have such rights but have to settle for more limited institutional rights. And managers go to great lengths to defend opposing rights of their own. All this casts doubt on the general validity of traditional theories, which portray collective goals as the primary orientations of organizational participants.

It might be more realistic to suppose that people who participate in organizations are intent, first, on advancing individual rights. These rights may be one's own or someone else's. They may be very abstract: rights to property, welfare, freedom, or whatever. They may or may not have legal status. And they may or may not have moral status. In any event, they form the foundation for working agreements concerning rules of organizational conduct, in which participants acknowledge more specific, mutual rights and obligations (what each one may, must, can, or cannot do). These agreements, in turn, may involve varying degrees of willingness; certainly, many are not altogether voluntary.[147] And they may give more substantial rights to one party than another. Allowing for such contingencies, the development of most organizations can be outlined as a series of right-conferring agreements made between a variety of participants at a variety of times.

In a firm, for instance, formal agreements can include articles of incorporation that specify rights of investors at the outset, employ-

---

[144]Quoted in Flathman (1984: 151).

[145](1972).

[146](1980).

[147]As pointed out in Chapter 1, many organizational agreements are "contracts of adhesion," which contain standardized terms designed by dominant parties for their own protection. While not necessarily voluntary, such agreements do signify a factual acquiescence to rules of behavior—which rules confer mutual (if unequal) rights. Problems of determining the voluntariness of agreements will be discussed at length in Chapter 5.

ment agreements that specify rights of workers and managers as the firm builds a labor force, supply contracts that specify rights of vendors and purchaser as other resources are acquired, dealer contracts that specify rights of distributors and manufacturer as products are marketed, sales agreements and warranties that specify rights of final consumers, and so on. As needs and opportunities arise, these formal agreements may be supplemented or modified by informal ones that provide greater specificity. Thus, according to Jensen and Meckling, "contractual relations are the essence of the firm";[148] moreover, through explicit and implicit contracting, "specification of individual rights determines how costs and rewards will be allocated among the participants in any organization."[149]

As mentioned, rights are not the only structural elements that guide behavior in organizations. One person's right (e.g., to manage certain affairs) may imply duties of another (e.g., to perform as agreed), and these duties may entail supporting goals other than one's own. But, in a right-based theory, duties and goals in organizations are derivative phenomena, ultimately stemming from *someone's* assumed right (say, to direct the use of capital, a right that may be assumed by different persons in different political or economic systems). To avoid losing sight of *whose* rights and interests particular goals really serve, it might be better to dispense with the notion of common, "organizational" goals entirely. Suggestions along these lines have become more frequent since Fox's attack on unitary views.[150] Alternative views cited previously—depictions of organizations as political coalitions,[151] exchange systems,[152] competitive arenas,[153] markets,[154] negotiated orders,[155] and the like—afford fresh perspectives on many

---

[148](1976: 310).

[149]Jensen and Meckling (1976: 307–308). See also Klein, Crawford, and Alchian (1978: 326); the authors propose treating the firm as a "set of interrelated contracts," adding that "the conventional sharp distinction between markets and firms may have little general analytical importance. The pertinent economic question . . . is 'What kinds of contracts are used for what kinds of activities, and why?' "

[150](1966).

[151]Allison (1971).

[152]Georgiou (1973).

[153]Cummings (1977).

[154]Pfeffer and Salancik (1978).

[155]Strauss (1978).

organizational processes by focusing on personal interest-seeking, instead of system goal-seeking. Nevertheless, older views have proved remarkably resilient. The traditional goal-based theories of Weber, Simon, and others are still invoked with reverence. And the source of this reverence is still a value judgment, one echoing back to Edmund Burke and the French conservatives. Right-based social systems, however much they "engage the affections of mankind," are just not very appealing to some theorists.

Traditional Objections

Recent attempts to downplay organizational goals have been criticized by theorists who feel that nontraditional views miss something of true significance: that there is more to organizations than the aims and behavior of participating individuals. Mintzberg, for example, disparages "political" views—notably Georgiou's[156]—as "rigid and closed" approaches that reveal only "inputs to a bargaining process in the form of the goals of the actors...but no outputs in terms of common goals."[157] Mintzberg maintains that objective outputs are obvious characteristics of organizations, which "can be conceived of as living systems that exhibit consistencies of their own, consistencies that cannot always be expressed as the sum total of the personal goals of their individual participants."[158] Mintzberg is surely right that organizations exhibit such consistencies; but he is hasty in concluding that they are evidence of organizational goals, and he is wrong in implying that other interpretations commit one to a crude sort of methodological individualism.

Recall the distinctions drawn in the prior chapter between three concepts: consequences *of* an organization, goals *for* an organization, and goals *of* an organization. Consequences *of* an organization are any outcomes of joint behavior. Goals *for* an organization are preferences of people for a certain subset of outcomes. Goals *of* an organization, in standard accounts, are not mere personal preferences but outcomes somehow preferred or intended by the organization itself. We can reject the third concept, the idea that organizations have goals of their

---

[156](1973).
[157]Mintzberg (1983: 19–20).
[158](1983: 248).

own, without giving up the first and second. And we can do so without losing any descriptive insights.

Organizations produce all kinds of objective outputs, both positive and negative, that are consistent consequences of collective action and not just summed characteristics of individuals (e.g., profits, goods, services, pollution, discrimination, etc.). Not all of these consequences can be counted as goals, though. Some, like profits, we may want to include; others, like employment discrimination, we want to exclude—but such classifications are problematic. It is a radical reification to assume that an organization ("living system" or not) can itself prefer one consequence over another. *People* prefer organizational consequences; and different people will often prefer different things. Therefore, it is actually more informative to suspend faith in goals *of* an organization and to concentrate on the diverse preferences that participants have *for* an organization. Examples abound in law, where treating the corporation as a goal-oriented actor is an expedient legal fiction in some situations, but misleading as a general rule. When dealing with questions of liability, misuse of company funds, and other sticky issues, courts have found it prudent to "pierce the corporate veil" to determine whose goals and rights are in fact being asserted under the corporate name.[159] "Organizational" goals hide a lot about personal interests, in a lot of settings: from labor relations[160] to economic behavior of the firm[161] to international affairs.[162]

Yet, there *is* something lost by abandoning organizational goals: not descriptive information, but normative information. Collective goals are values. Traditionalists like Simon and Mintzberg presume they are empirical phenomena as well. While this is contestable, organizational goals remain important "ethical premises" for administrative science. They express a belief in, and a value judgment in favor of, some common good over and above the private goods of social participants. As in the post-Enlightenment era, the validity of such a value judgment is self-evident to many theorists (a "given" for Simon), even if it is disputed by ordinary people (who can be dismissed as not "organizationally rational" or not real "members" of an orga-

---

[159]Hamilton (1971).
[160]Storey (1980).
[161]Jensen and Meckling (1976).
[162]Allison (1971).

nization if they do not share its goals). Theorists view lack of collective purpose in organizations as disorderly, wasteful of resources, an aberration of natural relationships, and otherwise generally disfunctional. Though the phrases are Mintzberg's, they are hardly exceptional and they all mean the same thing: lack of collective purpose is plain bad.[163] Organizations without common ends are likened by Mintzberg to "a bucket of crabs, each clawing at the others to come out on top,"[164] just as in society at large, where pulling toward private ends (a pluralist "political arena") "will be found in the breakdown of any form of government, under conditions typically described as anarchy or revolution."[165] Edmund Burke could not have said it better.

Mintzberg's picture is no fairer than Burke's, however. To reject common ends as fundamental values is not necessarily to invite selfishness. People can still respect other persons' interests and goals *for* an organization even if they recognize no impersonal, collective interest or goal *of* an organization. It is precisely such respect for persons that is entailed in the idea of individual rights.[166] As alternative values for social conduct, rights foster concern for the welfare of individuals besides one's self, if not for the well-being of some abstract social entity. Contractual theories stressing rights do the same. Critics, from Saint-Simon on, have often supposed that contractualists' lack of respect for social abstractions implies some kind of *egoism*.[167] This is a mistake. Participants in social relations might care about (a) themselves, (b) other natural persons, and/or (c) social systems. An egoistic theory would recognize only (a), thereby discounting altruism. Few right-based theories do so. Most, instead, simply devalue (c), portraying so-

---

[163]Mintzberg employs a Durkheimian twist in granting that private interest-seeking can be functional if it furthers the organization's long-term goals, but he clearly grants it no independent value and expresses general disdain for conflict over ends: "The purpose of an organization is, after all, to produce goods and services, not to provide an arena in which the participants can fight with one another" (1983: 446–447). The British industrial practices discussed previously have been particular targets of such complaints (see, e.g., Maitland, 1983).

[164](1983: 421).

[165](1983: 462).

[166]Dworkin (1978).

[167]Macpherson (1962) has been among the most prominent modern promoters of this view. Lessnoff (1986) reviews related objections to contract theories and provides a detailed response.

cial systems as but instruments for the benefit of natural persons. This is a far cry from egoism.

As Minogue argues, it is historically implausible that self-serving perpetrators of the Enlightenment,

> to conceal their rapacities, hit upon a doctrine of natural [individual] rights which led, within a generation or two, to the Clapham Sect and the abolition of the slave trade, the setting up of Sunday schools, the infestation of prisons with reformers, and a host of other activities arising from the growing eighteenth-century conviction that suffering was a bad thing. . . . It would be difficult to point to any evil that came into the world direct upon the heels of the doctrine of natural [individual] rights and easy to point to some that went out as a reasonably direct consequence of it.[168]

Governments based on belief in individual rights may be a bit disorderly, but they can be reasonably good systems; so can organizations. In reality, the welfare of *all* participants is likely to get *more* consideration in a right-based system than in a goal-based one, wherein the fate of specific individuals is not of prime importance. This applies especially to "nonmember" participants who comprise an organization's "external environment" (e.g., gullible consumers or "enemies" of the State). If we extend Mintzberg's analogy, crabs in a bucket who suddenly discovered a common objective might be even nastier to handle than before; crabs who suddenly acknowledged rights could be far more pleasant to deal with.

Admittedly, some alleged rights can be as controversial as some alleged goals. But certain rights—say, moral rights to equal concern and respect[169] or legal rights to avoid personal harms[170]—seem to be every bit as reputable as any goal. And the main point is that there are plausible alternatives to collective goals as ultimate ethical premises for organizational behavior and inquiry. Mintzberg at least imagines the possibility, whereas Simon does not. Simon assumes that normative choices in organizations can be reduced to questions about *which* goals organizations should have.[171] He assumes further that normative

---

[168](1978: 30).
[169]Dworkin (1978).
[170]Eser (1966).
[171](1957).

choices can be avoided in administrative science by leaving such questions to politicians or managers, by accepting their choices as ethical givens, and by focusing analysis on means to these given ends. In other words, a value-neutral science results from studying how organizational goals in general can be attained. The flaw is that normative choices are not confined to matters of goal *selection*. The value of goal attainment *itself* is debatable, and an administrative science that takes this value for granted can be a very biased science indeed.

Epistemological Implications

There is nothing inherently wrongheaded about beginning inquiry with a hypothesized value orientation, hoping that the world turns out to be as good or perfectible as one would like to believe. As Hesse demonstrates,[172] both natural and social scientists have historically drawn on normative beliefs as a source of theories and propositions about how things, in fact, work. And this chain of inference from *values* to *theories* to *facts*—from "ought" to "is"—is perfectly all right, so long as facts are not forced to fit one's conjectures but are allowed to modify them. (The reverse chain of inference—from "is" to "ought"—is highly suspect, of course; post-empiricist philosophers of science caution that facts cannot conclusively establish the validity of scientific theories, much less pre-theoretical values.) In natural science, pre-theoretical values have usually concerned the general beauty, harmony, or predictability of the universe. In social science, they have concerned the proper normative orientation of social actors. In both cases, the adoption of a guiding value can lead to discovery of empirical truths; but an eccentric value can lead one away from discovery of other, possibly more important, truths.

I have argued that, as a primary normative premise, the value of organizational goal attainment is eccentric: it is attractive mainly to a group of theorists and organizational managers. The value is useful to the latter in legitimizing their goals *for* an organization (in getting them accepted as goals *of* an organization). And it is useful to the former in developing knowledge relevant to managerial interests. But it tends to be not so relevant to the interests of "lower" organizational participants.

---

[172](1978).

Notice that, in operationalizing collective goals, researchers often rely on powerful persons (e.g., a "dominant coalition") to articulate an organization's objectives. This practice is not considered biased, for it is supposed that the goal set of a dominant coalition must represent the interests of remaining participants to elicit their support or discourage their interference. Thompson states that members of a dominant coalition are free to prefer any goals but only certain choices are rational, namely, goals that fit with the preferences of persons whose cooperation is required to attain them: for instance, "When the core technology of an organization must be employed on dynamic human objects, the outcome is in part determined by those human objects; and if they hold opposing outcome preferences, some compromise is likely."[173] "Compromise" of this sort can be very one-sided, as Thompson illustrates: "In prisons with therapeutic objectives...conflicting outcome preferences of prisoners force the prison to add custody as an outcome preference. A similar conflict among objectives often occurs in mental hospitals, although to the extent that tranquilizing drugs render patients cooperative, therapeutic objectives may gain priority over custodial ones."[174]

In effect, Thompson claims that, if dominant participants prefer some goal that they call "therapeutic" and if other participants balk at their idea of therapy, it is *organizationally rational* for the dominant coalition to compromise by incapacitating these "dynamic human objects." Perhaps powerful individuals do adopt strategies of this kind. But it is deceptive to describe them as logical means of furthering joint goals. And it is hardly impartial to direct most research toward ways of attaining "organizational objectives" that can be such thinly disguised assertions of power. Certainly, activities like custody in a prison or therapy in a hospital can be assertions of *right* as well, and interesting things to study. Reframing events in terms of rights, however, reveals the possibility that all participants have them, raises questions of why some have more than others, and suggests research of broader scope and wider relevance (e.g., comparative studies of prisoners' or patients' rights, which might interest litigants or legislators, besides standard studies of technical efficiency that interest administrators).

---

[173](1967: 137). See also Donaldson (1985: 91–92).
[174](1967: 137–138).

While preoccupation with managerial interests in organizational theory has not gone unchallenged,[175] it is commonly met with resignation or defended by insisting that we have little choice in deciding what aspects of organization to emphasize in theory-building and research. According to Meyer: "The attitude of scientific neutrality may, depending upon the questions asked, serve only the interests of those in control of organizations. But to use social science for ameliorative purposes is to compromise the scientific enterprise itself."[176] Why is it more scientific, though, to ask questions that address the concerns of organizational controllers, rather than questions pertinent to people who might suffer adverse consequences of control? And what could be more compromising than to base an entire science of organizations on a value that steers research into parochial subject areas?

There is nothing inevitable about a pro-managerial line of inquiry and nothing inevitable about underlying, goal-based theories of organization. Alternative, right-based theories can contribute to a less partisan administrative science, and their construction does not require any novel form of logic or epistemology. We can proceed by following Simon's general approach,[177] merely substituting rights for goals in basic assumptions:

> Assume that persons are oriented toward ends, which constitute ethical premises for social behavior and normative components of organizational structure: now, individual rights in lieu of collective goals.

> Assume that individual rights, in the abstract, are proper ends of association (as claimed in classic political declarations, as opposed to corporate reports).

> Assume that, as social scientists, we leave the specification of which rights people *should* have to social participants themselves: to lawmakers, interest-group representatives, organizational contractors, etc.

---

[175]See Krupp (1961); Albrow (1968); Benson (1977).
[176](1977: 78).
[177](1957).

Assume, finally, that we take at face value, or as given, the rights asserted by these various participants and focus attention on how, empirically, they are institutionalized, contested, promoted, or undermined in specific social settings.

Methodologically, this approach is no different than Simon's, but it may yield more value-neutral information. It is conceivable that the interests of individuals who have the most power to institutionalize personal rights (in law, organizational policies, or informal agreements) might still receive disproportionate attention in a right-based theory. However, theorists would no longer be able to conceal this tendency behind concern for some imagined common interest, and professional credibility could be hard to maintain were inquiry limited to a very narrow set of rights—say those of property owners or their agents. Imbalances of power and privilege are readily exposed by a right-based theory. And, historically, exposing of these imbalances has led to questioning of them. Organization theorists may well want to engage in this kind of questioning themselves, as in recent "critical theory."[178] If not, others outside the discipline will continue to do so, and they may question one's motives for remaining aloof.

Clearly, it is a departure from a positivist ideal of science to question the value of particular institutional rights, or to speculate about which allegations of moral rights deserve to be taken seriously. Again following Simon's approach, one would have to step out of a pure fact-finding, social scientist role and assume the role of political philosopher. Yet, why is this not legitimate on occasion? Surely, philosophy ought not replace science; but to decree that we cannot employ philosophical or ethical analysis to augment science is highly arrogant. It implies either (1) the belief that anything besides empirical fact finding is nonsense or (2) the belief that, if not nonsense, any other intellectual activity is irrelevant. Such beliefs are presumptuous because science itself is a social practice that has effects on people, whose well-being can be as important as the search for empirical truth.

The point is most obvious in the case of experimentation with human subjects. As noted at the outset, it is widely accepted that human beings have some rights limiting how they may be treated for scientific purposes. These rights may not be empirically verifiable; issues

---

[178]Fischer and Sirianni (1984) provide examples.

of *which* rights subjects ought to have in what situations elicit considerable debate.[179] But most scientists would probably deem it unprofessional to disregard the potential rights of subjects on that account. And virtually all would condemn certain research programs that acknowledged no moral rights or only prevailing institutional rights (e.g., the infamous biomedical experiments of Nazi researchers). If it is scientifically responsible to consider the moral rights of laboratory subjects and to allow these considerations to affect the course of empirical research, it is also responsible to consider the moral rights of the subjects of organizational theory and to allow the latter considerations to affect the course of theory development. This does not mean that theorists must adhere to some rigid ethical code, but that they should be free, for instance, to investigate violations of controversial "human" rights without facing charges of muckraking or sentimentalism.

I have tried to show that it is the age-old yearning for collective goals that is sentimental. In the next chapter, we will look at further implications of a right-based theory for some special organizational problems.

---

[179]Beauchamp et al. (1982).

4. Applications

This chapter will focus on various practical implications of a right-based, contractual theory of organizations. The question I intend to pursue is: What difference does it really make, for the design and control of organizations, whether we base theories on individual rights or collective goals?

It is worth reemphasizing at the outset that a right-based view does not imply disinterest in traditional topics of organizational theory and research: say, productive processes that result in profits, goods, services, and other social consequences. Such things are certainly important in actual organizations and deserving of continued study. A right-based theory, however, depicts the production of social consequences as an instrumental activity—a way of furthering individual interests—and not the ultimate purpose of organizations as goal models suggest. This approach broadens our perspective on organizations and our research concerns.

Consider, for instance, some of the broad implications of a contractual model mentioned earlier. The model encourages inquiry into events prior to production, such as how organizational participants decide which consequences to promote. Organizational goals are not regarded as "ethical givens,"[1] but as objects of negotiation that remain subject to dispute.[2] The model encourages inquiry into events concurrent with production, such as how some participants manage to legitimate personally preferred consequences. Alleged goals *of* an organization are not seen as natural system properties,[3] but as symbolic elements which dominant persons invoke to legitimize their defi-

---

[1]As in Simon (1957).
[2]As in Cyert and March (1963).
[3]As in Selznick (1957).

107

nition of the situation, their goals *for* an organization.[4] And a contractual model encourages inquiry into events subsequent to production, such as how organizational consequences impact individual participants. The ideal "end" of organizations is not viewed as the efficient attainment of selected outcomes,[5] but as the fair imposition of all outcomes: a just distribution of the benefits and burdens of cooperation.[6] This serves to focus attention on *who gets what* (and who pays) versus *what gets done*.

In effect, a contractual model subordinates production and system-maintenance processes to political processes. It acknowledges the utility of the former—the practical value of making cars, selling hamburgers, loaning money, and many other things that modern organizations do. At the same time, it reminds us that organizations do more important things. At their best, they increase opportunities for personal choice and the realization of one's chosen plans. At their worst, they destroy personal options and, literally, lives. Choices and lives, as subjects of rights, remain fundamental in a contractual view.

Is it really fair, though, to imply that other views discount lives, that goal-based models reflect more concern for the production of hamburgers than the welfare of human beings? Critics of utilitarian views have argued as much. Sen presents a practical demonstration in his study of famine,[7] which illustrates both empirical and normative advantages of a right-based approach.

Right-Based Analysis

There are few goods whose production is as critical as food. Without food, people die. In famines, they die in very large numbers: approximately 3 million, for example, in the Bengal famine of 1943. Sen provides some interesting facts about this disaster. It was quite discriminating in its effects, claiming mainly rural victims in specific occupational groups. The most affected rural groups were fishermen, transport workers, and agricultural laborers; the least affected were

---

[4]As in Silverman (1970); Thompson (1980).
[5]As in Parsons (1956).
[6]As in Keeley (1978).
[7](1981).

peasant cultivators and share-croppers. Urban workers in Calcutta, who were important to the war effort, were protected from starvation through rice subsidies and government-controlled food-grain shops for city residents (many destitute outsiders trekked to Calcutta only to die in front of such shops).

A variety of factors might have contributed to the famine. A cyclone in October 1942 was followed by torrential rains in several sections of Bengal. Rice imports from Burma were interrupted by the Japanese occupation of that area. British decisions to keep boats and rice from the advancing Japanese (who never showed up) hampered fishing and reduced coastal food stocks. Still, the most interesting fact is that these events did not materially decrease overall food availability in Bengal, which should have been adequate in 1943. While food output and total supplies declined somewhat from the record levels of the previous year, Sen notes, "current availability of food grains was at least 11 per cent higher in 1943 than in 1941, when there was nothing remotely like a famine. Even in per capita terms the current availability was 9 per cent higher in 1943.[8]

Sen shows that what changed dramatically in 1943 was not aggregate food *production* but individuals' *entitlements* to food, that is, legal rights to command food. Certain persons suddenly found themselves without property or skills of sufficient market value to trade for bare necessities; and they were without effective rights to obtain food through nonmarket means, such as state assistance. The price of rice increased sharply in 1943, due to inflationary pressures of the war (massive military and civil expenditures were financed largely by printing money), because of speculation in food grains (producers and traders withheld some stocks from market, anticipating higher prices and profits), and through general mismanagement of food supplies by the British and Indian governments (interprovince grain movements were periodically prohibited). Simultaneously, the purchasing power of various workers was sharply reduced, accounting for the differential effects among rural groups. Common agricultural workers, who had only labor to exchange for rice, saw their rate of exchange fall by two-thirds. Fishermen, who depended on selling fish to buy grain-calories, suffered not only from declines in the fish-rice exchange rate but from

---

[8](1984: 461).

the smaller catches occasioned by the boat-denial policy. In contrast, farmers, peasants, and share-croppers, who grew rice for exchange and consumption, maintained their purchasing power and food entitlements.

Other famines have been similar in achieving selective starvation in the midst of aggregate food sufficiency.[9] Famine occurs when particular people do not *have* enough to eat. This is different from a situation where there *is not* enough to eat.[10] The latter is a problem of production (including import and transportation). The former is generally a problem of impoverished entitlements: individual persons lack ownership rights to food—and the means to obtain those rights (income, trade opportunities, statutory welfare entitlements, etc.). Naturally, production failures can cause diminished entitlements and, in turn, famine. But they represent only one possibility; individuals may lose entitlements to food for any number of reasons. Unfortunately, both theoretical and practical attention has focused primarily on the production problem, which simplifies matters at no small risk to potential famine victims. As Arrow observes:

> Most people are convinced that the basic cause of a famine is not poverty but a failure of food supply relative to the population. A localized famine is commonly thought of as resulting from a local failure of crops that is not mitigated by importing food, as happened in the Sahel region of Africa in the late 1960s. Countries where hunger is widespread are frequently blamed, moreover, for allowing excessive population growth. The simple Malthusian ratio of food supply to population is further simplified so that the cause of misery is often seen as a matter of overpopulation alone; and we even hear advocates of "lifeboat ethics," by which countries should be abandoned to their fates.[11]

This approach has already been adopted, Arrow adds, in the form of low foreign-aid allocations by the United States.

While Arrow's claim might be a bit strong, Sen's evidence of traditional government insensitivity to food-entitlement problems is persuasive. At the onset of the Bengal famine, for example, British and

---

[9]Tilly (1985).
[10]Sen (1981: 1).
[11](1982: 24).

Indian officials relied on aggregate food availability estimates (which were not alarming) and minimized the threat of famine until it was too late to control. The Bengal government responded to the crisis with an inept propaganda drive, asserting that "the supply position did not justify the high prices prevailing"[12] and predicting that prices would soon come down. Afterwards, the official Famine Inquiry Commission concluded that the famine's primary cause was "the serious shortage in the total supply of rice available for consumption in Bengal as compared with the total supply normally available."[13] From beginning to end, policymakers viewed events in terms of a goal-based theory emphasizing overall food production, a theory that had serious consequences indeed: according to Sen, "the Malthusian focus on food output per head powerfully contributed to the absence of public policy to counter the famine" and "literally killed millions."[14]

The point of all this is certainly not that food output per capita is *never* important (different famines have different characteristics). It is not that production processes should be ignored. The moral is simply that production—or any aggregate outcome—is too narrow a concern. There is no necessary connection between total food output and the amount available to individual persons. Whether individuals can command sufficient food is contingent on rules of the particular society and organizations they are involved in. These rules specify (among other things) one's rights with respect to various goods and activities: who "owns" a good or is otherwise entitled to use it, what precise uses are permitted, how entitlements are created (e.g., through employment contracting), lost, exchanged, and so forth. By focusing on institutional rules, resulting entitlements, and shifts in those entitlements, famines become not only more understandable, but more manageable. Famines might be better anticipated, for instance, by monitoring entitlement-related variables, like unemployment among specific groups, rather than concentrating on gross food totals. Famine assistance might be accelerated by establishing entitlements where most needed, such as through cash relief to increase the purchasing power of severely affected persons, rather than awaiting mobilization of indiscriminate food relief efforts. Perhaps most significantly, the very oc-

---

[12]Sen (1981: 76).
[13]Sen (1981: 53).
[14](1982: 450).

currence of famine might be decreased through public entitlement policies combining anticipation and need-sensitive benefits, as in programs of unemployment insurance.[15]

It is worth keeping in mind that, while public policy proposals are prescriptive by nature and thus may presuppose *moral* rights, a right-based explanation of famine is descriptive and draws only on *conventional* rights. In Sen's entitlement approach, the emphasis is on legal rights as determinants of hunger and as mechanisms through which other factors operate: production processes, market forces, etc. Sen's analysis clears up a number of empirical questions (e.g., why particular people become famine victims), and it should dispel any remaining suspicion that goal-based views are somehow more scientific.[16] Famine, of course, represents an especially devastating failure of social organization and an especially dramatic illustration of the failure of goal-based theories. It is by no means a unique phenomenon, however, or a peculiar organizational application of a right-based theory.

There are many situations in organizations that exhibit features of the famine problem. These situations are symptomized by serious personal distress, caused by a shift in some command system (market, law, organizational policy, administration, or the like) against certain individuals. As in the famine case, this shift entails a loss of entitlements—which may or may not stem from, but is often blamed on, deficiencies in aggregate resources. Classic examples would include the legal imposition of industrialization costs, such as the burden of personal injuries or land damages, on various groups during the nineteenth century.[17] Instructive instances in recent years involve corporate "disinvestment" and "concession bargaining."

Industrial Applications

Disinvestment refers to the movement of capital away from existing facilities through such strategies as suspension of modernization

---

[15]Sen (1982) argues that social insurance programs are not as impractical in developing countries as others have imagined.

[16]An entitlement approach can be extended to account for a wide range of historical facts relating to food problems. It is used by Tilley (1985), for instance, to explain why organized food protests in eighteenth- and nineteenth-century Europe were most prevalent in food-producing regions: for one reason or another, wage earners in those regions lost capacity to buy food and had no other legal rights to it.

[17]Horwitz (1977).

and maintenance, relocation of equipment, subcontracting of operations, or outright plant shutdown. Bluestone and Harrison estimate
that "between 32 and 38 *million* jobs were lost during the 1970s as the
direct result of private disinvestment in American business."[18] Some of
these jobs were transferred to other regions of the country; many left
the United States altogether. During the 1970s, Bluestone and Harrison note, "GE expanded its worldwide payroll by 5,000, but it did so
by adding 30,000 foreign jobs and reducing its U.S. employment by
25,000. RCA Corporation followed the same strategy, cutting its U.S.
employment by 14,000 and increasing its foreign workforce by
19,000."[19] More comprehensive surveys by the U.S. Department of
Labor substantiate the present magnitude of the problem: 10.8 million adult American workers had their jobs abolished between 1981
and 1986; 5.1 million of these workers had been at their jobs for at
least three years and are conservatively counted as truly *displaced.*[20]

Despite disinvestment gains to new hires, shareholders, and perhaps other oganizational participants, the costs to displaced workers
have been considerable. It is difficult to specify the "typical" costs of
labor displacement, since effects vary from case to case. Nevertheless,
some very rough generalizations are possible. In introducing legislation to mitigate the effects of plant closings. Representative William
Ford (D-Mich.) summarized relevant findings of Congressional hearings on the matter:

> Whereas the median duration of unemployment in the United States
> is 10 weeks, studies have found that 40 percent of workers laid off in
> major plant closings are unemployed for 40–60 weeks and a quarter
> are unemployed for more than one year. . . .
>   Victims of plant closings typically suffer from hypertension, ab-
> normally high cholesterol and blood sugar levels, a higher incidence of
> ulcers, respiratory diseases, unduly high propensities to gout and dia-
> betes, and hyperallergic reactions. The mental health effects can be
> even more critical: Depression, anxiety, substance abuse and aggres-
> sive feelings frequently translate into spouse abuse, child abuse,
> crime, or suicide.

---

[18](1982: 9).

[19](1982: 6).

[20]U.S. Department of Labor Task Force on Economic Adjustment and Worker
Dislocation (1986).

Not only do workers lose their jobs in a plant closing, along with health benefits, pensions, and other fringe benefits, but the new jobs they eventually get do not provide as much income or status. Careful long-term studies show that 6 years after a plant closing, workers in the automobile, steel, meat packing, and aerospace industries still earn an average 12.5 to 18.1 percent less than before the shutdown. Over a lifetime, this income loss can total $40,000 or more per worker.[21]

Given these and other potential costs (e.g., loss of savings, home, and remaining personal assets), it may be little consolation to a displaced Detroit autoworker that his/her sacrifice permits creation of a new job in Smyrna or Singapore.

Plant closings, like famines, have hit some people harder than others. Among the most severely affected have been production workers in capital-intensive, basic manufacturing industries. When displaced, such workers "have nowhere to go except lower paid, more labor intensive (and less unionized) operative jobs, or into unskilled service work."[22] Craft workers, on the other hand, possess skills that are less industry-specific and stand a better chance of finding comparable employment. In general, women have suffered more than men, blacks more than whites, and older more than younger workers. Women, for instance, remain unemployed for longer periods,[23] minorities are overrepresented in declining industries,[24] and older workers experience greater annual income losses.[25] What displaced workers as a group have lost are *entitlements* (organizational if not legal rights) to ordinary benefits of employment; this is the immediate cause of their distress. Indirect causes are subjects of some controversy.

It is commonly assumed that disinvestment is a consequence of some deficiency in resources, some economic hardship confronting an industry or firm as a whole. Such hardship is usually attributed to uncontrollable forces and/or extraneous events. Reflecting this popular

----

[21]From the *Congressional Record* of May 2, 1983. For more detailed discussions of plant-closing effects, see Ferman and Gordus (1979); Gordus, Jarley, and Ferman (1981); Bluestone and Harrison (1982); Martin (1983).

[22]National Council on Employment Policy (1983).

[23]Gordus et al. (1981).

[24]Squires (1982).

[25]Holen et al. (1981).

conception, F. M. Lunnie of the National Association of Manufacturers has stated before the U.S. Congress:

> Because of the current economic conditions facing this nation, conditions which for the most part are beyond the control of either management or labor, this problem [of plant closings and mass layoffs] has become more pronounced. . . . [The] changing realities of the marketplace have necessarily resulted in revised corporate strategies and, in some cases, disinvestment in outmoded and/or uncompetitive facilities and industries.[26]

Lunnie maintains that governmental restrictions on closings would be counterproductive and that proposed legislation, requiring advance notice and assistance to displaced workers, "ignores the underlying causes of plant closings and focuses only on the symptoms of the problem." In Lunnie's view,

> The real problems we face include a range of factors such as a sluggish economy only slowly beginning to recover from the worst recession this country has experienced since World War II, a shift in the character of and therefore, the opportunities in the manufacturing sector, lagging growth in productivity and fierce competition in a global market that is unparalleled in our history. . . . Until we are able to effectively address these problems and restore the economy to a sound footing, significant improvements in the incidence of business failures and plant closings are not likely.[27]

The idea that worker displacement necessarily stems from deficient productivity, or profits, or some other aggregate outcome, is simplistic. And it has not gone unchallenged. Bluestone and Harrison question whether a firm such as General Instrument Incorporated *must* decide to cut costs by moving production of cable TV equipment from Massachusetts to Mexico, at the same time reporting: "Our cable TV group had its best year by far, with a record year-to-year world-wide revenue gain and a profit increase of $23 million."[28] Whyte

---

[26]U.S. House Subcommittee on Labor-Management Relations: Worker Dislocation (1984: 278).

[27]U.S. House Subcommittee on Labor-Management Relations: Worker Dislocation (1984: 278–279).

[28]Bluestone and Harrison (1982: 172).

and colleagues have documented other cases in which large corporations have abandoned profitable facilities.[29] Sperry-Rand, for example, announced plans in 1976 to liquidate a Northeastern furniture plant "which had been operating with a healthy furniture industry profit during its years as a subsidiary."[30] The plant merely failed to hit the high profit target (22%) decreed by management of the parent conglomerate. Closing was averted through purchase of the plant by employees, who were able to find local investors with more modest expectations. Not only have conglomerate managers sometimes shut down economically viable operations to seek higher rates of return elsewhere, but they have deliberately eroded the viability of some facilities by, for instance, forgoing improvements and diverting cash flow to fund new acquisitions.[31] Prime examples can be found throughout the American steel industry, long one of the most productive in the world but now weakened by years of disinvestment.[32]

In short, while plant closings may be economically motivated, not all are economically inevitable. Strategic choices—voluntaristic decisions of human beings, as opposed to deterministic effects of environmental forces—are important if often overlooked aspects of organizational behavior.[33] Compared to independently owned companies, large multiestablishment firms seem to account for more than their share of shutdowns and job losses.[34] This suggests that much disinvestment results not from the demise of weak (resource-poor) businesses, but from the policy choices of dominant (resource-rich) ones. To be more precise, the fate of many establishments is determined by corporate officials who manage great concentrations of capital and have great prerogatives—legal powers—to transfer capital in order to further their goals *for* an organization (e.g., greater capital accumulation). This is not in itself an indictment of such managers or prerogatives. Certainly, some facilities deserve to close and managers should have some rights to decide which ones. The issue is simply that it is more accurate to view closings as assertions of rights than casual-

---

[29]Whyte, Foote, Hammer, Meek, Nelson, and Stern (1983).
[30]Hammer and Stern (1980: 83).
[31]Bluestone and Harrison (1982).
[32]U.S. Congress, Office of Technology Assessment (1980).
[33]Bourgeois (1984); Kochan et al. (1986).
[34]Hochner and Zibman (1982); Harris (1984); Yago et al. (1984).

ties of natural selection processes, resource shortages, or the like. Even where closings do originate from economic imperatives, certain individuals must exercise rights to actually switch off the lights (say, by petitioning a bankruptcy court). And other individuals suffer the effects of closings through lost entitlements, due in turn to their thin legal rights to object. By focusing on participant rights, one avoids prejudging the legitimacy of shutdowns, and one is led to ask more sophisticated questions about them.

As Lustig states, "The real question is not whether closedowns will occur but who is empowered by social institutions to initiate them, why they are permitted to occur, and how society permits their burdens and benefits to be distributed."[35] A right-based perspective raises the latter kind of questions and exposes a variety of possibilities to public scrutiny and debate. It calls attention to the *human* agents of shutdowns—and to the possibility that some agents may act out of self-interest instead of concern for the "common good." It calls attention to the essentially *legal* justification for shutdowns—to the possibility that corporate agents need have only enabling rights, not necessarily compelling economic reasons, to close operations. It calls attention to the vulnerability of *particular* persons to shutdown costs—and to the possibility that these costs can be allocated more fairly, or at any rate differently, as in other industrialized nations.

Western European nations have recently experienced even more severe economic shocks than the United States. The former are more dependent on exports and hence more affected by growing international competition.[36] During the seventies, European countries sustained more serious employment loss than the U.S. (where losses in declining sectors were at least numerically offset by gains in service and other jobs); Harrison notes that "among the largest member countries of the European Community (EC), negative rates of growth across the private sector prevailed everywhere, and overall employment decline would have been even worse if not for the efforts of governments such as those in France, Belgium, and Denmark to create large numbers of public service jobs."[37] Despite global economic pressures, European workers have enjoyed greater protection against their

---

[35](1985: 137).
[36]Martin (1983).
[37](1984: 390).

personal effects than most Americans. Europeans have a more expansive social safety net, providing, among other things, more generous unemployment compensation and continued health care through national delivery systems.[38] Employer obligations toward displaced workers are also considerably different in Europe than in the United States. Whereas American employers have broad legal rights to lay off or dismiss employees at will, European employers have what amount to conditional legal privileges in this area. Laws in nearly every Western European country require employers to give advance notice of facility closings;[39] prenotification periods range from two months in Belgium to twelve months in West Germany. Moreover, employers must generally present an economic justification for mass layoffs to workers' councils, which can further delay closings by appealing the decision to governmental boards or courts. According to Martin, "The advance notice requirement and appeal options give workers facing dismissal a limited job property right that employers are willing to buy out with severance pay to induce quits."[40] Though European employees and unions are not altogether satisfied with such limited rights,[41] they have enabled European workers to better cope with disinvestment and displacement.

It is conceivable, of course, that strong worker rights may *cause* low growth rates, more displacement, and more personal distress in the long run;[42] but they may not, either—depending on how public policies are structured.[43] The key point, as in the famine case, is that there is no direct connection between overall economic growth, productivity, wealth, etc., and the resources available to particular people. While aggregate outcomes are not unimportant, whether individuals can command income, health insurance, or a job tomorrow is contingent on rules of the society or organizations they are involved in. These rules, by assigning rights and duties to various parties, allocate the gains and costs of social change. Public policies giving corporate managers strong rights to shift capital and shutdown operations do not

---

[38]Martin (1983).
[39]Harrison (1984).
[40](1983: 85).
[41]Harrison (1984).
[42]As Lawrence (1983) suggests.
[43]As Blakely and Shapira (1984) argue.

necessarily enlarge the economic pie, creating wealth that spills down to everyone. They may serve merely to rearrange wealth, at times perhaps benefiting investors at the expense of workers. Regressive redistribution of this sort can happen through "paper entrepreneurialism," whereby some managers pursue profitability through merger, acquisition, or financial wheeling and dealing rather than technological innovation.[44] It can happen through "deunionization," whereby some managers divert assets to nonunion facilities rather than negotiate over their use.[45] Or it can happen through regional "whipsawing," whereby some managers threaten communities and states with disinvestment rather than accept the local social wage—the assortment of welfare programs, government regulations, and worker entitlements that figure in the cost of doing business.[46]

Study of the rights and entitlements of different organizational participants alerts us to other possibilities concerning related events. To save their jobs, for example, employees in large numbers have lately agreed to reductions in wages and benefits, to less advantageous work rules, and associated contract concessions. As with plant closings, concession bargaining is commonly viewed as an adaptive response to low overall goal attainment, traceable to deficiencies in organizational resources and "economic hardship in many industries."[47] Mindful of rights, one might suspect there is more to it. American employers have substantial legal privileges to seek a more favorable bargain. These appear to have grown over the last decade, while the bargaining power of employees and labor unions has decreased.[48] Accordingly, Cappelli and McKersie find evidence that "in many cases firms are asking for concessions and striving to engage unions in this process when in fact the economic situation is not adverse and employment is not threatened."[49] Other research indicates that at least some concessionary agreements may just further the redistribution of resources from workers to investors.[50]

---

[44]Reich (1983).

[45]Kochan et al. (1986).

[46]Bluestone and Harrison (1982).

[47]Carrell and Heavrin (1985: 420).

[48]See, generally, Kochan et al. (1986). These trends will be discussed in more detail later.

[49](1985: 228).

[50]Becker (1987).

It is difficult to gauge the degree to which employers are simply taking advantage of labor's weak position to demand nonessential concessions. An oft-cited 1982 *Business Week* poll of major corporations showed 19 percent admitting to the seeking of unneeded concessions,[51] but such self-reports obviously must be treated with caution. If anything, they probably understate the extent of corporate opportunism. Firms can induce concessions in many subtle ways: for instance, by engaging in disinvestment to reduce the competitiveness of certain plants, by trading on ensuing fears of layoff to exact givebacks from workers at those plants, and by expanding these local agreements to gain concessions at other, healthier plants.[52] Here again, concession bargaining *may* stem from genuine economic necessity; and even if it does not, there may be nothing wrong with hard-nosed negotiation. However, it is more revealing to describe the process as a shift in rights and entitlements, which shift could result from any number of factors besides resource deficiencies or goal underachievement—for example, recent pro-employer interpretations of labor laws by the National Labor Relations Board. The idea that political systems, apart from economic systems, may have tilted against workers seldom surfaces in goal-based analyses. But it is worth serious consideration and it opens more options for public policymakers to explore in dealing with employment problems.

In the end, a right-based theory does not mandate specific public policies. As in the famine illustration, a right-based explanation of plant closings and concessions entails only empirical, *conventional* rights: legal or organizational rights are seen to be the devices through which market trends, corporate strategies, governmental administrations, and other forces affect people. Nothing directly follows regarding *moral* rights, rights persons should have. Nevertheless, a right-based view highlights the fact that workers with meager actual rights have fared rather poorly, even in prosperous organizations—as evidenced in early industrial practices involving child labor, female outworkers, workplace accident victims, and various minority groups. And such a view suggests that, as with past problems of industrialization, present difficulties might be eased by legislation *creating* worker rights: rights, perhaps, to increased protection of collective bargain-

---

[51]June 14, 1982.
[52]Cappelli (1985).

ing,[53] to advance notification of plant closing or to dislocation assistance,[54] and to community participation in plant relocation decisions,[55] among others occasionally proposed.

Institutional Design

The thought of addressing organizational problems by legislating rights has a certain commonsense appeal. But it has rarely occurred to organization theorists, who have tended to adopt a fairly narrow approach to the design of social systems.

Standard goal-based theories pose design questions from the perspective of persons in power (e.g., "Is there an optimal span of control?" or its current counterpart, "When should control be delegated?"). This approach takes for granted prevailing authority relations. A right-based approach would pose design questions from a broader, societal perspective that takes authority relations as contestable. Let me clarify the difference.

Division of Labor vs. Division of Power

There is a long history of interest in design issues among organization and management theorists. And there is a common interest that characterizes this tradition. Such an interest is reflected in Henri Fayol's work on general management functions and the *specialization of labor*,[56] in Frederick Taylor's work on scientific management and the *specialization of labor*,[57] in Chester Barnard's work on cooperative action and the *specialization of labor*,[58] in Mooney and Reiley's work on principles of organization and the *specialization of labor*,[59] and in other classic literature.

In fact, the specialized division of labor has been a preoccupa-

---

[53]Weiler (1983).
[54]Bluestone and Harrison (1982).
[55]Lustig (1985).
[56](1949).
[57](1911).
[58](1938).
[59](1939).

tion of social architects ever since Plato—and a focus of organization designers specifically, at least since Adam Smith.[60] Smith's famous illustration concerns the advantages of specialized tasks in the making of pins: one worker draws out the wire, another straightens it, a third cuts it, a fourth sharpens it, a fifth grinds the top, several more make the head, attach it, whiten the pins, put them into paper, etc. Smith identifies about eighteen distinct operations in the production of this simple item. He estimates that, properly specialized and organized, workers could produce about 4800 pins per man-day. Working separately, he maintains, they could produce at most 20 per day—maybe not even one. Allowing Smith some literary license, his point is reasonable: Big production gains can be achieved by dividing labor along functional lines. What is less reasonable is the suggestion of many later theorists that functional division of labor is the most basic if not the sole problem in structuring organizations.

Mintzberg claims, for instance, that "the structure of an organization can be defined simply as the sum total of the ways in which it divides its labor into distinct tasks and then achieves coordination among them."[61] "Coordination" is here understood as the integration of tasks to accomplish given objectives (through such customary devices as direct supervision, mutual adjustment, and standardization of work processes or output). Similarly, in Galbraith's view the whole idea of organizational design is "to bring about a coherence between the goals or purposes for which the organization exists, the pattern of division of labor and interunit coordination and the people who will do the work."[62] What if, however, the ultimate purposes for which an organization exists are in dispute? What if some people view certain outcomes as an organization's reasons for being (say, wages and benefits), while other people view these as mere costs of attaining different outcomes (say, goods or profits)? How is work to be divided when what work is *for* is unclear?

The traditional solution is to leave the job of selecting goals to superior group members, to leaders who are supposed to specialize in such tasks. In the case of societal design, this was Plato's approach and that of the early sociological masters—e.g., Saint-Simon[63] and

---

[60](1776).
[61](1979: 2).
[62](1977: 5).
[63](1821).

Comte.[64] It was also the approach of thinkers who shaped modern organizational theory—e.g., Selznick[65] and Thompson.[66] Surveying the field twenty-five years ago, Wolin observed that nearly all writers on organizations assumed that "the world created by organizational bureaucracies is and should be run by elites."[67] Things have not changed a lot since. A typical contemporary view is expressed by Daft:

> The formal hierarchy in organizations focuses the responsibility for governance on executives at the top of the hierarchy. They are responsible for governance decisions that define the goals, strategy, and well-being of the corporation.[68]

This approach, though, raises more questions. What is to prevent top managers from defining goals, strategies, and "organizational" well-being in an arbitrary way? What is to stop them from using their power to enhance the well-being of particular participants (including themselves) at the expense of others?

Several replies are conceivable. One invokes internalized constraints on managerial selfishness. Simon[69] and Gross,[70] for example, have suggested that processes of socialization over time elicit loyalty to the organization as a whole; eventually, members develop organizational or bureaucratic personalities which restrain egoistic impulses. This has been criticized as simplistic. Organizational managers are for the most part nice men and women; but reliance on their loyalty is as naive as trust in their benevolence. Adam Smith recognized that it is not good will but the self-interest of butcher or baker that puts dinner on our table. And self-interest is no less apparent among modern CEOs. I am reminded of a recent news item reporting massive selling of personal IBM stock by senior executives—including IBM's chairman and president—prior to public disclosure of reduced company earnings.[71] Disloyal? Of course; but hardly exceptional.

An alternative made popular by Adam Smith is to assume that those who direct organizations are disciplined by competitive, envi-

---

[64](1851–54).
[65](1957).
[66](1967).
[67](1960: 414).
[68](1986: 471).
[69](1957).
[70](1969).
[71]Chicago *Sun-Times*, July 20, 1986.

ronmental constraints. Following this strategy, Thompson,[72] Pfeffer and Salancik,[73] and others stress controls on managers imposed by markets for labor, capital, goods, and services. If workers, investors, or customers are unhappy, they can take their business elsewhere, thereby threatening an organization's resource supply and the security of persons in power. This is more plausible, but contingent on everyone's voluntary participation and their freedom to discontinue participation. For some participants, leaving the organization can be a very costly option, and it may not work to restrain powerholders anyway. Imagine that a student comes to you, describes an incident of sexual harassment by a university administrator or professor, and asks for your advice on what to do. Who would be callous enough to tell her to go to school elsewhere if she did not like it? Who could feel confident that this solution would generally prove more effective in curbing abuses of power than a more direct means of challenging authority (say an impartial grievance procedure)? It seems neither practical nor fair to expect all participants to express their preferences with their feet.

A third possibility is simply not to worry about these things. Whether managers wield power arbitrarily might be dismissed as an unscientific question that calls for an unfounded value judgment. According to empiricists like Mintzberg[74] and Meyer,[75] social scientists should avoid such questions and stick to describing organizations. However, it may not be feasible to deal with organizational design in a thoroughly nonprescriptive way. Starbuck and Nystrom point out that, in analyzing social structures,

> no one can regard everything skeptically and challenge every premise; some properties of current social systems have to be taken as stable givens, and unchangeable properties easily become desirable properties. For example, it is objectively true that some organizational members are called managers and that these managers control resources, determine strategies, and supervise other organizational members. Nearly all organization theorists assume that managers will continue

---

[72](1967).
[73](1978).
[74](1973).
[75](1977).

to exist indefinitely and to perform activities close to the ones they do now. But there are very fuzzy lines between saying managers will exist and saying managers ought to exist, between saying managers will supervise and saying managers ought to supervise. Nearly always, organization theorists cross those lines.[76]

The line is crossed, consciously or not, when we presume that the problem of conflict over organizational goals can be set aside. It is crossed when we presume that the problem of controlling organizational authorities can be set aside. And it is crossed when we presume that the really interesting problem of organizational design concerns the division of labor.

Recognizing the difficulties of explicitly justifying ruling elites or implicitly accepting their inevitability, some theorists have abandoned the traditional approach to organizational design. They suppose that "organizational" goals are controversial and that leaders may succeed in taking advantage of weaker participants—unless constraints are built directly into the structure of organizations. Proposed constraints have taken a variety of forms, including increased shareholder control of proxy machinery,[77] multiconstituent boards of directors,[78] employee bills of rights,[79] works councils,[80] and more conventional collective bargaining.[81] All these mechanisms are intended to increase organizational democracy, raising an age-old political design issue. The question now is how *power*—not just *labor*—can be divided.

The relevance of this political question to "private" associations, like corporations, has been challenged. Traditionalists believe it stems from a false analogy between governmental and corporate social systems.[82] Perhaps the analogy *has* been pushed too far by those who claim that modern corporations are actually "minigovernments" by virtue of their large size and scope of activities.[83] Ewing's argument that General Motors has more members and a bigger budget today

---

[76](1981: xii).
[77]Eisenberg (1976).
[78]Stone (1975).
[79]Garson and Smith (1976).
[80]Asplund (1972).
[81]Derber (1970).
[82]See various contributors in Johnson (1978).
[83]For instance, Miller (1976); Ewing (1977).

than any of the thirteen American colonies in 1776 does not necessarily establish that the political ideas of the Founding Fathers apply to GM. Nevertheless, these ideas *are* relevant to organizations—not because governments and organizations resemble one another in any superficial way, but because the same *problems* arise in their design.

As suggested earlier, persons may disagree over ends. They may place their own interests ahead of the common good. They may engage in conflict over resources. They may use power to exploit others or to force their views on them. And they may inflict all sorts of specific harms on one another. These problems are not unique to either governments or nongovernmental organizations; they cannot be classified as "public" or "private." They are general *social* problems, liable to show up in any kind of social system. In Western societies, it has been formal systems of government that have taken the lead in dealing with such problems: as in the framing of the American Constitution, in subsequent legislation regarding antitrust, labor relations and civil rights, in judicial modification of the common law (most recently, with respect to employment-at-will), and so forth. But governments and constitutions have not eliminated the underlying problems or freed organizations from concern about them. The very question that so engaged the Framers of the U.S. Constitution—how to protect individuals by dispersing power throughout society—is as pertinent today as two hundred years ago. It is now a question of organizational as well as governmental design. And to the extent that organizations themselves fail to respond, governments may be justified in continuing to force the issue.

Political Design: The Case of the American Republic

To understand better the interdependence of organizational and governmental design, it is helpful to look more closely at political theories of power separation. As a political doctrine, the idea of separation of powers has ancient origins. It is associated with early notions of government as a compact for securing individual interests.[84] Primitive forms of the doctrine stressed separate representation of various social classes, as in Cicero's view:

---

[84]Davis (1978).

I hold it desirable, first, that there should be a dominant and royal element in the commonwealth; second, that some powers should be
granted and assigned to the influence of the aristocracy; and, third,
that certain matters should be reserved to the people for decision and
judgment.[85]

Such a view developed into theories of "mixed" government, for instance in seventeenth-century English versions which sought a balance
between King, Lords, and Commons. Mixed theories were further
developed in American colonial governments but were eventually rejected as difficulties with England increased. Vile notes that, in America, mixed government came to be seen as a disguised form of tyranny
because it did not ensure a true "balance" of power and because it
presumed a continuing, legitimate role for an unwelcome monarchy
and aristocracy.[86] The alternative embraced after the break with England was to divide governing powers among different semifunctional
bodies—a federal executive, legislature, judiciary, and their state
counterparts—to better safeguard the personal rights and liberties the
Americans considered fundamental. Of greatest significance was not
the particular allocation of functional duties (which were not, in fact,
all that cleanly separated) but the distribution of sovereignty between
rival governmental forces.[87]

The principle adopted in designing the American Constitutional
system was *noncentralization*,[88] not *decentralization* as in prior mixed regimes (and in "organic" organizational designs). The latter implies a
central authority who delegates, at pleasure, responsibility to others;
the former involves a diffusion of power that is shared, by right,

---

[85]*Commonwealth,* cited in Gwyn (1965: 24).

[86](1967).

[87]In reality, there has always been a considerable mixing of functions between
branches of American government. Huntington (1959: 198) remarks that "the President legislates as much as he executes; Congress probably administers as much as it
legislates and not infrequently adjudicates as well; the Supreme Court seldom decides a major case without legislating." What distinguishes each branch, then, is not
a wholly separate *function* but a separate source of *power.* Indeed, the system of government fashioned by James Madison and adopted in 1788 (described below) is
based on the premise that different governmental units will act like competitive suppliers of comparable services. Thus, "the separation of power has been achieved by a
blending of processes" (Huntington, 1959: 198).

[88]Elazar (1981).

among independent agents. The Framers' zeal in diffusing power is well described by James Madison, chief architect of the Constitution, in *Federalist* No. 51. The first division is between "two distinct governments," state and federal, which vie to control one another. Within each government, then, power is "subdivided among distinct and separate departments," which have wills of their own, reflecting the desires of member-officials to maintain or enlarge their personal authority. Madison comments:

> Ambition must be made to counteract ambition. The interest of the man must be connected with the constitutional rights of the place. It may be a reflection on human nature that such devices should be necessary to control the abuses of government. But what is government itself but the greatest of all reflections on human nature? If men were angels, no government would be necessary.[89]

Further divisions are required, however, since "it is not possible to give each department an equal power of self-defense" against encroachments by others. The legislature is especially prone to dominance and so its power is divided again between two houses. Still other checks and balances, such as an executive veto, may be needed as backup devices for preserving, in practice, the departmental independence prescribed on paper.

Madison's compounding of separations has seemed excessive to some critics, who complain that it weakens national resolve, hampers unified action, or thwarts majority wishes.[90] But the Framers were willing to tolerate effects of this sort as costs of solving more basic problems. The important question is whether the Framers really solved the problems they *tried* to address. Madison recognized two great tasks in designing a government: "to guard the society against the oppression of its rulers" and "to guard one part of the society against the injustices of the other part."[91] It turns out that the first was handled much more carefully than the second.

The delegates who convened in 1787 to draw up a constitution for the United States were very conscious of group-on-group injustices that had occurred in many localities under the loose Articles of Con-

---

[89]*Federalist* No. 51: 322.
[90]E.g., Dahl (1956); Burns (1963); Sundquist (1986).
[91]*Federalist* No. 51: 323.

federation. Burns points out that "the main purpose of the convention [was] to set up a strong national government and hence check the power of local majorities to invade the rights of others."[92] Madison was particularly concerned about this "violence of faction." He explained the problem in a famed speech at the Constitutional Convention, which warrants extended quotation:

> All civilized societies would be divided into different sects, factions, and interests, as they happened to consist of rich and poor, debtors and creditors, the landed, the manufacturing, the commercial interests, the inhabitants of this district, or that district, the followers of this political leader or that political leader, the disciples of this religious sect or that religious sect. In all cases where a majority are united by a common interest or passion, the rights of the minority are in danger. What motives are to restrain them? A prudent regard to the maxim that honesty is the best policy is found by experience to be as little regarded by bodies of men as by individuals. Respect for character is always diminished in proportion to the number among whom the blame or praise is to be divided. Conscience, the only remaining tie, is known to be inadequate in individuals: In large numbers, little is to be expected from it. Besides, religion itself may become a motive to persecution and oppression. These observations are verified by the histories of every country ancient and modern. In Greece and Rome the rich and poor, the creditors and debtors, as well as the patricians and plebeians alternately oppressed each other with equal unmercifulness....We have seen the mere distinction of color made in the most enlightened period of time, a ground of the most oppressive dominion ever exercised by man over man....The lesson we are to draw from the whole is that where a majority are united by a common sentiment and have an opportunity, the rights of the minor party become insecure. In a republican government the majority if united have always an opportunity. The only remedy is to enlarge the sphere, and thereby divide the community into so great a number of interests and parties, that in the first place a majority will not be likely at the same moment to have a common interest separate from that of the whole or of the minority; and in the second place, that in case they should have such an interest, they may not be apt to unite in the pursuit of it.[93]

---

[92](1963: 14).
[93]June 6, 1787; quoted in Padover (1953: 17–18).

Notice several things about Madison's analysis. He is, first of all, talking not about how to control government but other social groups. Thus, public concern with harmful consequences of "private" associations is not something stirred up by misguided modern liberals; it was much on the minds of the American Founders, and Madison above all. Furthermore, it was precisely the feature of groups that came to be so prized by organization theorists—united pursuit of a common interest or goal—that Madison so feared (for precisely the reason suggested in the last chapter: the potential of goal-oriented groups to violate individual rights). Now how to control self-interested groups? Madison considered traditional remedies:[94] One might, for example, attempt to remove the causes of faction. However, this would require enforcing uniform opinions and interests within an entire community, which is impractical, or denying persons the liberty to pursue narrow interests, which is just as oppressive as factional violence. Madison rejected such cures as worse than the disease and, so, opted for trying to control the effects of faction instead of its causes. His solution, as stated at the convention and made more explicit in *Federalist* No. 10, was (a) a republican government of elected representatives (vs. a pure democracy managed by all) to "refine and enlarge the public views," and (b) a bigger unit of government (vs. small, provincial states) to "take in a greater variety of parties and interests." How this would resolve the problem of faction is not altogether clear.

Like more recent pluralists, Madison seems to have assumed that countervailing interest groups would naturally flourish and check one another in a large republic, thus relieving government of much of the responsibility for actively balancing them. Unlike other prominent thinkers of his own day, he did not propose to institutionalize any specific group interests in the basic structure or divisions of government. Off in London, in contrast, John Adams urged the Americans to try once more the European structure of class-based governmental divisions: national bodies representing aristocrats and common people. From Paris, Thomas Jefferson wrote in favor of purely functional and locally autonomous divisions, accountable for specialized activities to separate geographical constituents (envisioned as an otherwise homogeneous class of yeoman farmers organized around small townships).

---

[94]*Federalist* No. 10.

In Philadelphia, where the work of actually drafting a constitution was going on, Madison sought a more flexible structure, responsive not just to existing European classes or a longed-for agrarian one, but to all manner of possible interest groups.[95] Hence, he advocated competitive divisions—state vs. federal, state vs. state, branch vs. branch—that could reflect and moderate whatever competing interests might emerge in society at large.

In Madison's scheme, government was designed to represent interests almost as a market responds to consumer preferences: through enterprising departmental officials (of whom there are many thousands elected to legislate or appointed to head agencies at various levels of government). These officials exchange their political influence for the support of particular groups, thereby advancing both their own careers and the causes of their constituents. A neglected group creates an opportunity for officials to build a base of support or add to their current base. A dissatisfied group can shift their allegiance to numerous contenders for it. In theory, then, virtually any interest group has a way of achieving representation, but no one group is likely to capture enough centers of power to subjugate opponents. In fact, though, some minority groups may find it extremely difficult to achieve *effective* representation without institutionalized protections or legal guarantees. The obvious example in the early American republic was the group of slaves, who experienced much factional violence (in "private" agricultural organizations) and who suffered for many decades, until Constitutional immunities were finally offered.

Some analysts have supposed that Madison tried to mitigate factional, group-on-group tyranny with his elaborate arrangement of checks and balances.[96] But, as Carey argues,[97] checks and balances were directed toward a different problem: that of governmental tyranny. While Madison may not have seen how interest groups in a large republic could amass enough political power to oppress one another, he recognized that a governmental department could ultimately garner sufficient power to oppress any group. Once a noncentralized, competitive system of government is set in motion, departments will behave much like firms in a market. Over time, some will be more cre-

---

[95]Huntington (1959).
[96]E.g., Burns (1963).
[97](1978).

ative, aggressive, and do a better job of representing interests than others. Such departments will prosper, acquiring more supporters and more power (as in the ascendancy of national over state bodies, which have been slower to respond to new demands). Up to a point, this process is beneficial: less efficient units will be eclipsed by more efficient ones, and as the latter grow, their policies will become more moderate to accommodate an increasingly broad range of constituents. But what is to reverse the process, should a department so consolidate power that officials need care no longer about satisfying constituents (and turn instead to satisfying themselves)? An *economic* monopolist might have to face new entrants into the market and price competition, whereas a *governmental* monopolist has the police power of the state to deter challengers. Interdepartmental checks and balances were designed as prudent barriers to a governmental monopoly. As such, however, they afford little protection against nongovernmental factions; indeed, they may pose barriers to any governmental action, including efforts to aid victimized minorities.

To summarize, government to the Framers was the product of a constitutional compact for the purpose of securing individuals' fundamental rights. In framing this compact and resultant government, Madison believed that two things were essential: "You must first enable the government to control the governed; and in the next place oblige it to control itself."[98] Madison showed great ingenuity and persistence in tackling the problem of controlling government, that is, in providing the constitutional machinery of divided sovereignty, checks and balances, and the like. But Madison, and the Framers in general, tended to finesse the equally important problem of controlling the governed, that is, deterring societal factions from violating individual rights. Here, Madison relied mainly on a "multiplicity of interests" to provide *social* checks and balances in an expanded republic. These emergent social checks, he reasoned, would prevent one interest group from completely dominating the republic. Yet they do not prevent a group from dominating a *part* of the republic—which can be nearly as bad. Madison remarks on the issue in *Federalist* No. 10, where he outlines relevant advantages of a broad American republic: "The influence of factious leaders may kindle a flame within their particular states but will be unable to spread a general conflagration through the

---

[98]*Federalist* No. 51: 322.

other states." For instance, "A religious sect may degenerate into a political faction in a part of the Confederacy; but the variety of sects dispersed over the entire face of it must secure the national councils against any danger from that source."[99] But what comfort can persons harmed by a local faction like the KKK take from the fact that such a group is unable to seize national councils? And does Madison really take the problem of factional violence seriously enough in worrying about a "general conflagration" while allowing flames to kindle in specific states, or communities, or organizations?

Perhaps it is unfair to fault Madison personally for failing to devise better protections of many embryonic human rights. Along with other delegates to the Philadelphia Convention, perhaps he did the best he could under the political circumstances of the time. There was significant opposition to the proposed Constitution and the new powers it bestowed on the national government. To give national units even more authority to intervene in local affairs might have made ratification by the states impossible. For example, to press prohibition of slavery in 1787 could have meant a quick end of the Union.[100] Nevertheless, slavery, among other abuses, eventually *did* have to be prohibited by national authorities. And the structure framed in Philadelphia *did not* secure the rights of individuals against invasions by local factions and private interest groups, which Madison himself considered the primary source of oppression in society. The original structure has been amended occasionally to add various securities—beginning just after ratification with enactment of the Bill of Rights. But Constitutional amendments, with the notable exception of the thirteenth (outlawing slavery), have mostly addressed the same problem as checks and balances: the infringement of rights by government, not by self-interested factions. Anticipating this, Madison privately disparaged suggested bills of rights as "parchment barriers" that would be ineffective against the "real power" in a community. This power, as well as the main threat to rights, he wrote Thomas Jefferson, "lies in interested majorities of the people rather than in usurped acts of the Government."[101]

---

[99]*Federalist* No. 10: 84.

[100]Though the Constitution need not necessarily have been so conciliatory toward slavery; see Robinson (1971).

[101]Padover (1953: 255).

Jefferson replied that "half a loaf is better than no bread. If we cannot secure all our rights, let us secure what we can."[102] And so they did, with Madison leading in drafting the Bill of Rights—which guaranteed some important rights against the federal government but left future generations to fight for the rest of the loaf, security of individual rights against other powerful groups.[103]

Contemporary Implications

Placed in historical context, recent calls for a bill of rights in nonpublic settings like the workplace do not seem so absurd.[104] More peculiar sounding is the common counterclaim, that such "political" things have no applicability to "private" organizations.[105] From the outset, the restriction of rights-guarantees to acts by government was a compromise, not something the Founders took great pride in. Nor would it be a tradition worth preserving in any event.

Numerous writers have pointed out that individual rights remain insecure against modern organizations.[106] Large corporations in particular possess far more power than the factions Madison imagined, and they are certainly no less prone to violate rights. This does not mean that corporate officials are determined evildoers, but simply that in the current pluralist arena big firms resemble "elephants dancing among chickens," as Hacker puts it.[107] In such a dance, someone is liable to get hurt, even if the participants try to be careful. Take, for instance, rights to occupational safety and health, which most people today would consider central to individual well-being. Underscoring their importance, one corporate observer has advocated the policy "that *all* accidents and illness from exposure to known hazards can be prevented." A company must not accept "any predictable level of injury or illness in any manufacturing unit." In short, "if a product cannot be made and used safely, it ought not be made at all." These are

---

[102]Rutland (1983: 197).

[103]Including state governments, whose conduct was not affected by the Bill of Rights until 1925.

[104]E.g., Garson and Smith (1976); Ewing (1977).

[105]E.g., Martin (1978).

[106]E.g., Hacker (1965); McConnell (1967); Lindblom (1977); Coleman (1982).

[107](1965: 7).

not radical moralist claims but statements of a chairman and chief executive officer of Du Pont, Irving Shapiro.[108] Unfortunately, despite well-intentioned leadership, the chemical industry as a whole has been less than safe.[109] It has occasioned some of the most glaring rights violations in recent years (such as the Union Carbide accident at Bhopal, which claimed thousands of lives). And it is not even among the most dangerous industries.[110]

Over the past two centuries, of course, progress has been made in reducing and compensating harms. To some extent, organizations have taken remedial action on their own. To some extent, the adverse effects of organizations have been controllable through the competitive and adaptive system of government Madison did conceive; many injured and disadvantaged groups have gradually gained enough political influence to win protective legislation, regulation, or judicial relief. Workers, for instance, now have statutory rights to a safe workplace, unions of their choice, equal employment opportunity, and claim-rights to damages for all kinds of employer misconduct. Still, these are relatively fragile rights, not guaranteed in the same way as rights against government. Without constitutional protection, they remain objects of negotiation in the political marketplace: subject to swings in public opinion, economic fluctuations, changes of administration, and so on. The idea of a bill of rights is to secure some basic rights of individuals from much of this political pulling and hauling.[111] And it is not a bad idea in any social setting.

An illustrative worker right that has lately undergone serious erosion in the political arena is the right to union representation. Labor problems became major American concerns after the slavery issue was resolved in 1865.[112] As industrialization progressed, working con-

---

[108]Quoted in Bradshaw and Vogel (1981: 211–216).

[109]Ashford (1976).

[110]Perrow (1984) discusses related issues. He argues that it may be impossible to prevent accidental harms stemming from malfunctions of complex technologies (like nuclear plants). This does not imply, however, that these technologies must be tolerated or that the costs of accidents must be borne by their victims.

[111]This is not to suggest that bills of rights are iron-clad. The U.S. Bill of Rights, for example, contains a right to petition the government for a redress of grievances; for historical, political reasons this right has lost most of its original meaning and force (Higginson, 1986). Nevertheless, Constitutional rights have been more immune to such deterioration than other legal rights.

[112]Derber (1970).

ditions remained generally nasty even for highly skilled workers, prompting considerable labor unrest and organized moves for reform.[113] The struggle for significant worker rights culminated in the 1930s with passage of the Social Security Act (providing for old-age assistance, state unemployment compensation, and other social welfare benefits), the Fair Labor Standards Act (providing for a minimum wage, maximum hours, and the abolition of child labor), and especially the National Labor Relations Act (giving employees the legal right to form or join unions and prohibiting unfair, antiunion practices by employers). The chief architect of the NLRA, Senator Robert Wagner, picked up where Madison left off. He argued that it was time for Congress to project "into economic affairs the essence of true democracy, by outlining a system of checks and balances between industry and labor, crowned by governmental supervision and advice."[114] Wagner stressed that "the national labor relations bill does not break with our traditions. It is the next step in the logical unfolding of man's eternal quest for freedom."[115] This step was to expand democracy from

---

[113]Toward the end of the nineteenth century, for example, the railroad industry was one of the largest employers in America. Gutman (1976: 297) outlines common grievances of railroad workers:

> They often complained that employers withheld wages from them for several weeks or even months. Certain Wisconsin roads made them trade in company-owned stores.... Workers at the large Susquehanna Depot repair shops of the Erie Railroad said that many of the "best and oldest" workers were discharged "without assigned cause" and that "utterly unskilled" laborers received the same wages as some skilled mechanics. Engineers and firemen on the Pennsylvania system charged that when engines were damaged the workers paid the repair cost regardless of the cause.... Many engineers lost as much as 3 months of work every year because company officials did not supply them with new engines when their cabs were in repair.

Work was not only erratic and arduous but extremely dangerous. Licht (1983) notes that accidents were such a normal feature of jobs that, in 1889, roughly 1 in 35 railroad employees was injured in service and 1 in 350 killed. Certain occupational groups were particularly at risk. Illinois Central data for 1874–84 reveal that 1 in 7 workers in "switching service" suffered disabling injury and 1 in 90 was killed. Such conditions gave rise to some of the most serious industrial violence, legendary strikes, and militant labor organizations in American history.

[114]Derber (1970: 319).

[115]Derber (1970: 321).

governmental to industrial relations by extending to workers rights of
expression, assembly, due process, and election of representatives—all
through the bedrock right of collective bargaining which, to Wagner
and other lawmakers, was just as vital a check on twentieth-century
organizations as Madison's checks on eighteenth-century government.

In the eyes of many workers, however, the promise of the Wagner
Act has yet to be fulfilled. Far from "encouraging the practice and procedures of collective bargaining," which the Act declared "to be the
policy of the United States," labor law has "become an impediment."
This is the conclusion of the U.S. House Subcommittee on Labor-
Management Relations after extensive hearings on the NLRA's effectiveness.[116] Its report states: "Perhaps the most striking evidence of the
law's failure is that, in recent appearances before the Subcommittee,
virtually every labor union leader testifying called for repeal of the
law." The Subcommittee found it ironic that "Unions, which exist to
engage in collective bargaining, are calling for repeal of the law that is
intended to encourage that process." To be sure, union leaders are not
above political posturing before Congress; but it is clear that "workers
and their unions now view the labor laws with disillusionment and bit-
terness" and that "the effectiveness of labor law has declined dramatically."[117]

Reasons for this decline are several. Over the years, legislatures
have reduced workers' economic weapons, prohibiting union shops (in
right-to-work states), secondary boycotts, etc.[118] Courts have restricted
workers' rights to strike and to litigate breaches of labor contracts.[119]
The agency created to administer the NLRA, the National Labor Relations Board, has taken positions that now seem to encourage employer resistance to unionization, at odds with the Act's objectives.
(Chairman Dotson, a former management attorney, once wrote that
"collective bargaining frequently means labor monopoly, the destruction of individual freedom, and the destruction of the marketplace as

---

[116]U.S. Congress, House Subcommittee on Labor-Management Relations:
Failure of Labor Law (1984: 2).

[117]Failure of Labor Law (1984: 4).

[118]Weiler (1984).

[119]Stone (1981).

the mechanism for determining the value of labor.")[120] While the political context of labor-management relations has shifted rightward and unions have lost support among key governmental bodies, the economic context has become adverse as well. As noted earlier, unions have lost bargaining power due to the growing competitiveness of global product markets and the increasing mobility of capital.[121] The upshot is that organized labor today begins the bargaining process with diminished entitlements and may find it difficult to deal with employers on an equal footing, despite Wagner's pledge to restore such equality.

No doubt, some people (and many management theorists) would rejoice in the continued weakness of organized labor. This fact obviously limits the possibilities for securing worker rights to collective bargaining. There is little reason to think that corporate managers will one day gladly acknowledge these rights and voluntarily share power with unions. There is also little reason to think that unions will soon build enough public support in the United States to acquire constitutional protection of bargaining rights. If an Equal Rights Amendment to safeguard rights against sexual discrimination is not politically feasible, the prospects for any worker bill of rights are slim indeed. The trouble is that constitutional protections are not so essential for popular rights (say, rights of white people to political representation in antebellum America) as for unpopular rights (say, similar rights for blacks). But unpopular rights—precisely because they are unpopular—are not likely to gain such protection without some really wholesale social change. At least in the short term, then, worker rights will probably remain vulnerable to the winds of politics, trade, intellectual fashion, and the like. And the most realistic chance for greater security would seem to involve further tinkering with the shaky framework of labor law (as in the defeated Labor Law Reform Bill of 1977). Specific suggestions for legal change will be discussed a bit later. First, I would like to clarify why labor law is worth discussing at all, why unions deserve more than passing mention in organizational theory.

---

[120]Elsewhere, he added: "Unionized labor relations, shortsighted demands, greed, and debilitating work rules have been the major contributions to the decline and failure of once healthy industries." (Quotes are from U.S. House Subcommittee on Labor-Management Relations, Failure of Labor Law, 1984: 15). Examples of recent NLRB policies will be provided in the next section.

[121]See also Edwards and Podgursky (1986).

Unions, surely, are not the most noble organizations ever devised. Neither, however, are the corporations that spawned them. There is a certain logic to unions that derives from Madisonian pragmatism. Suppose we were to follow Madison and try to design institutions, taking into account human beings as they are, not as we would like them to be. Madison and the delegates to the Constitutional Convention did not suppose that people were Hobbesian brutes, incapable of selfless acts; but the Framers were practical men (planters, lawyers, merchants, and politicians all) whose wide experience indicated that self-interest was a fairly common motive. Madison's premise that men and women are not angels has held up rather well over the past two hundred years—not only in capitalist societies, where this belief might have self-fulfilling aspects, but in socialist societies premised on more optimistic views of human nature.[122] Government, accordingly, is a necessary evil. It is *necessary* because, unconstrained, self-interested persons may intentionally or inadvertently violate the rights of others. Government is an *evil,* at least potentially, because self-interested persons may wind up running it. And government, therefore, is wisely *limited,* for instance by checks and balances.

Some who accept all this (including, again, many management theorists and many of the staunchest supporters of an economic system based on private interest seeking, limited government, and free markets) would now have us believe a startling proposition: that self-interested persons, when participating in economic organizations, are somehow transformed into cooperative creatures, motivated to peaceably pursue collective goals. At times, perhaps, corporations do have a remarkable civilizing effect on people; but if we take *organizations* as they are, not as we would like them to be, it appears that self-interest remains a common motive and that persons running organizations have often been no more angelic than their governmental counterparts. Consequently, unions also may be necessary evils. They can be necessary to restrain reckless or self-serving corporate factions (such as "dominant coalitions"). They can be evils, since unions too may develop reckless or self-serving elements. But they can be preferable to vesting more oversight powers in reckless or self-serving departments of government.

---

[122]For a discussion of related controversies, see the contributions by Hofstadter, Diamond, and Goldwin in Horwitz (1986).

In sum, unions can contribute to the division of power within organizations and the noncentralization of power within government—effects consistent with the strategic aims of the Framers to avoid tyranny, public or private. Moreover, there may be many tactical advantages of relying on collective bargaining to control current corporate conduct. With respect to occupational health, for example, Bacow outlines reasons why unions could be more effective in guarding workers than state agents like OSHA.[123] Workers typically have more contact with union leaders than agency officials, and more influence over them (through elections). Labor-management negotiators can more readily design work rules tailored to local conditions than can drafters of federal standards. Enforcement procedures differ in important ways: "Collective bargaining agreements are enforced by the workers they are designed to protect, whereas regulations are enforced by relatively disinterested inspectors. The union's presence in the workplace is continual and pervasive; OSHA's is severely limited. Unions can vary and escalate their threats and sanctions; OSHA cannot."[124]

Of course, to say what unions *can* do is not to say what they, in fact, do. And to demonstrate a logic to unions is not to show that they are really institutions worth encouraging. Aren't unions frequently corrupt or obstructionist? Don't they wield monopoly power to secure excess wages for a few at the expense of the many? Why, in any case, should they enjoy special legal protections not afforded to other groups of organizational participants? Let me try to deal with these questions and tie labor unions to some more traditional concerns of organization theorists.

Labor Organizations

Unions have not gotten very good press of late. They are routinely portrayed in the media as greedy and undemocratic. They are often portrayed by academics as either irrelevant or socially harmful. Milton and Rose Friedman, among others, contend that "all of us, including the highly unionized, have indirectly been harmed as con-

---

[123](1980).
[124]Bacow (1980: 57).

sumers by the effect of [restrictive practices and] high union wages on the prices of consumer goods"; "unions were clearly not a major reason for the improvement in the lot of the worker in the United States."[125] Freeman and Medoff, however, have recently assembled quite a bit of evidence that the economic ill effects of unions have been overstated, in contrast to the benefits of unions as channels of employee voice.[126]

What Unions Do

Drawing on many different data sets (e.g., Census and BLS studies, National Longitudinal and Quality of Employment Surveys, NLRB reports, and extensive personal research), Freeman and Medoff find that, in general, unions positively affect productivity, reduce income inequality, and foster workplace democracy—all of which run counter to popular stereotypes. Comparing organized and unorganized workers, the authors find more specifically that unions raise wages (especially for younger workers) and fringes (especially for older workers). At the same time, unions tend to increase firm efficiency by reducing turnover, enhancing work-force skill levels, and prompting more technically rational management. Unions tend to equalize employee income within firms and industries by narrowing the earnings gap between white- and blue-collar workers and by encouraging standardized pay classification plans. Most significantly, unions tend to be representative institutions, responsive to the interests of members, as well as potential members.

Freeman and Medoff argue that "the picture of unions as nondemocratic institutions run by corrupt labor bosses is a myth."[127] Certainly, unions are not exempt from wrongdoing, but they seem no more prone to it than other organizations. Surveys of union members, data indicating frequent changes in leadership, and infrequent (if sometimes sensational) reports of impropriety in elections of officers suggest that members enjoy substantial access to union policy-making machinery—a key aspect of institutional democracy—particularly at the local level. Regarding abuses of power, Freeman and Medoff point

---

[125](1980: 235, 228).
[126](1984).
[127](1984: 22).

out that "while there is still some hand-in-the-till corruption in unions, the amount of union corruption is no more than, and probably
less than, business corruption....Crime involving violence is relatively rare, and it seems to be concentrated in four industries—local
trucking, longshoring, hotel and restaurant, and contract construction."[128] Neither can unions honestly be characterized as public-be-
damned cartels. For instance, strikes, according to Freeman and
Medoff, have small impact on the economy and public at large; costs
fall mainly on direct participants. In the national political arena, unions have been most effective not in securing legislation for their own
benefit, but in promoting the cause of workers generally and the welfare of lower income segments of society:

> As cases in point, the last major piece of legislation regulating collec-
> tive bargaining and unionism, the Landrum-Griffin bill, was enacted
> in 1959 over the vociferous opposition of unions, while...the mild
> 1977 Labor-Law Reform bill strongly favored by unions failed to clear
> Congress. By contrast, organized labor has been active and successful
> in pushing for major pieces of legislation which can be best called "so-
> cial" in nature, such as the Public Accommodation Act of 1964, the
> Civil Rights Act of 1964, the Voting Rights Act of 1965, anti-poverty
> legislation, and the Occupational Safety and Health Act of 1971.[129]

Freeman and Medoff conclude that unions provide "an important voice for some of our society's weakest and most vulnerable
groups, as well as for their own members."[130] This is not to say that unions don't also do nasty things, such as exacting inflated wages or bul-
lying nonunion "scabs." This is not to imply tolerance for crooks,
such as infamous Teamster officials. Harms caused by unions are
rightly condemned, like harms caused by any other organizations.
But, as with other organizations, unions normally do more than
harm. They constitute sources of power for the protection of individual worker rights. By negotiating work rules, they check managerial
privileges to issue arbitrary directives. By establishing grievance-
arbitration systems, they prevent managers from interpreting rules in
their own favor. And by giving employees a voice, an alternative to

---

[128](1984: 220).
[129]Freeman and Medoff (1984: 192).
[130](1984: 5).

voting with their feet, they inhibit injustices in the labor market. Freeman and Medoff ask us to "consider, for example, a firm that decides
to fire senior workers immediately before they become eligible for
pension rights. In the nonunion setting, a firm may be able to get
away with such a maneuver; in a union setting, it is unlikely to have
such power."[131]

Examples of this sort suggest problems with the traditional economic mechanism by which organizations are supposed to register
participant preferences. As described by Hirschman,[132] this economic
mechanism is *exit:* people leave the organization (or refuse to join)
when their expectations are not met. Dissatisfied members quit or
customers stop buying a firm's products, thereby calling attention to
declining organizational performance and the need for corrective
action. Unless firms take such action, they may experience further deterioration, loss of resources, and finally replacement by more effective organizations. Hirschman notes that the exit mechanism is
relatively neat, yielding a simple go/no-go signal that is impersonal,
quantifiable, and consistent with economists' fondness for Invisible
Hands. Exit, however, may be *too* simple. It generally affords little relief to particular people who bear the brunt of organizational
malfeasance—as in the case of workers fired just before acquiring pension rights. Exit is precisely what they would like, and arguably deserve, to avoid.

Hirschman contrasts exit with an alternative feedback mechanism (favored by political vs. economic theorists), which he terms
voice.[133] Applied to firms, customers or members use this option in expressing their dissatisfaction directly to management, its agents, or
outside parties—as in shareholder resolutions, consumer complaints,
employee grievances, and other forms of protest. Voice has a number
of advantages over exit. Hirschman discusses benefits to the organization, such as the ability of quality-conscious and creative participants
(who are often the first to exit) to help management solve problems.
Still more important benefits may accrue to individual participants,
insofar as exit is personally expensive. Hirschman supposes that voice
is more costly, if sometimes more effective, than exit. But more costly

---

[131](1984: 11).
[132](1970).
[133](1970).

to whom? Clearly, things like grievance systems, customer relations departments, and other instruments of voice are costly to the organization. It is unclear, though, whether this cost exceeds the aggregate cost of exit to those separate individuals who would otherwise have to leave the organization to remedy their displeasure (e.g., victims of age discrimination, who would incur costs of job search and lost earnings; drivers of "lemons," who would incur costs of vehicle replacement and excess depreciation; etc.). And it is not clear whether *total* cost considerations are very relevant anyway. Even if voice were more costly altogether than exit, it could be more equitable.

Bear in mind that voice and exit have at least two functions. They give individuals alternative ways of relieving dissatisfaction. And they give organizations alternative ways of obtaining useful performance information. Individuals (i.e., ordinary members or customers) and organizations (i.e., persons who manage them) may not prefer the same option.[134] Of the two, exit and voice, managers have generally preferred exit since it lessens the firm's costs. But this option permits firms to improperly "externalize" system-maintenance costs by shifting these to exiting individuals, who may prefer (and, in fairness, deserve) a voice.

Justification of exit as a preferred feedback mechanism entails some dubious assumptions. Either one must assume that exit is costless for participants or one must accept a utilitarian value judgment: namely, that the short-term sacrifices of exiting participants are out-

---

[134]In fact, managers may wish that other participants had neither option. Hirschman (1970: 124) observes:

[T]he short-run interest of management in organizations is to increase its own freedom of movement; management will therefore strain to strip the members-customers of the weapons which they can wield, be they exit or voice, and to convert, as it were, what should be a feedback into a safety valve. Thus voice can become mere "blowing off steam" as it is being emasculated by the institutionalization and domestication of dissent. . . . And exit can be similarly blunted. . . . [O]rganizations and firms that are ostensibly competing and are normally sensitive to exit can learn to play a cooperative, collusive game in the course of which they take in each other's disgruntled customers or members.

The long-run survival of an organization, on the other hand, and the longer-run strength of an economy depend on some feedback mechanism.

weighed by long-term advantages to future participants (who may benefit from the improved performance of specific organizations or the economy at large). Neither proposition is very attractive. Exiting the organization *is* obviously costly for certain people. And it is *not* obviously right to require these people to subsidize a response mechanism for the sake of organizations or other individuals. Recall the example of sexual harassment mentioned earlier. Students, employees, and other participants may be able to escape practices like sexual harassment by leaving organizations. Their exit may eventually stimulate organizations to tighten up policies, resulting in better treatment of subsequent participants and a fitter system overall. But why should anyone have to leave an organization, at any personal cost, to avoid sexual harassment? Why should the victims of harassment be expected to pay the price of inducing organizational improvements from which others profit? Wouldn't it be more fair to allow victimized participants a means of influence that might improve their own conditions and equalize the cost of keeping organizations responsive? Voice has exactly these effects.

While the cost of exit may fall heavily on persons who leave, the cost of voice to the organization is apt to be shared, to some extent, by all participants. The latter seems more just, despite implications of slightly lower profits for owners, slightly higher prices for consumers, or however else voice instruments are financed. Those who gain from an organization (and stay)—not those who suffer from an organization (and exit)—ought to pay for its upkeep, including the cost of devices that supply valuable performance feedback. It is not that exit is *never* an appropriate feedback mechanism. At times, exit *is* relatively costless for participants, say customers who stop for gas at the corner station. In such situations, the inequity of imposing exit costs on innocent people is not so worrisome. But, as costs of exit increase, so do objections. The more costly exit is to individuals, the more organizations may externalize feedback expense, the more inequity this may cause, and the more appropriate voice becomes. As with other negative externalities, where exit is very costly, legal intervention may be warranted to override market forces that encourage reliance on exit. Dealer relations or labor legislation, which enhance opportunities for voice, are cases in point.

In the case of labor, exit can be costly indeed—for workers with firm-specific skills, for those in remote communities, for those with pensions at stake, etc. It is because of high exit costs that issues of dis-investment and plant closings touched upon previously have stirred so much controversy (controversy traceable, again, to utilitarian claims that the distress of job losers can be offset by dividends to *other* people: job winners or investors or consumers). To workers who find exit costly, and involuntary besides, a voice option is desirable. Voice does not mean the ability to dominate policy making; it does not mean the power to veto plant closings. It implies, rather, the right to state an opinion, to have some say in decisions affecting one's welfare, and to ask for alleviation of personal exit costs (as in calls for job buy-outs funded by those who profit from sudden capital redeployment). In offering such rights, *unions* are primary instruments of voice. As Freeman explains,[135] they not only provide direct channels of communication between workers and management, but they give workers the confidence to use them. Through these channels, through collective bargaining and resulting grievance systems, workers can express discontent usually with less fear of retaliation than unorganized employees. Organized workers, of course, also stand a better chance of being listened to. And, in the process, management obtains better information about employee preferences.

One might grant all this, but still question whether governmental backing of unions is a good idea. Doesn't legislation giving unions special protection undermine the freedom to contract of employers and individual workers? Legitimacy aside, are laws really *necessary* to preserve labor's access to voice? The first question must be deferred until the next chapter, where it can be dealt with in depth. Freedom is a slippery concept that has caused much confusion in theories of contract. In the end, notions of freedom seem to depend on what basic moral rights persons are presumed to have, and rights to a voice in the workplace may be as plausible as any competing rights (e.g., rights to unrestricted accumulation and use of property). With regard to the second question, it does appear, unfortunately, that labor laws are not only necessary to ensure voice in the workplace, but that current U.S. laws are far from adequate for this purpose. This conclusion is supported by recent developments in labor-management relations.

---

[135](1976).

Responses to Unions

The extent of unionization in the United States has declined dramatically since the mid-1950s: from around 39 percent of private sector, nonfarm workers in 1954 to about 24 percent in 1980 and under 20 percent today.[136] This decline is even more striking when viewed against a pattern of rising unionization in other Western nations (and rising unionization among public employees in the United States). It is difficult to account for American trends on the basis of structural changes in employment, such as shifts from manufacturing to service jobs.[137] Many of the same changes have occurred in countries like Canada, where union density has increased.[138] It is also difficult to account for American trends on the basis of attitude changes. Public opinion polls show less approval of unions today than a couple of decades ago; but they show a similar erosion of confidence in business, and a solid majority of Americans still feel that unions are needed to prevent employers from taking advantage of workers.[139] Whether or not managers would take such advantage, most would clearly welcome the demise of unions; and a number of analysts have identified more aggressive managerial opposition as a primary cause of union decline in the United States.[140]

Managerial antagonism toward unions is understandable. Despite their positive effects, unions cost firms money and they complicate administrators' jobs. The productivity gains cited before frequently do not make up for the higher wages of organized workers, and therefore unions tend to reduce company profits (especially monopoly-level profits available to firms in highly concentrated industries).[141] Unions obviously curb managerial authority as well (especially arbitrary uses of authority), limiting one's discretion to fire, discipline, change work rules, etc. In response, employers have

---

[136]Dickens and Leonard (1985).

[137]Farber (1985).

[138]Meltz (1985).

[139]Lipset and Schneider (1983).

[140]E.g., Weiler (1983, 1984); Freeman and Medoff (1984); Rose and Chaison (1985).

[141]Freeman and Medoff (1984).

recently become much more active in discouraging union organization—legally, through hard campaigning in certification elections and, illegally, through dismissal or intimidation of union supporters. The latter tendency is most troubling. Weiler has documented a sharp rise in charges of unfair labor practices against employers over the years.[142] Between 1960 and 1980, such charges increased by 400 percent (from about 7700 to over 31,000), while the number of certification elections remained fairly constant.[143] Evidence is strong that this increase is not due to greater employee propensity to file charges, but to greater employer misconduct. The proportion of charges found meritorious by the National Labor Relations Board also increased significantly between 1960 and 1980, and the number of workers ordered reinstated (because of unlawful termination) jumped from under 2000 to over 10,000. Taking into account the numbers of workers involved in representation elections, Weiler estimates that "the current odds are about one in twenty that a union supporter will be fired for exercising rights supposedly guaranteed by federal law a half-century ago."[144]

One might ask why managers would risk illegal activities and associated sanctions. Freeman and Medoff reply:

> One reason why firing workers for union activity has become increasingly popular is that the penalties for such activities are slight. Employers who are found guilty of firing union workers are forced to reinstate the workers and to pay them limited back pay (the wages they would have received minus whatever income they received on other jobs), often several years later. In addition the employers must post a notice that they will not engage in such illegal activity again. Such notices are jocularly referred to as "hunting licenses"; rather than convincing workers that management will forego such tactics in the future, they warn workers of how far management is willing to go to defeat unionism. Another reason for the growth of illegal management opposition is that it is an exceedingly effective way to chill an organizing campaign.[145]

---

[142](1983).
[143]Up less than 15 percent, from around 6400 to 7300.
[144](1983: 1781).
[145](1984: 233).

The authors argue that an employer's actions in the time period between union filing of a representation petition and actual voting by
workers are critical. By delaying the vote and by vigorously campaigning against the union, management can reduce the odds of union success. By firing instigators, management reduces the union's chances
substantially. Illegal termination of union supporters has the immediate effect of preventing them from casting votes, which could be decisive in a close election; it excludes them from company premises,
where they might campaign effectively; and it may convince enough
others that a union is just not worth the trouble (once more, a small
number of intimidated voters could be decisive).[146] Freeman and Medoff calculate that as much as half of the decline in union organizing
may be due to unfair labor practices by managers in certification elections.[147]

Weiler further notes that, even when unions win elections, employers increasingly are refusing to deal with them.[148] American labor
laws do not require employers to reach agreement with unions on a
contract, but only to bargain in "good faith." Between 1955 and 1960,
86 percent of newly certified bargaining units eventually secured a collective agreement. In 1980, the percentage was only 63 percent; if one
excludes the 10 percent of units in companies having other unionized
workers, newly unionized firms avoided a first contract almost half the
time. Weiler adds: "Combining the certification-victory rates and
first-contract-achievement rates indicates that the ultimate 'yield' for
unions from the overall NLRA representation process had actually
dropped in 1980 to approximately a third of what it was in 1955."[149]

Federal labor laws not only encourage anti-union tactics through
cumbersome representation procedures and minor penalties for foul
play, but through a politicized administrative agency. Responsibility
for enforcing the NLRA lies with the National Labor Relations
Board, which is highly susceptible to partisan influence. During the
Reagan administration, the Board has issued a series of policy rever-
sals strengthening management's hand in transactions with workers
covered by law. NLRB decisions over the past few years have, for ex-

---

[146]See Weiler (1983).

[147](1984).

[148](1984).

[149](1984: 355).

ample, expanded managerial rights to question employees about union sympathies,[150] allowed employers more opportunity to claim "business justifications" for terminating union activists,[151] curtailed the rights of individual employees to challenge unsafe work assignments,[152] and limited the obligation of employers to bargain over various topics.[153]

The point is that labor laws are significant determinants of the degree of unionization and the rights that people subsequently enjoy in the workplace. Without effective enabling legislation, workers may have the will but not the strength to organize in the face of opposition by more powerful employers. Again, a Canadian comparison is relevant. Meltz observes that union membership in Canada and the United States historically followed similar trends until the early 1960s.[154] At that time union density, the percentage of nonfarm workers belonging to unions, stood at about 30 percent in both countries. Since then, however, trends have diverged sharply, American density declining to below 20 percent and Canadian density increasing to almost 40 percent. A prime reason for this disparity is the legal climate for organizing.[155] Compared to American labor law, the Canadian system is more decentralized, with legislation differing from province to province. On the whole, though, Canadian laws are more conducive to unionization; provincial labor codes include, for instance, in British Columbia "provision for the imposition of first agreements in the event of [union-employer] inability to agree on a first contract," "in Quebec an anti-strike-breaking law, and in Ontario the imposition of compulsory dues checkoff for union members and nonmembers."[156] Possibly the most important feature of the Canadian system involves procedures for union certification.

As suggested above, American laws specify a relatively cumbersome process of certification. A union must, first, get prospective members to sign "authorization cards" indicating an interest in rep-

---

[150]*Rossmore House,* 269 NLRB No. 198 (1984).

[151]*Old Tuscon Corp.* 269 NLRB No. 88 (1984).

[152]*Meyers Industries, Inc.,* 268 NLRB No. 73 (1984).

[153]*Milwaukee Spring II,* 268 NLRB No. 87 (1984).

[154](1985).

[155]Rose and Chaison (1985).

[156]Meltz (1985: 323).

resentation. Once the union receives signed cards from 30 percent of the eligible workers, it can petition the NLRB to hold a certification election. For its part, the NLRB reviews the petition, decides on the appropriate bargaining unit, and tries to ensure conditions for a fair election. Meanwhile, union and employer wage vigorous campaigns to win employees' votes. When the election is finally held—usually about two months after the union's petition[157]—the union becomes the employees' official bargaining representative, if so chosen by a majority of those voting. As Weiler reports,[158] this complex process allows much opportunity for intimidation of workers, especially by an employer determined to remain union-free (and especially when the NLRB is sympathetic to such employers). The Canadian approach, in contrast, streamlines the process and reduces incentives to harass union supporters. This approach is, quite simply, to do away with extended election campaigns, which spawn unfair labor practices, and to certify unions on the basis of the authorization cards alone. In most provinces, the responsible labor relations board will certify a union as the bargaining agent for a group of workers once a majority signs cards authorizing the union to represent them. Weiler's experience as chairman of the Labour Relations Board of British Columbia indicates that, under this procedure, organization can be accomplished quickly, confidentially, and free from the sort of managerial interference common in the United States. He concludes: "The antidote to employer intimidation, then, is not a heavy battery of regulations and sanctions, but rather a simple change in the legal environment—a change that by making coercive tactics fruitless, eliminates the temptation to use them."[159]

Unlike proposals to import unique experiments in labor relations from exotic places (such as Mondragon in the Spanish hills), reforms patterned after the Canadian approach are not difficult to envision in the United States. Certainly, the political difficulties of labor reform in America are serious; but there do not appear to be major economic or cultural barriers to adoption of the Canadian system, which has proved workable on a large scale in a society very similar to

---

[157]Weiler (1983).

[158](1983).

[159](1983: 1806). Since 1983, revisions in the British Columbia code have made it less progressive, relative to laws in other provinces.

the American. In fact, the Canadian approach has already gained a foothold in the United States, as Weiler explains:

> In return for the significant monetary concessions granted by the United Auto Workers in the 1982 negotiations, General Motors agreed to recognize the UAW as bargaining agent for production workers in its nonunion plants whenever the UAW presented an independent arbitrator with authorization cards signed by a majority of the employees. . . . Less than six months after the adoption of this procedure, the UAW had secured bargaining rights at three Southern General Motors plants where it had been unsuccessful for the previous six years under the normal NLRB procedure.[160]

The object of legislation, of course, ought not be to guarantee the organization of every GM plant, or to maximize membership in unions, but to give workers a free choice in deciding who, if anyone, will represent them. Weiler finds it hard to see why *employers* should have a say in this choice—why they should have legal rights to participate in the process by which employees elect representatives to deal with them. A card-based certification process has the potential to expand workers' freedom of choice in dealings with both employers *and unions*. Under current U.S. law, employees who wish to get rid of an unresponsive union must follow another cumbersome ritual entailing a formal decertification election. It would be possible, however, to handle decertification as well as certification on the basis of cards alone (or some such written statements of intent, with the outcome determined by the will of the majority in the bargaining unit).[161] A simpler decertification procedure of this type would increase members' control over their union by decreasing their cost of exit. As discussed previously, where exit is not so costly, it is an appropriate response mechanism— perhaps more effective than voice in this situation.

A card-based system of representation, then, is a particularly interesting innovation in that it can simultaneously enhance worker access to voice vis-à-vis employers, and exit vis-à-vis unions, thereby enlarging worker influence over each. It is but one example of a legal

---

[160](1983: 1808).

[161]Canadian law is generally more cautious with regard to decertification. Ontario, for example, requires a decertification election in addition to written statements of opposition to the union.

change that might improve the quality of worklife. There have been many other suggestions for reforming labor law: increased penalties for unfair labor practices, systems for expediting NLRB case handling, first-contract arbitration to help newly certified unions reach agreement with obstinate employers, etc.[162] Debate over the respective merits of these proposals must be left to others, but I hope organization theorists will contribute to it.

My purpose has not been to establish the superiority of any specific reform, like card-based certification. More generally, I have tried to show the validity of questioning prevailing legal rules and resulting authority relations in organizations. Organization theorists have not done much of this. I do not believe the reason is necessarily a conscious desire to defend managerial privileges, but rather a natural reaction to the misdirection involved in received goal-models of organization.

Conclusion

Recall the opening theme: What does it matter, for the design and control of organizations, whether we base theories on individual rights or collective goals? Throughout this chapter, I have illustrated the difference it makes. We saw in the famine case that a focus on production *goals* may emphasize the wrong problem; victims have died because their legal *rights* were not substantial enough to command food. Despite the aggregate level of economic or organizational output, individuals' entitlements to that output are more immediate causes of human well-being and misery. Similar logic may apply to cases of plant shutdowns, worker givebacks, and other distressful events in industrial societies. The implication is that such problems might be addressed, at least in part, through institutional changes that strengthen rights of disadvantaged parties (e.g., through labor unions, which afford workers a voice in job or income losses, and which can lessen exit costs where opposing voices predominate). If organizational changes are blocked by parties in charge, legal changes could sometimes be warranted to overrule them (e.g., labor-law amendments or plant-closing legislation).

---

[162]See Weiler (1984); Cooke (1985).

This line of analysis is foreign to traditional thinking about organizations, which takes for granted the value of collective goals and their prevalence in social systems. Traditional theories also take for granted the legitimacy of managerial authority, since it is often functional for goal attainment (*by definition*, in theories that entrust managers with responsibility for setting "organizational" goals). These theories tend to direct research attention to a narrow set of design questions, having to do with the proper division of labor in organizations. Broader issues, concerning the division of power, are supposed to be for the political process to resolve and political scientists to discuss. But political processes have not settled matters—because, for instance, the American Founders passed the buck with their half-a-loaf plan of government. And political scientists typically look to organizational theory for guidance about what organizations are *for* in the first place.

If one assumes organizations are basically *for* advancement of individual rights, instead of collective goals, a number of distinctive things emerge. The whole point of organizational design is no longer differentiation and integration of duties; we dare now consider how dispersal of power might safeguard participants from exploitation. Managerial authority is no longer unquestioned; we dare now utter words like "union." And the political arena is no longer off-limits to inquiry; we dare now ask whether some organizational problems can have (Good Lord!) governmental solutions.

The sort of inquiry suggested, while different in content, need not be peculiar in method. Nothing here implies abandonment of the no-nonsense empirical work that organizational researchers prize. What is rejected is the mostly nonsense idea that only empirical work of practical value to managers is real administrative science. Freeman and Medoff's studies of what unions do, for example, are as empirical and rigorous as anything produced by mainstream students of organization. And they do have practical value. It happens, however, that their implications are of value to a wider audience than managers:

> All told, if our research findings are correct, the ongoing decline in private sector unionism—a development unique to the United States among developed countries—deserves serious public attention as being socially undesirable. We believe the time has come for the nation to reassess its implicit and explicit policies toward unionism, such as it has done several times in the past. And we hope that such a reassess-

ment would lead to a new public posture toward the key worker institution under capitalism—a posture based on what unions actually do in the society and on what, under the best circumstances, they can do to improve the well-being of the free-enterprise system, and of us all.[163]

One might ask, finally, what *free enterprise* has to do with any of this. Proposals for more governmental protection of workers and unions may seem to show little respect for liberty, or contract. Some have argued against even weak labor legislation on grounds that it deprives persons of freedom to contract on their own terms. Reynolds, for one, claims:

> Federal labor regulations clearly harm liberty. . . . Restrictions on the liberty of employers are obvious, including infringements on their first amendment rights of free speech, their right to offer higher wage rates to their employees (e.g., during a union organization drive), their right to participate in a company-sponsored labor organization, and more generally, their human right to employ people on whatever terms the free marketplace may dictate. Similarly, employees are prevented from accepting voluntary private arrangements that would otherwise be available for the mutual benefit of both themselves and employers.[164]

Notice, though, that liberty appears to be derived from more fundamental concepts, namely, presumed moral rights: rights of speech, rights to set wage rates, etc. In other words, labor laws are coercive to the extent that one accepts a "human right to employ people on whatever terms" the marketplace may dictate. But such a human right is disputable, to say the least. And the liberty of employees, when confronting powerful employers on their own, to enter into any one-sided, take-it-or-leave-it arrangement that comes along is a debatable freedom.

This point is not exactly self-evident, and it is important enough to devote the next chapter to its defense. Freedom is a key but frequently misunderstood concept in contractual theories. Our main interest in this chapter has been the analytic uses of conventional rights. We turn now to uses of moral rights.

---

[163]Freeman and Medoff (1984: 251).
[164](1986: 233).

5. Freedom

Milton and Rose Friedman believe that

> market competition, when it is permitted to work, protects the con-
> sumer better than do the alternative government mechanisms that
> have been increasingly superimposed on the market.... If one store-
> keeper offers you goods of lower quality or of higher price than an-
> other, you're not going to continue to patronize his store. If he buys
> goods to sell that don't serve your needs, you're not going to buy
> them. The merchants therefore search out all over the world the prod-
> ucts that might meet your needs and might appeal to you. And they
> stand back of them because if they don't, they're going to go out of
> business. When you enter a store, no one forces you to buy. You are
> free to do so or go elsewhere. That is the basic difference between the
> markct and a political agency. You are free to choose.[1]

However, Rakoff contends that

> the consumer's experience of modern commercial life is not one of
> freedom in the full sense posited by traditional contract law, but rather
> one of submission to organizational domination, leavened by the abil-
> ity to choose the organization by which he will be dominated....
> Strong competition, far from ameliorating the situation, will only ex-
> acerbate it.[2]

Such are opposing positions in an important debate. While
stated in the extreme, these positions ought not be dismissed as merely
the harangues of right- and left-wing ideologues. The Friedmans' view
has a respectable tradition among thoughtful economists.[3] Rakoff's

---

[1](1980: 222–223).
[2](1983: 1227–1229).
[3]See Knight (1947); Hayek (1960); Buchanan (1969).

view has a respectable tradition among equally thoughtful legal scholars.[4] Moreover, these positions should not be dismissed as trivial arguments over one's degree of freedom at the grocery checkout. Although the debate is frequently conducted in terms of consumer choices, it concerns all sorts of exchanges in modern organizations. It has, for instance, particularly interesting implications for the employment transactions discussed in the last chapter.

The *big* issue is how much freedom people actually enjoy in capitalist markets for goods, services, labor, investment, etc. I do not intend to address this question—it is too big to resolve here. There is a related question, however, that is more manageable and even more basic: How can we tell whether the discrete agreements that comprise market systems, indeed any social systems, are truly free or voluntary? A plausible social-contract theory must have something to say on this score. One of the most objectionable features of contractual approaches, from the seventeenth century to the present day, is their tendency to gloss over the problem of distinguishing voluntary behavior. In this chapter, I will try to show why it is a problem and how it might be dealt with.

The Problem of Freedom

Virtually everyone is in favor of freedom. Freedom has been extolled as a key social value by historic champions of both individual rationality (e.g., Locke) and state supremacy (e.g., Hegel). It is enshrined in various political declarations, both liberal and socialist. And it is invoked to justify all manner of social policies (even conflicting policies, like the legislation or abolition of a minimum wage). Such universal appeal suggests not only that freedom is a fundamental value, but also that it is so vague a value as to mean all things to all people.

With respect to the opening quotes, freedom certainly means something different to the Friedmans and Rakoff. The Friedmans claim that consumers in competitive markets are free in that no one forces them to buy things they do not want at prices they are not will-

---

[4] See Llewellyn (1931); Kessler (1943); Mueller (1969).

ing to pay. Rakoff claims consumers are unfree in that they cannot ordinarily alter the terms (apart from price) of doing business with major firms—terms including disclaimers of liability, limitations of warranty, prerogatives of creditor, and miscellaneous legal boilerplate found in common "contracts of adhesion" (i.e., standardized sales agreements, leases, and other form contracts drafted for the protection of the organization). Both claims have an element of truth; their relative credibility does not hinge on empirical fact but on how one interprets the concept of freedom.

There is a long record of dispute over the real meaning of freedom.[5] The classical liberal view conceives of freedom in a "negative" sense, as the absence of restraint by other people. The American Bill of Rights, for example, enumerates a variety of negative freedoms (of speech, press, religion, assembly, etc.) that are generally immune to restraint by governmental agents. This view has been criticized as too narrow. According to critics, negative freedom *from* interference with public speech, say, may be meaningless without reasonable access to communication media, without the freedom *to* have opinions heard (as held by the U.S. Supreme Court in sanctioning governmental measures to promote fairness in broadcasting).[6]

Theorists have proposed several alternative views of freedom, conceived in a "positive" sense of opportunity *to* act in a certain way. The most extreme conception stems from the organic analogies of social systems fashioned by Plato, Rousseau, Hegel, and their followers. Here freedom is defined as self-mastery, meaning control over one's own impulsive desires and fulfillment of one's proper role in society. Just as uncontrollable action by a part of the body is not true freedom but a symptom of disease, so undirected action by individuals is not true freedom in the social organism but license or anarchy or anomie or something similarly unhealthy. In effect, this view equates freedom *with restraint*, with submission to authority (as in Rousseau's famous

---

[5]Cranston (1953) provides a helpful survey.

[6]*Red Lion Broadcasting Co. v. FCC*, 395 U.S. 367, 377 (1969). The fairness doctrine has remained controversial, of course, since its adoption by the Federal Communications Commission in 1949. It was recently abandoned by the FCC; Congress voted to enact the doctrine into law; President Reagan vetoed the bill; Congressional support continues. Stay tuned.

dictum that one may be "forced to be free")—all of which is a bit far-fetched.[7]

In more moderate views, positive freedom is defined as self-determination or control over one's destiny, rather than self-mastery or control over one's desires.[8] This conception is closer to the classical negative idea—quite close, in fact, to what some modern writers call negative freedom.[9] It differs from the classical idea chiefly in expanding the set of barriers seen to limit freedom. Positive freedom is understood as the absence of a wide range of obstacles to effective choice: not only direct interference by others, but possibly exploitive economic practices, educational disadvantages, physical disabilities, and so forth. Views of this kind have been criticized as too broad. Almost anything can serve as an obstacle to effective choice (given the diversity of conceivable human aims), making positive freedom a potentially hollow concept.[10]

Some theorists, such as MacCallum[11] and Feinberg,[12] have argued convincingly that the traditional distinction between positive and negative freedom is not all that productive. But there is an associated distinction that is well worth pursuing. At the risk of some oversimplification, the main controversy over the nature of freedom can be reduced to the question of which conditions count as genuine impediments to freedom and which constitute mere inabilities to act, choose, or become.[13] Nearly everyone would agree that one is deprived of freedom by an armed robber, but not by the inability to deflect bullets with one's bare hands. Most interesting cases fall somewhere in between, and the problem is where to draw the line. This is a theoretical problem with a great deal of practical significance—for example, for determining criminal or civil liability, and especially for deciding which organizational agreements are *voluntary* contracts, deserving of moral respect, personal commitment, or legal enforcement. (In dis-

---

[7]Berlin (1958); Raphael (1981).
[8]See McCloskey (1974).
[9]E.g., Berlin (1969).
[10]Benn and Peters (1959).
[11](1967).
[12](1973).
[13]Miller (1983).

cussing organizational applications, I will treat "freedom" and "voluntariness" as essentially equivalent concepts.)

Freedom and Organizational Exchange

Corporations and other organizations were described earlier as series of contract-like agreements on rules of behavior (see Chapter 2). These agreements may be formal or informal, explicit or tacit. They are made between various participants at various times. They link together investors, managers, workers, suppliers, distributors, customers, and other parties through exchanges of mutual rights and obligations. *Mutual*, however, does not necessarily imply *equal*. And agreement to organizational rules does not necessarily imply willing, voluntary consent (but need only involve acquiescence in a lesser evil, as Llewellyn[14] observed).

It is often simply assumed that organizational agreements are freely entered into, that business firms in particular rely on voluntary exchange among participants. Hessen, for instance, states that "at every stage throughout its growth, a corporation is a voluntary association, based exclusively on contract."[15] Even social scientists sensitive to power imbalances in organizational exchange have just *defined* exchange between participants as "voluntary transactions...for mutual benefit."[16] In principle, organizational contracts, agreements, or exchanges should be voluntary, but in practice they sometimes are not, as evidenced by the volume of litigation over their validity. Some libertarian writers assert that much of this litigation is misguided; Pilon declares that the courts have "no moral right to intercede on behalf of one of the parties to obtain for him a term that he could not obtain voluntarily from the other party."[17] This view, again, presupposes that agreements *are* voluntary, unless some flagrant procedural defect (e.g., fraud) can be demonstrated. And the crucial question remains: What specific defects do undermine the freedom or voluntariness of contract?

---

[14](1931).
[15](1979a: 43).
[16]Cook (1977: 64).
[17](1979: 1295).

Recent philosophical work on this question has yielded three general approaches to distinguishing voluntary from involuntary transactions. The first specifies that the criterion of voluntary or free behavior is necessarily a *normative*, moral principle concerning the nature of constraints on behavior. Nozick, for example, proposes that one's freedom is compromised by the actions of others, which they have no *right* to perform.[18] Obstacles to choice posed by natural phenomena or by other persons' rightful actions do not reduce one's freedom but, rather, one's ability to choose (say, flying over walking or the choice of a marriage partner). Similarly, Miller proposes that impediments to freedom are those obstacles for which other persons are morally responsible.[19]

Oppenheim, in contrast, typifies a second approach by defining impediments to freedom as obstacles for which others are causally responsible.[20] According to Oppenheim, any constraints attributable to human agency restrict freedom, while restrictions of ability arise from natural events alone. In this approach, the criterion of free or voluntary behavior is a *descriptive*, nonmoral principle.[21] A more sophisticated criterion of this sort is offered by Zimmerman, who suggests that persons restrict the freedom of others by certain objective, coercive acts (to be discussed later).[22]

The third approach is a *consequentialist* one that looks to the outcomes of transactions, instead of the types of constraints on the participants, in assessing freedom or voluntariness. Consequentialist principles may have both descriptive and normative features. They identify an empirical or potentially measurable social result that is presumed to represent a "good" state of affairs. Utilitarian (e.g., greatest happiness) and economic (e.g., minimum transaction-cost) criteria are illustrative; but perhaps the most persuasive example is Kronman's[23] use of a Rawlsian difference-principle as the criterion of voluntary exchange (explained below).

---

[18](1974).

[19](1983).

[20](1985).

[21]At least proponents assume that such a criterion can be descriptive in character. Nonmoral accounts of causality are problematic, though, and nonmoral accounts of coercion are troublesome indeed, as we shall see.

[22](1981).

[23](1980).

It is instructive to look more closely at typical views in each category. I will argue that the first approach is ultimately the most satisfactory. However, we can learn quite a lot from theorists who disagree.

Consequentialist Approach

In response to libertarian theories, which emphasize moral (property) rights as the basis of free exchange, Kronman tries to show that "the idea of voluntary agreement . . . cannot be understood except as a distributional concept."[24] In other words, whether an agreement is voluntary or not (and whether it merits legal enforcement or not) depends on its consequences, on how it allocates benefits among the contracting parties. This is contrary to traditional beliefs that the voluntariness of an agreement depends on its antecedents, on how it was reached. Kronman submits that, if one focuses only on the process by which an agreement is made, it is difficult to formulate a non-controversial principle for distinguishing voluntary from coercive bargains.

Imagine that I purchase a used car from an auto dealer and comply with ritual procedures, such as signing a sales contract. Is my purchase voluntary? Maybe, maybe not. There are circumstances under which I could reasonably claim coercion. Some obvious circumstances would involve use of physical force (the dealer's partner, Mongo, twists my arm until I sign) or threats (Mongo proposes to leave with my kids if I leave without the car). Although I could choose to walk away from the deal (armless or childless), few rational persons would do so and few would consider my agreement under the circumstances to be voluntary.

There are other conditions that may render my agreement involuntary; force or threats by themselves are rather arbitrary criteria of coercion. Suppose that, instead of employing physical intimidation, the dealer lies to me about the car, either in word (he claims, falsely, that the engine has recently been rebuilt) or in effect (he has turned back the odometer from 89,000 miles to 29,000). Such acts of deception are perhaps not quite as coercive as acts of physical force. Still,

---

[24](1980: 474).

most people would want to include them as impediments to voluntariness; even extreme libertarians have been so inclined.[25] Why, now, draw the line at explicit misrepresentation? Suppose that the dealer just misleads me (he truthfully states that the car had only one previous owner but avoids mentioning that the owner was Hertz) or withholds information (he does not inform me of a transmission defect) or merely capitalizes on my ignorance (he neglects to point out the unreliability of GM engines modified to run on diesel fuel). Cases of this sort are more problematic. Purchases under these conditions of nondisclosure might seem to entail an increasing degree of voluntariness, compared to cases of deliberate deception;[26] yet, it is hard to say exactly why they should be treated differently.

It could be argued that, in situations involving no explicit misrepresentation, I have myself to blame for jumping to conclusions and failing to take precautions (such as arranging for an independent inspection, which may reveal things like unusual wear, transmission defects, or maintenance problems). But it is not clear why the burden of self-protection should fall on the buyer here and not in cases of deception, or physical intimidation for that matter. One supposed reason might be that buyers cannot prevent the latter events. However, people can insure themselves against almost any eventuality. As Kronman notes,[27] one can take precautions against misrepresentation by insisting on (or purchasing) specific guarantees and even against force or threats by hiring a bodyguard. When buying a used car, such measures may be no more impractical than the prevention of stupidity. Another possible reason for treating deception or intimidation differently from nondisclosure may be simply that *active* advantage-taking is by nature more exploitive than *passive*. But this rule does not hold up either. A dealer who misinforms me that a car has rustproofing is not necessarily more exploitive than one who fails to mention a serious mechanical defect.

In determining the voluntariness of exchange, then, on what ba-

---

[25]E.g., Pilon (1979).

[26]The *Restatement (Second) of Contracts* states: "If the other is indolent, inexperienced or ignorant, or if his judgement is bad or he lacks access to adequate information his adversary is not generally expected to compensate for these deficiencies" (quoted in Fried, 1981: 82–83).

[27](1980).

sis do we decide that sellers may make the most of certain advantages over buyers (like superior intelligence), but not other advantages (like superior physical strength)? Going beyond elementary sales cases, how do we decide when *any* organizational participants (e.g., employers) may legitimately exploit *any* advantages (e.g., superior economic resources) in driving a bargain?

Kronman contends that there is no inherent difference between the exploitation of various advantages, no objective feature of exchange transactions that enables us to sort out legitmate (noncoercive) from illegitimate (coercive) uses of personal resources. We do frequently, and properly, distinguish coercive deals involving use of superior force from noncoercive deals involving use of superior information; but the grounds for making such a distinction must be an ethical premise, according to Kronman, not a descriptive criterion of "voluntary behavior."

Kronman rejects, as too controversial, ethical premises incorporating moral rights (i.e., persons have the right to exploit information but not physical strength). And he believes the most compelling premise is that voluntary transactions should result in beneficial outcomes for both parties. In other words, the exploitation of a given advantage is noncoercive and permissible if it works to the long-run benefit of the disadvantaged party, but not otherwise. Kronman admits that this principle might have questionable applicability in some individual cases, and he claims that it should be interpreted as a general rule, requiring merely that "most people" would benefit in the long run from transactions in which other parties exploit particular advantages. Thus, transactions based on force would tend to be disqualified, since weaker persons would not ordinarily benefit from them. However, transactions based on exploitation of information would often qualify as voluntary, since they may encourage investment in knowledge acquisition and thereby work to the long-term benefit of even poorly informed parties.

Kronman's analysis is convincing, up to a point. It demonstrates the ambiguity of the voluntariness concept and the arbitrariness of certain purely empirical definitions. It yields a principle that fits many of our intuitive judgments about whether transactions are voluntary or coercive. And it is certainly an improvement on other consequentialist approaches entailing principles of simple economic efficiency (which principles do not take outcome distribution into consideration). But Kronman's principle can have some very counterintuitive implications, as he acknowledges, and these count heavily against its practical value.

The principle of benefit-to-the-least-advantaged-party does not *flatly* rule out the use of force, for instance. This would not be a strange implication for a principle of justice, or efficiency, or some other general social virtue; but it is an odd implication for a principle of voluntary exchange. There are situations in which most people could benefit in the long run from forced transactions. It might even be rational for people to voluntarily grant a monopoly of force to designated agents, for example, elected state officials, in order to ensure beneficial transactions: payment of taxes for the common defense, public services, and the like. Yet, despite the prospective benefits of these transactions for most people, *some* persons might view their compliance as very *in*voluntarily (especially on April 15th). Organizational cases of this kind are rather common because, as Olson observes, "large or latent groups have no tendency voluntarily to act to further their common interests."[28] Groups must therefore rely either on selective incentives or compulsion to secure collective benefits. As in societal cases, compulsory arrangements may benefit most group members in the long run (e.g., members of union shops), but they may nonetheless be coercive (at least to free-riders).

In sum, while benefical outcomes might serve to *justify* compulsory practices like governmental taxation or union security agreements, they do not necessarily make such practices *voluntary*. And what Kronman seems to offer is a principle of justification—a rough rule of social justice[29]—not a means of determining the voluntariness of specific transactions. All consequentialist principles share this tendency to measure some overall social good apart from interpersonal freedom. Freedom or voluntariness appear to depend on something more than just the *outcomes* of transactions (whether evaluated in terms of cost efficiency or efficiency plus distribution). Were nothing else involved, Fried remarks, litigation concerning the validity of contracts might be greatly simplified "if courts sometimes took it upon themselves to decide particular cases on an ad hoc basis, free of the constraints of pre-

---

[28](1965: 165).
[29]After Rawls (1971).

existing convention."[30] He adds, "But courts generally do not operate on such an ad hoc basis, and they rarely admit it if they do—which tells powerfully against theses such as Kronman's."

Fried argues that the way transactions come about, their conformity with established conventions of bargaining, cannot be ignored in deciding questions of voluntariness. Most philosophers and legal scholars would probably agree, but differ sharply over whether these conventions themselves presuppose moral criteria of freedom.

Descriptive Approach

A number of theorists have tackled the problem Kronman dismisses as intractable: that of devising a descriptive, nonmoral criterion of free or voluntary exchange. Recent work has focused largely on the reverse problem of operationalizing the concept of coercion. The notion of coercion directs attention to the sort of procedural concerns that consequentialist views neglect (prior restrictions of choice); and it gets at the basic question of freedom identified earlier (Which conditions count as impediments to freedom and which constitute mere inabilities to act or choose?). Perhaps theorists have also been drawn to coercion in the belief that it is somewhat easier to describe than volition; however, it has proved to be every bit as tricky.

In most interpersonal transactions, oné person's choice is motivated to some extent by inducements provided by others. In cases of coercion, inducement reaches the point where one is compelled to act against his or her will. The object is not necessarily to describe this point very precisely, but to specify criteria that produce no zany results in classifying coercive situations. Particularly problematic situations entail offers that bear some resemblance to threats. And much theoretical analysis has lately centered on ways of distinguishing (coercive) threats from (noncoercive) offers.

An early investigation along these lines is reported by Nozick.[31] His approach looks to be a descriptive one, although it is so loaded with qualifications that it's difficult to be absolutely sure (and Nozick switches to a purely moral approach in later work).[32] Nozick suggests

---

[30](1981: 84).
[31](1969).
[32]See Nozick (1974).

that the difference between threats and offers concerns how a person proposes to alter the consequences of another's behavior. In general, if a proposal "makes the consequences of [another's] action worse than they would have been in the normal and expected course of events, it is a threat; if it makes the consequences better, it is an offer."[33] To illustrate, a highwayman worsens a traveler's (normal and expected) consequences by proposing "your money or your life"—and thus issues a threat—whereas an employer betters an unemployed worker's (normal and expected) consequences by proposing a job in return for pay—and thus issues an offer.

Nozick does not rely on a consequentialist principle, since he deals not just with after-the-fact outcomes but with the manipulation of consequences by parties prior to an agreement. Nor does he seem to fall back on a moral principle, since the baseline for judging whether consequences are made better or worse—that is, the "normal and expected course of events"—has an empirical nature. Nozick mentions that "normal and expected" can mean either *empirically predicted* or *morally required*; but he states that, should these two not coincide, the appropriate baseline is the course of events *preferred* by the recipient of a proposal. The result is a mostly descriptive standard.

Unfortunately, Nozick's principle fails to properly distinguish even some unproblematic cases, as noted by several critics.[34] Suppose, for example, that a butcher usually sells me a cut I enjoy at $Y per pound (the normal and expected course of events). If the butcher raises his price to $Y+y, he worsens my consequences and, according to Nozick's formula, his offer becomes a coercive threat—he will withhold meat unless I come up with an extra y, which sounds peculiar. In attempting to correct Nozick's formula for such anomalies, Zimmerman presents what may be the soundest descriptive approach to be found in the coercion literature.[35]

Like Nozick, Zimmerman contends that a person, P, threatens another person, Q, by issuing a proposal that worsens Q's consequences, relative to some baseline course of events. Zimmerman, though, assumes the baseline course of events to be not what P normally does (e.g., sell meat at $Y per pound) but *"what Q would be able to*

[33]Nozick (1969: 447).

[34]See Frankfurt (1973); Lyons (1975); Zimmerman (1981).

[35](1981). Frankfurt, Lyons, and others join Nozick in eventually abandoning nonmoral criteria.

do for himself if P had not made his proposal"[36] (e.g., buy $X worth of food from anyone else wishing to sell). This is an important modification that throws ordinary price hikes into the noncoercive, offer category, where they appear to belong.

To handle different cases that have proved troublesome for descriptive approaches, Zimmerman adds another important qualification. He argues that some *offers* can be coercive if, prior to the offer, P places Q in a situation where Q can do little for himself. Imagine, for instance, that a nineteenth-century mill owner, A, buys up surrounding farm land and turns it to pasture, thus depriving tenant farmers of a livelihood. If the owner subsequently proposes to give the former tenants factory jobs, at subsistence wages, his proposals are genuine offers, since they improve the farmers' bleak prospects. Nevertheless, they are coercive on Zimmerman's account, since the mill owner caused the bleak prospects. In contrast, a nearby owner, B, who had no hand in the farmers' plight but simply exploited it by making similar employment offers, would not act coercively.

Zimmerman, then, asks us to compare the situation facing the recipient of a proposal before it is made, the "pre-proposal situation," to the situation he or she faces after the proposal is made, the "proposal situation." A proposal is coercive if (1) the recipient (strongly) prefers the pre-proposal situation to the proposal situation, or if (2) the maker prevents the recipient from enjoying other pre-proposal situations that would be (strongly) preferred to the proposal situation. Condition 1 represents a threat, condition 2 a coercive offer.

Compared to other descriptive principles, Zimmerman's formula deals successfully with a wide variety of routine cases. However, it still seems to deal rather arbitrarily with more problematic ones. Consider the previous factory example. Zimmerman's suggestion that an owner may grossly exploit workers without coercing them is highly questionable. Lyons comments:

> Suppose B [a factory owner who does not cause worker Q's vulnerability to exploitation] hires Q, makes Q do hard, degrading, unhealthy work for long hours, for a bare subsistence wage. What's more, B enjoys snapping orders to Q on the job, to make him jump. Of course, then B is forcing Q to undergo this humiliation! Of course he's using

---

[36](1981: 126).

coercion to extort these degrading performances from Q. Of course B is undermining, limiting Q's freedom.[37]

Clearly, owner A, who creates Q's vulnerability by driving him off the land, is more of a rascal than B, who just stands by and takes advantage of the situation. But this does not absolve B from coercion. While B does not decide that Q must leave farm for factory, B decides what conditions Q must work under, B decides to treat Q like a beast of burden, and B's decisions appear sufficiently unilateral to be called coercive.

Zimmerman's formula is subject to a crucial ambiguity: In distinguishing coercive offers, what is to count as "prevention" of a preferred pre-proposal situation? Zimmerman claims that prevention entails the active posing of obstacles to another's action, not merely failures to assist, and he attempts to clarify with another example:

> Suppose P quietly corners the market in penicillin and then offers to sell some to the infected Q at an outrageously high price. Is this just a case of monopolistic exploitation, or is P to be counted as preventing Q from having any of the commodity on better terms, and therefore as coercing him? I am inclined to say that this monopolist does coerce his customer. Contrast this with a case of "natural monopoly" in which all the penicillin in the world, except for P's, is simultaneously destroyed through no action of P, and he then charges the same outrageously high price. Here I am inclined to say that P exploits but does not coerce his customer.[38]

As Alexander notes,[39] the implied distinction is not so clean. Monopolists under both conditions actively prevent preferred pre-proposal situations—e.g., simple appropriation of the drug by Q. Any monopolist would presumably have to rely on personal force or some police power to prevent Q from just taking what he needs. Zimmerman responds that this kind of prevention does not count.[40] He fails to explain why not but, rather, falls back on the assertion that how a monopoly was *originally* acquired is more relevant than how it is perpetuated: that is, "P prevents Q [at time t] from obtaining some scarce

---

[37] (1981: 13).
[38] Zimmerman (1981: 137).
[39] (1983).
[40] (1983).

resource on his own if *P acted before t* to acquire all of the resource. If, on the other hand, *P* enjoys a natural monopoly [through chance, bequest, etc.], then *P* merely refrains from giving or merely prevents *Q* from taking, and is thus merely an exploiter."[41]

Such assertions look not only like *ad hoc* stipulations, but they look to contradict Zimmerman's interpretation in other cases. His notion of coercive offers was devised specifically to handle cases where *P* exercises seemingly wrongful control over *Q*—e.g., *Q* is a slave, *P* a slaveholder—and *P* proposes to loosen control in exchange for some service. Zimmerman wishes to sustain the coerciveness of these proposals without calling them threats (which would strain the imagination) or without referring to "wrongful" control (which involves a moral element). Hence, he talks of coercive offers wherein *P*, the slaveholder, prevents *Q*, the slave, from enjoying preferred situations, such as freedom from physical domination. In such cases, however, Zimmerman says that how slavery originally came about is *less* relevant than its perpetuation: "The slave-owner's proposal counts as coercive even if he did not do the original enslaving."[42] Here, it *does* count as prevention of a preferred situation if *P* merely refrains from giving *Q* what he wants or merely prevents *Q* from taking it. Zimmerman, again, fails to explain why cases of physical domination should be treated so unlike cases of economic domination.

In the end, Zimmerman's approach appears to incorporate a pseudo-descriptive criterion (prevention of a preferred situation) that can mean whatever one likes—whatever is necessary to produce conclusions that fit one's intuitions about the coerciveness of particular cases. Zimmerman's conclusion that slavery and monopoly should be treated differently may be reasonable, but the point is that this conclusion does not follow from his "descriptive" principle. It follows from different interpretations of his principle, which interpretations may conceal normative presuppositions. For instance, if one presupposes that a practice, such as slavery, violates persons' rights both at its inception and through its perpetuation, then it seems natural to view both inception and perpetuation as acts that prevent preferred situations and coerce. If, however, one presupposes that a practice, such as monopoly, violates persons' rights only at its inception, then it seems

---

[41]Zimmerman (1983: 168–169).
[42](1981: 136).

natural to view its inception, but not its perpetuation, as an act that prevents preferred situations and coerces. I suggest that moral presuppositions of this sort underlie Zimmerman's analysis.

The reason for looking at Zimmerman's scheme in some detail is that it represents a relatively well-developed descriptive approach. And it illustrates the tendency of these approaches to hide, rather than avoid, moral conceptions. Further development might one day yield other descriptive principles that are less objectionable. But I think this is unlikely. Over fifty years ago, Frank Knight argued that objective, nonmoral criteria of coercion or free exchange are illusions.[43] Knight did not *prove* that volitional criteria are necessarily normative. I don't know if "proof" is possible. Yet, it is safe to say that theorists have chased the vision of value-neutrality over the past half century without making obvious progress.

Normative Approach

According to the final approach to be considered, freedom, voluntariness, and coercion are all basically normative concepts. This does not mean that they have *no* descriptive content, but that they cannot be completely specified in empirical terms. They are dependent to some extent on moral judgments.

It will not do to directly associate freedom or coercion with very general, good/bad, moral values. Knight apparently had something like this in mind:

> Scrutiny of any typical case of unfree behavior reveals that the coercive quality rests on an ethical condemnation, rather than the ethical condemnation on a factually established unfreedom.... We say that the victim of a highwayman is coerced, not because the character of his choice between the alternatives presented is different from any other choice, but because we think the robber does "wrong" in making the alternatives what they are.[44]

Surely, though, a policeman may not do "wrong" in apprehending a criminal yet still act coercively.[45] As mentioned in connection

---

[43](1929).
[44](1929: 10–12).
[45]Dworkin (1968).

with consequentialist approaches, we cannot simply equate freedom with goodness, justice, or overall ethical approval of an act, since some decent transactions may be coercive and some lousy ones may not be (e.g., extremely dangerous wagers made just for fun). Whatever moral evaluation is involved in identifying coercion, Dworkin maintains, it must be "more subtle and complex than the judgment that what is happening is wrong."[46]

In line with our conclusions concerning Zimmerman's theory, the kind of subtle judgments entailed in ideas of freedom or coercion might best be expressed in the language of individual moral rights. Several theorists have taken this position. Nozick, for example, states that whether I am coerced or not depends on whether others act within their rights in influencing my choice.[47] Only if they do *not* is my resulting action nonvoluntary. Fried explains that a robber lacks the right to offer me my life in exchange for my money and therefore coerces, whereas a retailer does have the right to offer me a can of peas in exchange for 39 cents and thus does not coerce.[48] Such views have drawn much critical response,[49] but they have plausible aspects and furnish useful points of departure for devising a workable normative approach.

A right-based approach to volition not only reflects many of our commonsense convictions (toward, say, Fried's robber or retailer), but it accords well with more or less settled judicial opinions about duress in contractual dealings, voluntariness in criminal plea bargaining, and other legal questions.[50] It also accounts for some persistent *disputes* over the voluntariness of specific cases. Consider disagreements over the effect of minimum wage legislation on freedom of contract. If an employer in the United States were able, legally, to hire an unskilled worker at $1 per hour, would this transaction be coercive? Some liberals would think so, believing that a worker's consent to such a low wage must arise from desperation and be less than voluntary. Some libertarians would think otherwise. Is a similar transaction at $3.35 per hour (the current legally prescribed minimum) coercive? Some

---

[46](1968: 229).
[47](1974).
[48](1981).
[49]See Scanlon (1976); Cohen (1979); Reiman (1981).
[50]Werthiemer (1979).

libertarians would think so, believing that an employer's consent to a
state-imposed rate above what the parties could reach on their own
must be less than voluntary. Some liberals would think otherwise. At
bottom, one's stand on the issue will depend on what moral rights persons are presumed to have—and on the assumed priority of those
rights. If one grants priority to property rights, the fixing of wages at
$3.35 by legislators will tend to be seen as a coercive restriction on the
use of capital. If one gives priority to welfare rights, the fixing of wages
at $1 by employers (alone or jointly in markets) will tend to be seen as
a coercive restriction on personal well-being. To resolve such differences, we would most likely have to fall back not on some deeper notion of freedom but on yet more basic moral rights.

The bedrock moral rights upon which *real* freedom rests may not
be easy to uncover. This does not imply that they do not exist; I will
suggest some candidates presently. My purpose here, however, is not
to argue for any particular basic rights that might ultimately reconcile
divergent conceptions of freedom. My intent is to show that freedom
is problematic and to indicate a way of understanding statements
about freedom. Freedom, I propose, is an "essentially contested" concept,[51] *whose meaning is relative to observers' preconceptions of fundamental human rights.* In other words, freedom is not a commodity or objective
good, like income, that is pretty much the same stuff wherever it
comes from and whatever currency it is measured in.[52] It is an abstract
concept, more like quality-of-life, that refers to a lot of different things
lumped together under some general unifying theme: under quality-
of-life, we can lump enjoyment of wealth, health, etc.; under freedom,
enjoyment of various individual rights. In applying such concepts,
people may disagree over what things count and how much (though
there may be a nonrelativistic basis for evaluating separate components, e.g., the justice of wealth holdings or the validity of rights
claims). This subjective view of freedom avoids a controversial feature
of Nozick's theory[53]—namely, his pre-commitment to property

---

[51]Gallie (1956); Connolly (1983).

[52]Dworkin's (1978) argument against the commodity idea of freedom is especially persuasive; see his Chapter 12: "What Rights Do We Have?" He rejects a
right "to something called liberty as such" in favor of rights to specific liberties that
may be independent of one another.

[53](1974).

rights—without being merely evasive. It is enough for a theory to explain both the stability of certain judgments about freedom (as in cases of physical threats, where most people agree on rights) and the variability of other judgments (as in cases of wage fixing, where people disagree on rights). A theory of freedom need not produce conclusive judgments of its own in each and every case.

On the other hand, a credible theory should not produce very counterintuitive judgments. Consequentialist and descriptive views were criticized earlier for generating counterintuitive results, and a theory that ties freedom to moral rights could be vulnerable on this score as well. Not just any moral right will help to distinguish freedom and coercion, but only special types, commonly called *human rights*. The trouble with garden-variety moral rights is that they can be invoked to justify almost anything short of gross misconduct. In effect, they are roughly equivalent to "good reasons" for behavior. And, as such, they present the same problem as other broad ethical criteria of freedom: There are sometimes good reasons for coercion. It is reasonable to suppose that state agents have moral as well as legal rights to detain and prosecute murderers, thieves, and other wrongdoers. It is nonsense to suppose that they carry out these rightful activities of law enforcement without coercing anyone. Theorists advocating right-based views have tried to deal with this problem in various ways, none entirely successful.[54] A focus on human rights may resolve the difficulty.

Human rights are defined by Feinberg as "moral rights of a fundamentally important kind held equally by all human beings, unconditionally and unalterably."[55] Classical examples are rights to life, trial by jury, and others set forth in famous political declarations as universal and inalienable. The unique rights of state agents to enforce the law would not qualify. Terms like "unconditional," "unalterable," and "inalienable" are meant to convey that human rights are somehow *permanent* entitlements, not subject to cancellation or sale, not contingent on one's social status, role, etc. These terms need not, however, mean that human rights are *absolute*, that they are unlimited in application. Indeed, few if any rights could be absolutely exceptionless.

---

[54]See, e.g. VandeVeer (1977); Wertheimer (1979); Ryan (1980).
[55](1973: 85).

One's right to life, for instance, might conflict with another's right to life, and thus even this right may be liable to limitations.

Justified limitations of human rights are often explained by pointing out the "prima facie" nature of these rights.[56] The idea of prima facie rights involves, first, a presumption that the rights in question are always to be respected and, second, the recognition that they may nonetheless be overridden in unusual circumstances. This idea does not undermine the priority of fundamental human rights, so long as it is only other human rights (and not utilitarian considerations) that are seen as legitimate overriding factors. Extending Dworkin's trump analogy,[57] prima facie human rights might function somewhat like trumps in a game of pinochle. Special cards remain trumps, outranking any other suit played, but they may come into conflict with trumps held by others. In such situations, they may give way to higher trumps or (because there are duplicates of each card in pinochle) to another's identical trump. Similarily, human rights may be overridden by more basic human rights or by a human right of the same "face value." While not sure winners, an ace of trump or a prima facie right to life are still genuine trumps or rights, hardly trivial things to hold.

In the affairs of people, of course, the defeat of a trump *is* trivial compared to defeat of a right. As Melden remarks,[58] the overriding of a human right, even where unavoidable and justified, represents a *tragic* situation. Persons who believe in a human right to life might regard a variety of infringements as justified: perhaps capital punishment, taking an assailant's life in self-defense, or killing enemy soldiers in battle. But these are not happy events. Melden notes that, no matter how necessary or excusable, damage is done to someone when a human right is infringed. This damage is acknowledged in feelings of guilt or at least regret over the infringement of a recognized human right. And it is reflected in ordinary usage of the word *coercion*—which can be applied to any such infringement, legitimate or not.

Viewing coercion as dependent on the infringement of a human right has a number of advantages. It handles the main objection to a normative theory of freedom, that coercion is not always wrong. At

---

[56]Frankena (1955); Vlastos (1962); McCloskey (1984).

[57](1978).

[58](1977).

the same time, it is consistent with our intuition that coercion, if sometimes warranted, is normally bad. It deals successfully with specific cases that have proved troublesome for other moral conceptualizations, for example, the incarceration of criminals. If we assume that persons in general have a right not to be caged or locked up, if we assume that this is a human right which cannot be forfeited, then locking people up will constitute coercion—regardless of whether the keyholders are duly authorized jailers (and morally justified) or plain terrorists (and not justified). This approach explains why the term "coercion" is commonly, and properly, applied in both situations.

Finally, awareness that freedom and coercion are derivative concepts, subordinate to notions of human rights, may help us to better understand some disputed cases. Let me illustrate a few implications concerning employment transactions.

Implications

Nozick, in a much debated analogy, compares employment choices to one's choice of a marriage partner.[59] One cannot choose any partner one wishes; selection is limited by the rightful choices of others. These choices, while reducing one's options (possibly to the extent that alternatives are very unattractive), do not reduce the voluntariness of one's eventual marriage decision. Likewise, Nozick argues, rightful choices of others in the marketplace may reduce one's options for earning a living, but these do not make an unattractive wage bargain coercive. This conclusion has met with some skepticism.[60] Whether our sympathies lie with Nozick or his critics will depend on what we consider "rightful" under the circumstances and especially what *human* rights we are prepared to accept.

Most would agree with Nozick's analysis of the marriage case, because no plausible human rights are apt to be infringed in his envisioned market for partners. There have occasionally been some extraordinary things demanded in the name of human rights, but never have I heard anyone claim the right to an alluring mate. Few would

---

[59](1974).

[60]Scanlon (1976); Cohen (1979); Reiman (1981).

find coercive a marriage contract that failed to guarantee prescribed levels of excitement, status, wealth, or happiness (though a contract that allowed abusive treatment could well be coercive). Employment is another story. As suggested above, it is not unusual to suppose that workers have human rights to certain levels of income or well-being; and people might, on that account, find coercive many unattractive employment contracts.

In parts of the United States, for instance, some very unattractive contracts are entered into by migrant farmworkers. Employment arrangements are typically made with a crew leader, an independent labor contractor who, in turn, arranges with growers to supply labor for harvesting specified crops. For his part of the bargain, the crew leader may provide workers with transportation to a labor camp, wage advances to cover expenses en route, food and alcohol on site, spot credit or small loans when needed, and a piece-rate wage for fieldwork performed. Friedland and Nelkin show that such services act to enhance the control and income of the crew leader.[61] The leader's ownership of available transportation limits workers' mobility once they are hired; wage advances place migrants in debt before they begin working (which may be several days after arrival in camp); goods sold on site can cost far more than elsewhere; loans and charges must often be repaid in unitemized amounts, determined by the crew leader alone; and piece-rate compensation leaves workers to bear the expense of weather delays, equipment breakdowns, poor fields, and other problems. The work itself is unpleasant and exhausting: for example, hard-paced stoop labor under adverse conditions (under a hot sun, in contact with toxic pesticides, etc.). Labor camps offer equally dismal living conditions: for example, primitive sanitation and dilapidated housing (frequently lacking windows, heat, or indoor plumbing). As Dunbar and Kravitz document, wages are so low that some parents must put their children to work to make ends meet—and even then may barely earn enough to pay off indebtedness to the crew leader.[62] Continual downward pressure on wages is exerted by a steady stream of illegal migrants, trying to escape even worse conditions to the south and willing to work for almost anything. According to the U.S. Com-

---

[61] (1971).
[62] (1976).

mission on Civil Rights, the most desperate work without knowing their wage at all.[63]

Just how willing migrant farmworkers *are* is an open question. One worker states:

> I take my children north for the purpose to help me work. No, it's not good, but I don't have any choice because I don't make any money down here.[64]

Another explains the nature of choices sanctioned as forms of free enterprise:

> The free enterprise system works real good if you got money, education, or profession.... Now remember, the farm worker hasn't got money, we don't got profession many times, and we don't got education. So, by free enterprise, if I'm more hungry than you, I got to work cheaper than you.[65]

Deals in which one party's degree of hunger has a major (negative) effect on wages and working conditions seem rather unfree. They seem so, at any rate, to many citizens of liberal democracies, all of which have extensive regulations intended to reduce economic coercion. Are not these state regulations, however, themselves coercive, as libertarians like Nozick contend? Maybe so, at least in part; but it does not follow that states are the *only* or *most* coercive social institutions.

The mistake libertarians—and liberals—tend to make is to assume they have a corner on liberty. There is a wide variety of possible human rights. There is a wide variety of ways in which these rights might be infringed by individuals, organizations, governments, and economic systems. There is, consequently, widespread potential for coercion in social life. It is conceivable that both state restrictions on employment bargains and unrestricted labor agreements may infringe someone's human rights and be coercive. (The former could infringe farmers' rights to personal property, as libertarians claim; the latter could infringe farmworkers' rights to personal well-being, as liberals claim). In such cases, it is profitable to debate which are authentic human rights and which should take precedence when rights come into

---

[63](1978).
[64]Quoted in Dunbar and Kravitz (1976: 111).
[65]Quoted in Dunbar and Kravitz (1976: 1).

conflict. What is not profitable is to take human rights for granted: to presume that debates over human rights can be avoided in deciding questions of freedom or to presume that only a very narrow set of human rights can have any validity—e.g., eighteenth-century "natural" rights to life, property, or (of all things) liberty itself.

Machan illustrates a typical narrow view in asserting:

> Government regulation is wrong in principle because any bona fide instance of it...infringes upon human liberty, something to which everyone has a natural right, including members of the business and professional community, who are most thoroughly regulated.[66]

An alleged human right to liberty is highly suspect if, as proposed here, liberty cannot be defined independently but only in terms of other human rights. A right to liberty would mean, literally, a right not to have one's rights infringed, from which it is impossible to draw inferences about government regulation, or anything else. Theorists manage such inferences, of course, by ultimately invoking some more specific rights that regulation does appear to infringe (usually, property rights). What is most dangerous about this practice is not what is smuggled *into* the idea of liberty, but what is left *out*. Theorists tend to exclude enjoyment of rights that have inconvenient policy implications (e.g., welfare rights, which might support regulation) and, when pressed for justification, argue against such rights on grounds that their protection would impair liberty—which is about as circular as an argument can get. Though Nozick has been much criticized for this sleight of hand,[67] it is also employed by his opponents who advocate government intervention in the labor market. Preston maintains that capitalist market exchanges should be restricted since *they* are likely to infringe human liberty.[68] What they really infringe are assumed worker rights to basic resources. What of acquired property rights? These are rejected because their protection would impair liberty; and so the dance goes on.

The point is that theorists across the ideological spectrum are quick to perceive the coerciveness of some institutions that infringe some preferred rights. Yet they are slow to recognize that competing

---

[66](1983: 260).
[67]Scanlon (1976); Reiman (1981).
[68](1984).

rights might be just as valid and that the institutions they admire might be just as coercive. Libertarians may well be correct that states are often coercive. But liberals may still be correct that private corporations are often coercive. And socialists may be correct that the capitalist market system as a whole is often coercive. In short, coercion may be the central problem in all forms of social organization, as contractual theories of organization imply (see Chapter 1). In this view, it is the central task of organizational design to minimize coercion—not by definition (through narrow interpretations of liberty), not by oversight (through disregard for the difficulties facing weaker participants), but by minimizing those harms to persons that might infringe anyone's human rights.

The most plausible human rights are *rights that virtually any human beings would claim for themselves, regardless of their personal tastes or motives.* Very specific rights are more apt to meet this requirement than the grand, abstract rights of classical formulas. While we have good reason to be skeptical of a general right to liberty, for instance, human rights to specific liberties—privileges to express one's opinion, practice one's religion, and so forth—are relatively unobjectionable, as Dworkin observes.[69] We can increase our confidence in human rights by becoming even more precise in their specification. Feinberg suggests that rights to avoid particular harms, like torture, are the strongest candidates for the title of genuine human rights:

> If torture is still too vague a term, we can give exact empirical descriptions of the Chinese Water Torture, the Bamboo Fingernail Torture, and so on, and then claim that everyone has an absolutely exceptionless right in every conceivable circumstance not to be treated in any of those precisely described ways.[70]

Surely, almost anyone would claim for one's self rights prohibiting such treatment. To deny that all persons have human rights of this sort would go beyond the bounds of scientific detachment and verge on outright callousness. (One need not, however, agree with Feinberg that any human rights are absolute, always wrong to infringe. The issue now is whether their infringement would constitute coercion. This seems clearly the case with torture.)

---

[69](1978).
[70](1973: 87).

There are quite a lot of rights that virtually any persons in specific situations would claim for themselves. The right to a living wage is probably one—unless we suppose that not all workers care whether they earn enough to live on. The right to pay workers a subliving wage is probably not—unless we suppose that all employers care nothing for the well-being of their employees. No doubt, some property rights would qualify as human rights. Nearly everyone would claim rights to avoid armed robbery, frauds, and related things (following Feinberg, we could give more detailed descriptions of "armed robbery" and various "frauds," as recorded in criminal proceedings). It is not obvious, though, that from these specific rights we can derive a broad right to private property, which would be infringed by state acts such as wage regulations or the collective bargaining protections discussed in the last chapter. Certainly, someone who believes in a broad property right might find most government regulations coercive. But one may have a tough time convincing nonbelievers that one is not just being obstinate in opposing minimum wages and working conditions in cases like migrant farmwork. And one may have a tougher time yet showing that state labor regulations, even if coercive, are generally *more* coercive than the private, organizational regulations they replace and are, therefore, wrong on balance.

Conclusion

The aim of this chapter has been to demonstrate the usefulness of moral rights, not necessarily to catalog them.[71] Prior chapters have focused on the utility of *conventional* rights as descriptive concepts. Here I have tried to explain how other important concepts that are often presumed to be descriptive—for example, freedom or voluntari-

---

[71]As suggested earlier, a list of specific human rights might be derived from a hypothetical contract situation, similar to Rawls's (1971) imaginary setting for deriving principles of justice. The interesting theoretical question in this case would be: What concrete rights would self-interested participants agree to support if they were to negotiate a system of rules for mutual benefit (and if they were unsure of their own eventual positions in this rule system)? Further theoretical development of the more abstract "manifesto" rights, popular among some philosophers, could be useful as well. It might be worthwhile to work back and forth between specific and general rights to seek a kind of Rawlsian "reflective equilibrium."

ness—are ultimately dependent on *human* rights. Perhaps the most direct lesson for organizational theory is that voluntary behavior in organizations is much more problematic than usually assumed. At least since Chester Barnard,[72] organizations have been portrayed as systems of willing cooperation. According to Barnard and others, an organization can only survive so long as benefits to the diverse participants are satisfactory or good enough to induce their continued contributions. But, in practice, "good enough" can mean anything from thoroughly enjoyable to barely tolerable, depending on a participant's alternatives to cooperation (which may be very bad indeed, say in a system of slavery). We cannot, then, infer voluntariness from acts of organizational contribution or participation (Slaves participate!).

Nor can we infer voluntariness, I have argued, solely from the consequences of organizational agreements or the procedures by which they are arrived at. The consequentialist and descriptive approaches challenged here have historically failed to provide adequate criteria for determining the freedom of contracts. Through the eighteenth century, for instance, English and American courts tended to rely on the first approach, judging the equity of exchange in deciding the validity of commercial contracts. Horwitz mentions that in sales cases, "when the selling price was greater then the supposed objective value of the thing bought, juries were permitted to reduce the damages in an action by the seller, and courts would enforce an implied warranty in actions by the buyer."[73] As the arbitrariness of these decisions became more apparent, courts turned to the second (descriptive) approach in the nineteenth century; judges now sought to discover the expressed wills of the parties by reference to formal rules of contract formation. This approach, however, ratified mostly the wills of powerful business interests, as in adoption of the caveat emptor doctrine and the fellow-servant rule (which denied employer responsibility and put employees at risk for injuries caused by coworkers).[74] In our own century, the threats to freedom posed by principles like caveat emptor and assumption-of-risk in employment have become just as apparent. Who today would seriously choose to consume the contaminated food products that were once sold to "willing" buyers by unregulated deal-

---

[72](1938).

[73](1977: 167).

[74]See Horwitz (1977); Friedman (1985).

ers and processors? Who today would feel more free working without any promise of compensation for injuries on the job? Should one be inclined to tolerate such risks, who would still not question the voluntariness of a labor contract like the following (entered into by a Chinese immigrant in 1873)?

> An agreement to assist the woman Ah Ho, because coming from China to San Francisco she became indebted to her mistress for passage. Ah Ho herself asks Mr. Yee Kwan to advance her six hundred and thirty dollars, for which Ah Ho distinctly agrees to give her body to Mr. Yee for service of prostitution for a term of four years. There shall be no interest on the money. Ah Ho shall receive no wages. At the expiration of four years Ah Ho shall be her own master. Mr. Yee Kwan shall not hinder or trouble her. If Ah Ho runs away before her time is out, her mistress shall find her and return her, and whatever expense is incurred in finding and returning her Ah Ho shall pay. On this day of agreement Ah Ho, with her own hands, has received from Mr. Yee Kwan six hundred and thirty dollars. If Ah Ho shall be sick at any time for more than ten days, she shall make up by an extra month of service for every ten days sickness. Now this agreement has proof—this paper received by Ah Ho is witness.[75]

Even nineteenth-century legal minds could not maintain the pretense of voluntariness in such cases, no matter how correct the ritual of the contracting parties.

In recent years, courts have increasingly looked beyond the empirical formalities of contracting to see whose rights are really entailed in appeals to freedom of choice. And no longer are property rights always treated as high trumps (as Mr. Yee might have preferred). Legislatures in this century have also recognized a growing list of rights whose infringement is deemed coercive and unlawful: rights of workers to collective bargaining, rights of minorities to equal opportunity, rights of distributors to due process in franchise termination, etc. Some bemoan this state intrusion into private dealings.[76] Others take a certain glee in proclaiming the death of contract.[77] But what is dead, or dying, is mere formalism: trust in ceremonial procedures and

---

[75]Quoted in Baxandall et al. (1976: 99).

[76]E.g., Dorn (1985).

[77]E.g., Gilmore (1974).

magic words of consent, which mask vested interests and favor parties with the most legal cunning, or the wealth to hire it.

While our courts and legislatures may still make plenty of errors and allow a lot of injustices, they are less likely now to mistake behavioral displays of agreement for truly voluntary acts. Students of organization might avoid similar mistakes by paying closer attention to the potential for coercion in ordinary institutional practices—including practices most explicitly contractual. As a final example, recall Rakoff's opening comments about the possible coerciveness of "contracts of adhesion": standardized leases, sales agreements, and other form contracts, which are skillfully drafted by and for the benefit of organizations, and which are then offered to participants on a take-it-or-leave-it basis. Rakoff suggests that, contrary to popular belief, market competition may not prevent organizations from forcing terms on participants, but may actually encourage it.[78] In fact, it has not been monopolists but firms in highly competitive industries, like insurance, that have been notorious abusers of adhesion contracts (at least from the standpoint of prompting governmental re-drafting). Rakoff explains that competition drives firms to reduce transaction costs. One way to do this is to standardize agreements with customers, employees, vendors, and other participants. Standardization allows firms to stabilize their external environments by shifting the risks of nonroutine events to the adhering party.[79] It also provides an important means of control over internal operations. The form contract imposes discipline on salespersons, for instance, who might otherwise be tempted to ease sales terms in order to meet objectives or earn commissions. By denying discretion to operating personnel, who can themselves now be standardized and more easily replaced, form con-

---

[78](1983).

[79]Rakoff (1983: 1226) adds:

Many of the [standard] terms concern risks that in any individual transaction are unlikely to eventuate [but may prove very costly when they occur]. It is notoriously difficult for most people, who lack legal advice and broad experience concerning the particular transaction type, to appraise these sorts of contingencies. And the standard forms—because they are drafted to cover many such contingencies—are likely to be long and complex, even if each term is plainly stated. . . . The ideal adherent who would read, understand, and compare several forms is unheard of in the legal literature and, I warrant, in life as well.

tracts help authorities to preserve the existing power structure within an organization.

Everyday experience with complex organizations bears out Rakoff's contention that one cannot deal with them as if they were individual persons or small enterprises of the sort alluded to by Milton and Rose Friedman in their opening quote. Customers know they can negotiate only a few terms. If they try to bargain over the form terms, Rakoff notes, "the salesman will explain his lack of authority to vary the form. Haggling, the customer finds, requires penetrating the hierarchical structure of the firm in the hope of finding someone who will deal—a daunting and perhaps prohibitively costly endeavor."[80] Ah, but can't contract standardization simply reflect overall consumer preference for lower price versus flexibility of nonprice terms? Possibly—maybe as much as employers' standard disclaimer of liability for industrial injuries a century ago reflected the preference of employees for a decent wage versus workplace safety (as inferred by courts of the period). Possibly, though, there are some tradeoffs people should not have to make, some choices offered by organizations that are not freely made.

Particularly coercive offers in modern organizations, I have submitted, include the choice between employment and unionization. Certain terms of this kind have been overturned by law, as in "yellow-dog" contracts; others remain lawful, as in contracts with farm workers not covered by labor legislation; and many more cases have arisen lately despite the law, as discussed in Chapter 4. Organizational theory might have a more liberating influence if such choices were not taken for granted, but if researchers instead studied how both employment and union options could be kept open to workers through further legal innovations (such as the quick certification procedure proposed by Weiler[81]). By leaving these issues to lawyers (like Weiler and Rakoff), we forgo an opportunity to discover how organizations function empirically, and we may uncritically accept normative no-

---

[80](1983: 1225).

[81](1983). There is, by the way, nothing incongruous about asking how organizations can become more free through more law, just as there is nothing incongruous about asking how society at large can become more free through more law. Friedman (1985) provides a relevant analysis, describing the growth of law in America as a movement toward "total justice."

tions of freedom that serve the special interests of dominant participants.

The point is *not* that organizations are necessarily coercive. But it
is naive to suppose that they are never coercive. And it is more than
naive to suppose that almost any arrangement between nominally
consenting adults deserves legal sanction. In the end, a contractual
theory does not commit us to a determinate position on the voluntariness of organizations; the specific deals that comprise them may or
may not be considered voluntary, depending on what human rights
we acknowledge and whether those rights are violated. It follows that a
contractual theory also does not commit us to a determinate position
on the role of government. If we acknowledge only gross property
rights, we may wish the state to do no more than enforce whatever
terms contracting parties can negotiate on their own. If we acknowledge other human rights, however (and there seems no reason not to),
we may wish the state to supply terms to secure those rights. The most
appropriate conclusion concerning legal regulation of contract may
well be Havighurst's:

> The law of the contract, in that it partakes of the wills of the parties,
> leans toward equality for the strong; in that it partakes of the will of
> the judge and the wills of legislator and administrator, it leans toward
> equality for the weak. And with this blend of equalities, the contract
> institution leans toward liberty.[82]

---

[82](1979: 187).

6. Organizational Effectiveness

Since much research is carried out with the explicit or implicit aim of improving organizations, an evaluative concept defining improvement is desirable— if not essential. In organizational theory, the usual name for such a concept is *effectiveness*. This chapter will examine various formulations and describe the sort of evaluative criteria implied by a social-contract theory.

Recent studies of organizational effectiveness have emphasized the subjectivity of this concept. Whereas researchers have traditionally defined effectiveness in terms of objective organizational goals, some have lately attempted to define effectiveness from the subjective viewpoints of organizational participants or constituents.[1] This latter approach is consistent with a social-contract model of organizations; however, it requires development if it is to avoid objections and become a viable alternative to received views. Let us start with these views.

Traditional Views and Interactionist Alternatives

Goal-based definitions of effectiveness are still the rule in organizational theory;[2] as Etzioni has stated, "Effectiveness establishes the degree to which an organization realizes its goals under a given set of conditions."[3] Theorists, of course, use the term "effectiveness" to convey normative information. The term does not simply *mean* degree of goal attainment, which is potentially a matter of fact; but it expresses

---

[1]Cummings (1977); Keeley (1978); Pfeffer and Salancik (1978); Connolly, Conlon, and Deutsch (1980); Kanter and Brinkerhoff (1981); Zammuto (1982).

[2]Hall (1980).

[3](1975: 135).

a general and somewhat vague virtue of organizations, a matter of value. Steers's review indicates effectiveness is a broad construct that connotes positive value, that remains theoretically obscure, but that tends to be *operationalized* in the form of organizational goal attainment.[4] Steers also elects a goal-based formulation, advancing a common argument:

> The major advantage of the goal approach in evaluating effectiveness is that organizational success is measured against organizational intentions instead of against an investigator's value judgments (that is, what the organization "should" be doing).[5]

> [Thus] we can study within a more objective framework what an organization is actually trying to do—and how well it succeeds.[6]

It is questionable, though, whether a goal-based approach is really objective. In the first place, it is difficult to specify organizational goals or intentions objectively. As we have already noted, participants may disagree about these; so might independent observers. It is frequently suggested that one analyze actual policies and procedures to determine an organization's "real," operative goals,[7] but the purpose of organizational policies and procedures is generally ambiguous. In a manufacturing operation, for instance, policies and procedures may generate objective consequences, such as products, salaries, profits, pollution, etc. Some of these consequences are presumably goals, i.e., reasons for action; others are costs, i.e., expenses of action. Now, how does one categorize consequences like profits and salaries? Certain participants and observers (e.g., shareholders) may see the manufacturing operation as a profit maker, whose costs include salaries; some (e.g., workers) may see this operation as a salary maker, whose costs include profits; still others (e.g., taxing bodies) may consider both profits and salaries to be goals, or costs (e.g., customers). And there is ordinarily no objective test by which to resolve such differences. Ultimately, what are taken to be goals *of* an organization look very much

---

[4] (1977).
[5] (1977: 5).
[6] (1977: 12–13).
[7] Perrow (1961).

like subjective goals *for* an organization, as conceived by someone or other.

Furthermore, it is not obvious why organizational goals, ambiguous or not, are appropriate criteria of effectiveness. Why are criteria derived from organizational intentions any more objective, in the sense of having normative validity, than other evaluative standards (say, ones derived from individual rights)? Even if one could demonstrate that organizations really have goals (such as survival, integration, or other aims attributed to organizations in organismic models), one must still justify their status as criteria for evaluation. From the fact that an organizational goal exists, one cannot logically infer that it ought to exist and be attained. Perhaps organizations like the Ku Klux Klan do try to survive; it does not follow that they should survive or be judged on their survival capacity. In fact, the attainment of all sorts of goals of all sorts of organizations is regularly subordinated to other values in our courts, press, customs, and within many organizations themselves. Theorists have been reluctant to become entangled in debate over the value of organizational goal attainment,[8] but it is a mistake to think that it is not a matter for debate, that it is a self-evident good.

Subjective value judgments are inherent in evaluation,[9] and the question that a useful theory of effectiveness must address is *whose* values should count for how much. Goal-based theories often begin with a reasonable assumption, namely, that the values of organizational participants, not academic experts, should furnish the primary criteria of effectiveness. The researcher's task is merely to systematize the value judgments of the subjects of research. Although this assumption cannot yield an objective criterion, it may yield something almost as good—an impartial criterion, which respects the basic interests of persons who actually participate in organizations and which is free of researcher bias toward any special interests. Traditional goal-based approaches typically fail to achieve impartiality, however, because they incorporate a subsequent, less reasonable assumption: that organizational goals reflect the common values of our subjects, or at least the

---

[8]See, especially, Simon (1957).
[9]Campbell (1977).

values of persons classified as organizational members. Even a narrowly defined class of members may have no common interest in any particular goal.[10] Contrary to received doctrine, organizations need not entail shared purposes, but only shared activities, which serve the diverse and conflicting purposes of individuals—profits for some, wages for others, etc. Thus, any "organizational" goal may only reflect the values of some subjects, and the attainment of such a goal is hardly an impartial measure of system effectiveness.

To reduce bias, theorists generally no longer rely on single-goal measures of effectiveness, like profitablility or productivity. Many propose that organizations have multiple and opposing goals that represent the different values of specific interest groups.[11] Yet, the important question of whose goals (values) should count for how much remains.[12] Moreover, multiple-goal measures may still misrepresent the values of participants, because even those who share an interest in an organizational outcome may have no common interest in its overall *level* of attainment, as goal models imply. Employees, for instance, may all have an interest in increased wages, which are sometimes included in the goal set of an organization; but employees care about their *own* wages, and perhaps how they compare to those of others, not necessarily about the aggregate (or average) level of wages that an organization attains. If an organization increased its overall wage level by increasing the compensation of favorably situated individuals (relatives of officers, possessors of scarce skills or prestigious degrees), it is unlikely that many others would consider the higher wage level to be much of an improvement. The point is that goal-based measures of effective-

---

[10]Of course, one can narrow the definition of organizational membership to such an extent as to nearly force goal consensus. For example, one could regard only shareholders as true members of a corporation, whose goal is profit. Even in this extreme case, however, goal consensus is not assured. Some persons and activist groups hold stock in major corporations not for profit, but simply to challenge company policies. Moreover, as organizational boundaries are narrowed to include fewer participants as members and more as outsiders, the primacy of organizational goals vis-à-vis conflicting environmental expectations becomes more difficult to justify. Finally, no matter how narrow the set of members, their interests may not be impartially served by the attainment of a shared goal because of the distribution problem explained below.

[11]Van de Ven (1980); Scott (1981); Hall (1982).

[12]Cameron and Whetten (1983).

ness, whether single or multiple, are rather insensitive to the distribution of outcomes, whereas organizational participants usually care a great deal about how outcomes are distributed. It is only when persons feel that their own interests are protected by some equitable distribution principle (e.g., allocation of profits according to shares held, in the case of owners) that they may value the attainment of a collective outcome or goal.

By and large, goal-based theories are biased toward the values of participants who have the most to gain by attainment of a given goal. Such problems have led some theorists to challenge not only traditional notions of effectiveness, but traditional notions of organization itself. Despite the oft-drawn distinction between facts and values, there is a connection between how we conceptualize a thing and how we evaluate it.[13] It may not make much sense to continue to view organizations as systems for the attainment of collective goals if goal-based evaluation is so problematic.

The most serious challenge to traditional views involves the idea that organizations are negotiated interaction systems: instruments for the satisfaction of personal interests. Reflecting this idea are models that portray organizations as political coalitions,[14] games,[15] competitive arenas,[16] markets,[17] negotiatied orders[18]—and, more generally, *contracts*. All avoid anthropomorphic imagery that attributes intentions, needs, welfares, and other biological properties to organizations; instead, organizations are seen to be nonteleological structures composed of the interrelated behaviors of self-interested participants (constituents, stakeholders, etc.). In line with the contractual approach discussed earlier, interactionist models do not deny that a shared purpose may emerge among participants. But such a purpose is not assumed to be an essential aspect of organizations; it is an occasional feature requiring empirical confirmation. It is not assumed to be a goal *of* the organization as a personified entity; it remains a goal *for* the organization of natural persons. And it is not assumed to have

---

[13]Taylor (1967).
[14]March (1962).
[15]Allison (1971).
[16]Cummings (1977).
[17]Pfeffer and Salancik (1978).
[18]Strauss (1978).

any intrinsic value; it is but a means of furthering individual purposes for cooperation.

The descriptive credibility of interactionist models has been demonstrated elsewhere;[19] our concern here is with their normative implications. These models suggest that organizations are effective to the extent that they do, in fact, satisfy the interests of participating individuals. Such a broad criterion of effectiveness is, of course, subject to differing interpretations; and, like goal-based criteria, it lacks objectivity. But, unlike goal-based criteria, it has potential for impartiality over a wide range of circumstances. Typical interpretations have been classified by Zammuto into four distinct theories of effectiveness (entailing relativistic, developmental, power, or social justice "metacriteria").[20] While certainly not the only possibilities, these theories represent logical options for specifying effectiveness in terms of participant interest-satisfaction. How well these theories maintain impartiality is an important point of comparison.[21]

Relativistic Approach

Perhaps the most straightforward theory is the strongly relativistic multiple-constituency approach of Connolly, Conlon, and Deutsch.[22] The authors contend that no single statement about organizational effectiveness is possible nor desirable; they believe that judgments of effectiveness are inevitably contingent upon which indi-

---

[19]E.g., Dalton (1959); Allison (1971); Farberman (1975); Storey (1980); see also Chapters 2 and 3 above with regard to the social-contract model.

[20](1982).

[21]Impartiality is a reasonable, minimal standard for assessing theories of organizational effectiveness. A claim to something like impartiality is implied not only in theories that purport to identify an ultimate common good or collective goal, but also in theories that reject shared orientations and define effectiveness from the separate viewpoints of an organization's multiple constituencies. Impartiality is of special importance in defending the validity of normative theories to subjects of research. It may not be feasible to invoke criteria of empirical "proof," but demonstration that theories favor the basic interests of no particular persons is an appropriate response to anyone who would challenge the validity of an effectiveness conception. The meaning of impartiality will be clarified later in this chapter.

[22](1980).

viduals or groups (constituencies) supply the criteria for evaluation: "Individuals become involved with an organization (as owners, managers, employees, customers, suppliers, regulators, etc.) for a variety of reasons, and these reasons will be reflected in a variety of different evaluations. It appears somewhat arbitrary to label one of these perspectives a priori as the 'correct' one."[23]

The relativistic, multiple-constituency approach is intuitively plausible, but it contains critical ambiguities, one of which is whether there is any nonarbitrary justification for regarding a given constituency's perspective as more valid or correct than another's. Connolly et al. tend to dismiss attempts at justification, suggesting that each constituency's perspective is equally valid. This suggestion is defended only indirectly, though, causing further ambiguity concerning why each perspective is valid. It is true that the evaluations of different constituencies will generally vary;[24] yet, from this empirical fact, one cannot draw the normative conclusion that one evaluation is as valid as another. To reach such a conclusion, an implicit normative premise is required.[25] The premise relied on by Connolly et al., along with most relativists, seems to be that it is less ethnocentric, authoritarian, biased, or the like—and therefore *right*—to accept the validity of virtually any participant's judgments. In fact, the authors grant no special standing even to the perspectives of direct participants, but use the term "constituencies" "to emphasize the possibility that individuals and groups not directly associated with the focal organization may form evaluations of its activities."[26] Presumably, these evaluations are legitimate as well.

One might ask, now, whether it really is less biased, and thus right, to accept the validity of just about anyone's judgment regarding an organization. Some participants' perspectives may themselves be heavily biased against the basic interests of others, and it is questionable whether they should be granted the same validity as anyone else's.

---

[23]Connolly, Conlon, and Deutsch (1980: 212).

[24]Pickle and Friedlander (1967).

[25]Williams (1972) discusses related problems of logic in relativist theories. Hatch (1983) elaborates on the questionable impartiality of ethical relativism and describes its decline within anthropology, a discipline long associated with relativist thinking.

[26]Connolly, Conlon, and Deutsch (1980: 213).

A relativist might argue, for instance, that if owners prefer higher profits and workers prefer better wages or working conditions, it makes no sense to say that one preference is more deserving than the other. In some circumstances, it may indeed appear arbitrary to order these preferences—but not always.

In the nineteenth century, a good deal of public debate took place over the employment of children in the English textile industry. Mill owners vigorously opposed labor restrictions because they feared increased competition from foreign goods, as well as reduced profits. However, reports of the conditions to which children were exposed in the industry shocked others and eventually led Parliament to enact protective legislation despite the owners' objections. Testimony before Michael Sadler's Select Committee of the House of Commons in 1832 provides a vivid description of mill conditions.[27] One witness, Matthew Crabtree, reported starting in a mill at the age of eight, working regularly from six in the morning to eight at night (and from five to nine during brisk periods), performing operations that rubbed skin from the hands until they bled, running throughout the day to keep pace with the machine speed, suffering beatings with straps and clubs when fatigue diminished output, and being unable even to eat at the end of the day for anxiety about the next. Crabtree's testimony, and others', indicate that his experience was not unusual and was better than many. In considering mill conditions, in enacting the Factory Acts, the British Parliament *had* to choose between the preferences of owners for greater profitability and the preferences of children for health, education, and opportunity to escape poverty. Few today would regard the choice Parliament made as arbitrary or doubt that it signaled a genuine improvement in the factory system.

The drawback of an unqualified relativism is that it recognizes no limits on the validity of demands that organizational participants may place on one another. In attempting to avoid bias, it may unintentionally, but effectively, legitimate the most extreme demands, prejudices and, in some cases, outright cruelty—thereby calling into question its own claim to impartiality. Obviously, it is not always possible to order conflicting participant preferences with great confidence; and the task may only become easy with the advantage of

---

[27]Wing (1837).

considerable hindsight. Nevertheless, the task need not be an impossible one, as relativists allege, and it is a far more practical one than they usually admit.

The proposition that it is not necessary or desirable to rank constituency perspectives in accordance with a general effectiveness criterion contains a final ambiguity: not necessary or desirable *for whom*? For theorists, it may be convenient to adopt a thoroughgoing relativism, but not for those who actually take part in administering complex organizations (managers, regulators, judges, etc.). Connolly, Conlon, and Deutsch recognize that conflicts among perspectives are quite common in organizations and present serious problems for administrators;[28] still, their extreme relativism permits them to say little about means of resolution. The authors "feel no embarrassment" about leaving such conflicts unresolved, but they are convincing in disputing the importance of a preference-ordering criterion only in cases where different organizations are the subjects of conflicting evaluations. For example, they state:

> We would argue that the question "Is General Motors more or less effective than HEW?" is of the same order as "Is an elephant more or less effective than a giraffe?"...We see no particular merit in an obsessional search for the single measure of merit on which organizations can be compared.[29]

Administrators and other parties, however, want to know whether GM or HEW or a woolen mill is *itself* more effective at one time than another. These *are* important comparisons; participants will make them, and act on them; and theories of effectiveness that ignore them are impractical at best.

Developmental Approach

In response to the ambiguity of a strongly relativistic approach, Zammuto has advanced an "evolutionary" theory of effectiveness.[30] This theory is similar to the relativist view in normative outlook but

[28](1980).
[29](1980: 216).
[30](1982).

goes a bit further in identifying a direction for organizational improvement. According to Zammuto, "effectiveness stems from the ability of an organization to satisfy changing preferences of its constituencies over time."[31] He assumes that preferences will vary among constituencies and within the same constituency over time, but he does not assume that this variation necessarily results in unresolvable conflicts. A way of handling competing preferences is expressed in his evolutionary "meta criterion." This criterion "specifies that effective performance increases the adaptability of the organization/environment by changing the constraints on performance, allowing it to satisfy changing constituent preferences."[32] The idea is that organizations operate in niches, composed of physical, biological, and social constraints that "define what is possible and limit the alternatives available to organizations."[33] An effective organization is one that eventually expands its niche, the limits on what is possible, in order to better satisfy participants in the long run.

Although Zammuto's evolutionary theory is framed in the language of an organismic social model, its main argument is separable from such a model, and the theory is properly classified as a participant-interest view.[34] The argument might be put in other words by saying that organizations are not zero-sum games: Should conflicts among constituent preferences arise, these should be handled not by subordinating some groups or by redistributing outcomes among groups, but by imaginatively expanding the range of possible outcomes so as to permit the satisfaction of both current and emerging preferences—which is "the hallmark of effectiveness from [Zammuto's] evolutionary perspective."[35] Unfortunately, this approach does not

---

[31](1982: 82).

[32]Zammuto (1982: 78).

[33]Zammuto (1982: 72).

[34]The separability of Zammuto's argument from an organismic model is apparent from the normative implications of his theory. These are distinct from the implications of more naturalistic evolutionary models (e.g., Aldrich, 1979), which stress system versus participant well-being. Whether or not one agrees that Zammuto's model represents a true evolutionary theory, it is representative of the important class of economic developmental theories that qualify as participant-interest approaches. Earlier comments on goal-based theories and the following section on power-based theories address issues raised by other evolutionary models.

[35]Zammuto (1982: 147).

go far enough in specifying a clear criterion of effectiveness, for many situations may be zero-sum, or close to it.

As an example of relatively effective adaptation, Zammuto cites the strategy of General Motors during the 1970s. The company downsized its product line and strengthened its international operations by expanding its niche overseas. It remains to be seen, however, whether GM can devise a strategy that is effective in terms of satisfying current and emerging constituent preferences. From the viewpoint of many consumers, product and process innovations have not been sufficient to offset the higher labor costs built into domestic vehicles. Some American workers have already lost jobs and benefits through GM's attempts to adapt, and more are threatened. In short, the effectiveness of GM, assessed against Zammuto's criterion, is indeterminate. This case is not exceptional.

As Thurow observes, many changes in social systems result in gains for some constituents and losses for others.[36] Zammuto's metacriterion yields little information about these changes. The criterion strongly resembles a Pareto efficiency principle, though it is not altogether clear whether Zammuto has in mind a standard of *actual* or *potential* Pareto efficiency. The former standard lends approval to a social change only if someone is made better off and no one worse off; the latter lends approval to a change if it increases system potential to make someone better off and no one worse off, given hypothetical compensation for any losses. In any event, Pareto-like principles are notoriously inconclusive.[37] Thurow contends that, since *someone* is likely to be made worse off by virtually any large-scale social change, "nothing is [actually] Pareto efficient in the real world";[38] furthermore, changes that are only potentially Pareto-efficient conceal true conflicts between constituents' preferences, which simply cannot be ignored in the real world (where hypothetical compensation is small comfort). Thurow's view may be too pessimistic. There may be certain cases where a more-is-better-than-less approach is informative, but nontrivial cases for a theory of effectiveness are precisely those in which such an approach produces no decisive judgments—cases in

---

[36](1981).
[37]Little (1950); Rawls (1971).
[38](1981: 219).

which some constituents get more over time, some get less, and a choice must be made about whose preferences should have priority.

Zammuto assumes that this choice can be avoided if enough imagination is used in organizational design. In the final analysis, he says, "the evolutionary approach does not raise the question of whose preferences should be satisfied. Rather, it's a question of how preferences are going to be satisfied."[39] The first question is not so easily set aside. There are, after all, objective limits on organizational capacity to satisfy participants' preferences. And participants' subjective expectations tend to rise along with system capacity to meet them, suggesting that attempts to satisfy current and emerging preferences may entail a futile run on a "hedonic treadmill" (as Brickman and Campbell describe the phenomenon[40]). For practical purposes, it is often necessary to distinguish between more or less legitimate preferences, as in laws and other normative codes. Theories that make no such distinctions generate not only indecisive evaluations, but troublesome normative implications.

It is too much to ask that an effectiveness theory provide a conclusive evaluation of every conceivable social change. Some organizational changes are probably neither good nor bad, and an attitude of indifference toward them is appropriate. Still, a theory that equivocates over a very wide range of change has a decidedly conservative bent. Using Zammuto's criterion,[41] for instance, one could not even say for sure whether something like the abolition of slavery represented a real improvement in American plantation organizations. Many constituents were dissatisfied by the change, and it did not reduce constraints on the performance of many plantations or enhance their capacity to satisfy future preferences. Developmental theories may not directly endorse the status quo, but indirectly they can serve to support the most extreme patterns of social or economic advantage by implying that there are no good reasons for changes that redistribute system benefits (instead of expanding them).

In sum, the developmental approach, like the relativist approach, has value in emphasizing that the satisfaction of human interests is the basis of organizational effectiveness; however, it

---

[39]Zammuto (1982: 83).
[40](1971).
[41](1982).

underestimates the probability of collision between the interests of organizational participants. What is needed to address adequately the distributional issues raised by a participant-interest theory of effectiveness is a criterion for prioritizing conflicting constituent preferences. Two priority rules have been mentioned most often in recent discussions of the effectiveness concept: one ordering preferences according to participant power,[42] the other according to a liberal notion of justice.[43]

Power Approach

One of the most complete statements of a power-oriented approach to evaluation is provided by Pfeffer and Salancik.[44] The authors begin with an interactionist model suggested by Cyert and March[45]: organizations are conceptualized as coalitions of self-interested groups or participants. Coalition participants engage in exchange relationships through the medium of the organization, which remains viable to the extent that it supplies personal inducements sufficient to elicit participants' continuing contributions. In Pfeffer and Salancik's view, organizations function much like markets:

> There is no requirement for the participants to share vested interests or singular, paramount goals. Anything that justifies a participant's involvement is sufficient from an organizing point of view. . . . Organizational participants may come into the coalition when there is some advantage to be gained and leave when there is no longer any perceived advantage. The gains and costs are defined in terms of the individual participants or groups, not in terms agreed upon by all or promulgated by the organization's management.[46]

From this perspective, Pfeffer and Salancik develop a participant-interest theory of organizational effectiveness, in which effectiveness is a multifaceted concept reflecting the criteria and prefer-

---

[42]Pennings and Goodman (1977); Pfeffer and Salancik (1978).
[43]Keeley (1978); House (1980).
[44](1978).
[45](1963).
[46](1978: 26).

ences of various interest groups. The authors do more with this idea than most theorists. They recognize that balancing the diverse and competing demands of participant groups is a basic problem of administration, and they argue that not all demands are equally important. Some participants contribute more critical and scarce resources to the organization, and it is primarily those persons, who have the most power to affect operations, whom an effective organization must satisfy. Therefore, to assess organizational effectiveness, one must, first, identify relevant participants, considering what resources are critical to the organization and who could possibly provide them; second, weight the relative power of participants to control critical resources; third, determine the criteria by which various participants evaluate the organization; and, finally, assess the impact of organizational actions on these weighted criteria.

Pfeffer and Salancik advance both descriptive and normative claims for this procedure: it "represents both a model of organizational behavior and a prescription for managing organizations to ensure their continued survival."[47] The normative, if not the descriptive, claim is controversial. Perhaps some organizations do act so as to satisfy the most powerful participants. The question remains whether they should.

Pfeffer and Salancik offer a reasoned defense of their normative position. They do not rely on a simple might-makes-right justification, but assume that the rewarding of uncommon skills and material contributions can increase organizational capacity to provide benefits for all participants, including those who have less to bargain with. The ultimate justification, then, for a power-based system of incentives is that it can work to everyone's advantage, not merely to the advantage of the powerful. Early advocates of such systems, like Adam Smith and Frederick Taylor, were quite careful to stress their advantages to even "the lowest ranks."[48] Pfeffer and Salancik are similarly careful.

A power-based theory, of course, raises the problem of specifying

---

[47](1978: 89).

[48]Adam Smith says:

It is the great multiplication of the productions of all the different arts, in consequence of the division of labor, which occasions, in a well-governed society, that universal opulence which extends itself to the lowest ranks of the people (1776: 11).

just what *is* to everyone's advantage and, in turn, what resources are critical for its attainment. The acceptability of any meritarian theory of effectiveness depends largely on its ability to identify a mutually advantageous outcome. Smith[49] and Taylor[50] assumed that it was a collective goal, the production of aggregate wealth, that advantaged everyone. Unfortunately, the attainment of this goal, or any goal, may not benefit anyone but the powerful. Pfeffer and Salancik do better in supposing it is a general means (of attaining participants' own goals) that works to everyone's advantage. They propose that, while participants may have different preferences for organizational ends, all have an instrumental interest in perpetuating the organization itself: "It is in the interests of all coalition participants to have the organization survive, for their continuing participation in the organization indicates they are obtaining benefits they would like continued."[51] Hence, organizational survival serves as a common value, a basis for distinguishing critical resources, and a reason for giving priority to the demands of participants who control such resources.

Though organizational survival carries a heavy justificatory burden in power-based theories of effectiveness,[52] it may not be a sufficiently impartial value to bear the load. Pfeffer and Salancik's assertion that all participants have an interest in organizational survival is debatable. It is not consistent with their original theoretical model, which regards shared interests as unnecessary. Moreover, mere organizational participation does not indicate that persons are really obtaining benefits they want continued through system survival; Pfeffer and Salancik themselves demonstrate that

> organizations may purposely manipulate the illusion of satisfaction to avoid the open expression of some demands. Patients in a psychiatric

---

Taylor adds:

All that you have to do is to bring wealth into this world and the world uses it .... Nineteen-twentieths of the real wealth of this world is used by the poor people, and not the rich, so that the workingman who sets out as a steady principle to restrict output is merely robbing his own kind (1916: 10).

[49](1776).
[50](1916).
[51](1978: 47).
[52]See also Pennings and Goodman (1977).

hospital may be drugged to reduce their demands on the staff. At the same time, relatives may be told about all the fine therapeutic activity going on.[53]

As the example suggests, some people may participate in organizations because they have virtually no choice or because they are mistaken in their beliefs about the benefits of participation. Many participate in the *hope* of securing goods,[54] which may never materialize (e.g., a successful career promised to hard-working employees, social popularity promised to consumers of beauty aids) or which are eventually outweighed by accompanying ills (e.g., hidden product defects, a latent industrial disease). People may simply discover too late that the costs of organizational participation exceed the benefits, and the interests of such participants might have been better served had the organization not survived.

As Pfeffer and Salancik point out, it is not in the interest of a survival-oriented organization to pay much attention to disadvantaged participants, unless they acquire the collective power to withhold critical organizational resources. And organizations can do a number of things to diffuse this power. They may, for instance, make cosmetic accommodations to interest groups, giving participants a feeling of influence; Pfeffer and Salancik mention that "a consumer affairs department can deal with complaints about the product with a letter and a free sample, but the production and development departments remain unaffected."[55] While letters and samples may not fully relieve the regret over participation of former customers, they may be enough to prevent collective actions, such as calls for governmental regulation or warnings to new customers, that could endanger an organization's resource supply. Even regulations and warnings may pose ineffective threats to organizational survival and prompt little organizational concern for regretful consumers if potential customer-resources are plentiful (as in the tobacco industry).

From an impartial point of view, the objectionable feature of the power approach is that individual persons are ultimately granted only instrumental worth. Consumers, employees, and other participants take on importance only insofar as they can contribute to or threaten

---

[53](1978: 98).
[54]Hirschman (1970).
[55](1978: 274).

system survival.[56] The danger is that this approach may sanction harsh or deceptive practices that work to the organization's advantage—that is, to someone's advantage—but not to the advantage of all participants, which is the rationale for a power-based incentive system in the first place. This danger is present whenever a collective consequence (organizational goal attainment, system survival, revolution, or whatever) is adopted as a surrogate for individual interests and as the basis of participant value. An impartial theory of effectiveness cannot overlook the intrinsic worth of individual persons. Intrinsic worth implies that each participant has at least some claims that do not depend for their legitimacy on one's personal power to affect organizational well-being. Claims of this sort (say, rights to disclosure of information about the risks of investment, employment, or purchase) often appear just as deserving as more functional demands; they are certainly not trivial to many organizational participants. In order to allow for these claims, it is necessary to view individual participants as ends in themselves, not merely as resources for the organization's use. This shift in perspective underlies attempts to derive criteria of effectiveness from theories of justice.

Social Justice Approach

A final category of participant-interest theories includes approaches that invoke liberal principles of social justice as standards for organizational evaluation.[57] In this category, Zammuto places the the-

---

[56]With regard to employees, Pfeffer and Salancik (1978: 46–47) note: "A lawyer may be relatively unimportant until the organization is confronted with a major lawsuit that threatens its survival. In Crozier's (1964) example of the maintenance workers in a French factory, the workers were important only when and if the machinery broke down." Again, it is possible that some organizations do treat some participants as important only to the extent that they can influence system survival. Yet it is far from clear that such treatment respects everyone's interests and ought to be called "effective."

[57]Dahrendorf (1979: 96–97) clarifies the meaning of "liberal" in this context: "The moral element of liberal thought is the conviction that it is the individual that matters, and the defence of his inviolability, of the unfolding of his potential, of his life chances which follows from this conviction. Groups, organizations, institutions are never a purpose in themselves, they are instruments for the purpose of individual development."

; of Keeley[58] and House,[59] both of whom build on the ideas of John Rawls.[60] Such theories are not distinctive in applying philosophical notions of justice to problems of effectiveness, but only in making this application explicit. Justice and effectiveness are parallel concepts. Both represent a primary measure of social-system value: according to Rawls, "Justice is the first virtue of social institutions,"[61] just as, according to Hall, "Effectiveness is the ultimate question in any form of organizational analysis."[62] And both concepts require the same type of measure, one that fairly balances the interests of system participants: for Rawls, "Principles of social justice...provide a way of assigning rights and duties in the basic institutions of society and they define the appropriate distribution of the benefits and burdens of social cooperation";[63] similarly, for Pfeffer and Salancik, "The effectiveness of the organization is a sociopolitical question" concerning "who wants what and how important is it that the demand be satisfied? and what are the implications of the satisfaction of one demand for the satisfaction of other demands?"[64]

Organization theorists have not often realized that their conceptions of effectiveness fall within the broad scope of social justice, and some are uneasy about the overtly normative language of justice;[65] but recognition of the connection between these concepts permits us to draw upon a long tradition of philosophical thought. In fact, all the approaches to organizational effectiveness reviewed thus far have, in one way or another, been advanced by philosophers as theories of justice—goal-based approaches as forms of utilitarianism, power-based theories as meritarian theories, and so forth. Furthermore, these classic theories of justice have lately been subject to criticism on precisely the grounds that the corresponding theories of effectiveness have been criticized: they fail to respect impartially the basic interests of participants in a social system.[66]

---

[58](1978).
[59](1980).
[60](1971).
[61](1971: 3).
[62](1980: 536).
[63](1971: 4).
[64](1978: 11, 87).
[65]E.g., Connolly, Conlon, and Deutsch (1980).
[66]Rawls (1971).

To appreciate the demands of justice, we need a better understanding of impartiality. Central to the meaning of impartiality is respect for persons.[67] Such respect is entailed in the proposition that individual human beings are ends in themselves, not merely resources or means to organizational well-being. In explaining this proposition, Vlastos argues:

> Everything other than a person can only have value *for* a person. This applies not only to physical objects...but also to...an epic poem, a scientific theory, a legal system, a moral disposition. Even such things as these will have value only because they can be (a) experienced or felt to be valuable by human beings and (b) chosen by them from competing alternatives.[68]

Human beings, on the other hand, can themselves experience well-being or other emotions, choose plans, and respond to interests of their own. And it is this capacity to experience, choose, or value *for one's self* that sets persons apart as sources (rather than mere objects) of value, that makes persons ends in themselves.

Because social systems, such as states, organizations, or component groups, lack this capacity of persons, they can have only derivative value. McTaggart declared that the personification and attribution of independent worth to nation-states, for instance, amounts to a crude form of fetish-worship—compared with which "zoolatry is rational and dignified. A bull or a crocodile may not have great intrinsic value, but it has some, for it is a conscious being. The state has none. It would be as reasonable to worship a sewage pipe, which also possesses considerable value as a means."[69] For evaluative purposes, every organization is much like a sewage pipe; that is, it acquires worth from its functional value to persons, whereas persons have inherent worth.

From the notion of respect for persons, an impartial norm for evaluating social systems can be derived, subject to the following general requirement outlined by Paul Taylor:

> To be substantively impartial a norm must be such that, when adopted and applied, every person as a person is given equal consider-

---

[67]Paul Taylor (1978).
[68](1962: 48–49).
[69](1934: 109).

ation. This does not mean that everyone must always be treated in the same way. But it does mean that each person's total set of basic interests is regarded as making the same initial claim-to-fulfillment as every other person's. (Basic interests are here understood to include, first, whatever is necessary for preserving an individual's autonomy as a chooser of his own value system, and second, whatever is necessary for realizing those of a person's ends and goals that are of fundamental importance in his or her self-chosen value system.)[70]

In line with this requirement, an organization can be considered just or effective to the extent that the *basic* well-being of each participant is given equal consideration in policymaking and implementation. Equal consideration implies recognition that every participant has some unconditional rights to well-being, rights independent of personal resources or talents, organizational needs, etc. It does not imply, however, that any and all preferences have identical standing or that all participants must be treated alike.

Consideration for the basic well-being of different persons may in fact call for differential treatment. Vlastos remarks that if someone is threatened with murder, it is not partial or unjust—indeed, justice demands—that such an individual receive more than ordinary police protection to allow an ordinary level of personal well-being.[71] Similarly, persons with physical or economic handicaps may deserve special treatment to compensate for those handicaps. It may also be impartial and just to permit individuals with natural talents and resources to profit from these advantages, not because they are more worthy of rewards or because they have greater capacity to promote organizational welfare, but because the basic well-being of persons lacking natural advantages might be further diminished if incentives for social cooperation were denied to the more talented and resourceful. As Benn puts it, "It may be expedient, but not just, that one man should starve that others might grow fat; but there is no injustice if, in allowing some to grow fat, we can reduce the number that would otherwise starve."[72]

---

[70](1978: 49).
[71](1962).
[72](1967: 76).

Impartiality, then, boils down to treating persons as equals, in contrast to treating them the same.[73] The distinction reflects an assumption that some interests are more fundamental to human well-being than others—for example, immunity from physical attack, access to employment opportunities, security against frauds, and the like. These are the interests that deserve equal consideration. In a just social system an attempt is made to ensure the satisfaction of such interests for each and every participant. This means giving first priority to participants whose fundamental interests might be in jeopardy. Principles of justice expressing this priority include Benn's principle of equal consideration of interests, which "provides for the satisfaction of interests in order of urgency, every individual's claim being otherwise equal";[74] Rawls's difference principle, which provides for maximizing the expectations of the least advantaged participants in a social system;[75] and the author's earlier minimization-of-regret principle, which provides for minimizing the dissatisfaction of the most regretful organizational participants.[76]

For purposes of social evaluation, such principles are useful rules of thumb. They describe general directions for organizational improvement and fit many of our normative intuitions. Nevertheless, rough rules of thumb may yield very counterintuitive judgments in

---

[73]Dworkin (1978: 227) has discussed this contrast in some detail. He points out:

> There are two different sorts of rights [implied in the notion of equality]. The first is the right to *equal treatment*, which is the right to an equal distribution of some opportunity or resource or burden. Every citizen, for example, has a right to an equal vote in a democracy. . . . The second is the right to *treatment as a equal*, which is the right, not to receive the same distribution of some burden or benefit, but to be treated with the same respect and concern as anyone else. If I have two children, and one is dying from a disease that is making the other uncomfortable, I do not show equal concern if I flip a coin to decide which should have the remaining dose of a drug. This example shows that the right to treatment as an equal is fundamental, and the right to equal treatment derivative. In some circumstances, the right to treatment as an equal will entail a right to equal treatment, but not, by any means, in all circumstances.

[74](1967: 76).
[75](1971).
[76]Keeley (1978).

some cases, and they may be difficult to apply in others.[77] To better assess the appropriateness of various principles of justice for evaluating organizations, it might be helpful to compare alternatives within a wider framework of possible effectiveness theories.

Bases of Interpersonal Judgment

In developing a practical and impartial measure of organizational value, it is essential to recognize that the ends of participants can vary and conflict. Theorists have tried to simplify the problem of evaluating social systems by assuming uniformity of ends or lack of conflict among ends, or both. These simplifications restrict the applicability of theories and create potential for bias. Figure 6-1 classifies typical theories according to the degree to which they take seriously (1) the variability of participant ends and (2) the prospect of conflict among participant ends.[78] These dimensions are logically independent: people could have the same ends, but still experience conflict over the enjoyment of those ends (e.g., in competing for a poker pot); and people could have different ends, yet experience no conflict over their separate attainment (e.g., in an ordinary exchange transaction).

Collaborative Views

Theories in the lower half of Figure 6-1 treat conflict among ends as unproblematic or, at best, as of secondary importance. Examples of some of these views have already been discussed, and their shortcomings can be quickly summarized. In traditional single-goal models of organizational effectiveness, such as a profit-maximization view, it is assumed that participants share very specific ends and nonconflicting interests in higher overall levels of goal attainment. These are strong assumptions, empirically credible only in special cases (perhaps in small businesses or pressure groups, cults, etc.); extending these as-

---

[77]Nozick (1974); Strike (1979).

[78]Theories are categorized according to *primary* assumptions; some theories have secondary implications that could fit another category. Utilitarian and functional theories, for instance, have distributive implications, but these derive from more basic assumptions in the categories indicated.

sumptions to more complex organizations discounts legitimate interests in opposing outcomes as well as participant concerns over outcome distribution. Theories to the right in the figure represent attempts to circumvent such problems.

The credibility of single-goal models can be strengthened by supposing that participants have only the most general end in common: maximization of subjective welfare or utility, as in classical utilitarianism. By definition, welfare is a universal good, and a utilitarian measure like "the greatest good of the greatest number" could apply

Figure 6-1

Assumptions of Effectiveness/Justice Theories

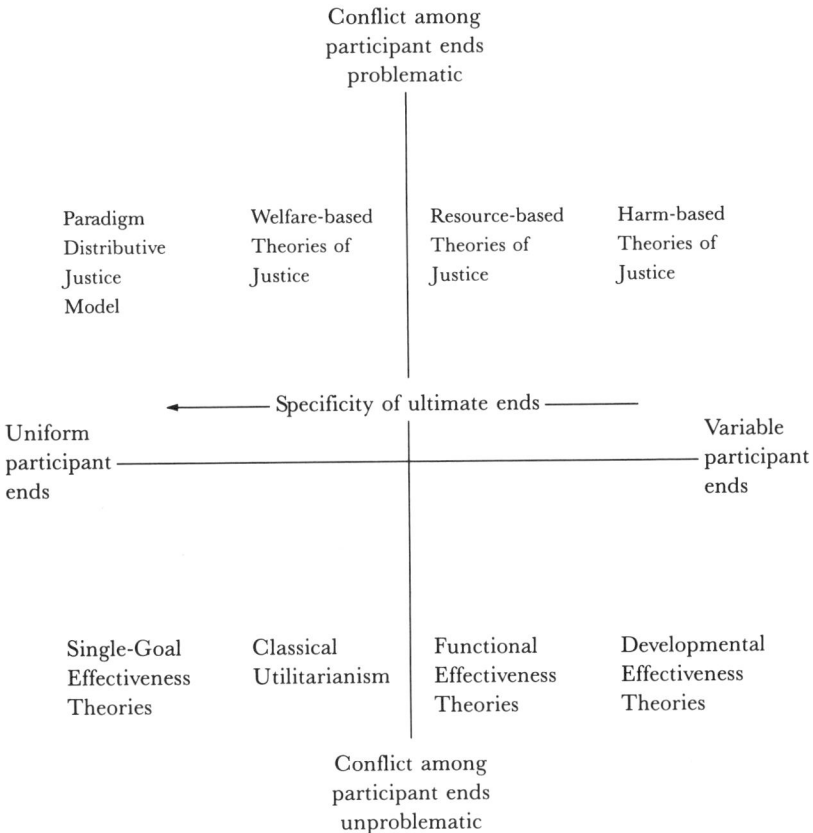

Conflict among
participant ends
problematic

| Paradigm Distributive Justice Model | Welfare-based Theories of Justice | Resource-based Theories of Justice | Harm-based Theories of Justice |

——— Specificity of ultimate ends ———

Uniform participant ends   Variable participant ends

| Single-Goal Effectiveness Theories | Classical Utilitarianism | Functional Effectiveness Theories | Developmental Effectiveness Theories |

Conflict among
participant ends
unproblematic

to almost all organizations. In aggregating utility, moreover, utilitarianism appears to avoid bias by giving each participant's welfare equal weight, according to Bentham's maxim of "everyone to count for one, nobody for more than one." However, it is still assumed that conflicts over whose welfare goes up or down in the process of social change can be disregarded; as long as total (or average) welfare in a system increases, a change is for the better, even if some individuals experience significant welfare losses. This assumption is questionable. Social participants normally care very much about their own welfare, and welfare losses especially; by ignoring these interests, utilitarianism fails to respect the separate worth of individual persons, as Rawls notes.[79] Hart adds that, because persons count only as data points in calculations of aggregate utility, controversial implications result: given the same overall level of welfare, "the situation in which a few enjoy great happiness while many suffer is as good as one in which happiness is more equally distributed."[80]

In functional effectiveness theories, the assumption of common participant ends is relaxed somewhat; the ultimate ends of participants are viewed as variable. It is nevertheless assumed that participants share interests in aggregate organizational consequences, which constitute very general means to everyone's particular ends. The distinguishing feature of functional theories is that these consequences are nondivisible or otherwise immune to conflict over their distribution. The theory of Pfeffer and Salancik,[81] which posits a commonly valued consequence of organizational survival, is typical.[82] Such theories take no account of the fact that a given consequence may have widely differing impacts on individual participants. Some may benefit a great deal from organizational survival, for instance; others may benefit more from dissolution and sale of assets; still others may benefit most from a consequence in between—takeover, reorganization, divestiture, or something else. To choose one consequence as *the* appropriate means to participants' ends seems rather arbitrary and serves to conceal conflicts among these ends. Functional theories divert attention toward conflicts over participants' instrumental value to

---

[79](1971).

[80]Hart (1979: 830).

[81](1978).

[82]See also Yuchtman and Seashore (1967); Pennings and Goodman (1977).

the organization, which is easier to manage (e.g., by prioritizing claims on the basis of power) but which is harder to reconcile with the intrinsic worth of persons and impartial respect for their own outcome preferences.

Developmental effectiveness theories allow for more variability in participant ends. As illustrated in Zammuto's evolutionary model,[83] no constraints on preferences are imposed; instead, a rate of organizational or economic development sufficient to satisfy both current and emerging desires is assumed. Thus, conflicting ends are theoretically avoided by growth in the benefits of cooperation. This approach is a bit utopian, given limits on the capacity of cooperative systems to provide benefits and given the tendency of expectations to rise along with economic development. Conflicting expectations are not so readily dismissed, and, operationally, developmental theories often revert to functional or goal-based views (as in supply-side economics).

Distributive Views

Theories in the upper half of Figure 6-1 treat the problem of conflicting participant ends more seriously. In these theories, social systems are evaluated on the basis of how fairly they balance and satisfy participant interests. Again moving from left to right in the figure, the paradigm model of distributive justice addresses the question of allocating some specific, uniformly valued good (like a pie that must be divided). Presumably, all individuals prefer more rather than less for themselves, and their conflicting outcome preferences require a distributive principle to evaluate alternative allocation policies. Various principles have been advanced: distribution according to need, desert, strict equality, etc.[84] Most such principles find some application in everyday life; yet, none is unobjectionable as a criterion of organizational justice or effectiveness, because of disagreements over the ultimate object of distribution (not everyone cares for pie).

For the sake of argument, imagine a very simple organization: a cooperative formed by a group of persons to buy (at wholesale markets) perishable commodities for home consumption. Suppose that all participants have roughly the same disposable income and need for

---

[83](1982).
[84]Vlastos (1962); Leventhal (1980).

food. Suppose that all have comparable skills and contribute equally of their time to the project; perhaps they take turns visiting the wholesale markets in the early morning and, subsequently, allocating their purchases. Suppose, finally, that an equal share of food is distributed and an equal share of its cost is assessed to all. While this arrangement may satisfy a variety of principles of distributive justice, it may not satisfy requirements of impartially. Participants could have two distinct reasons for joining a cooperative—some, mainly to save money on food; others, mainly to obtain better quality, fresher goods than those available elsewhere. Assuming that shopping in the early morning will maximize quality and freshness, the economy-minded could legitimately complain that this shopping policy favored the others, that by shopping later they might get bargains on leftovers and minimize cost. Neither an early nor a late shopping policy would equally respect the interests of all. Of course, alternative policies that do so might be devised, but the point is that simple models of distributive justice, which ignore the variability of participant ends, do not guarantee impartiality.

Welfare-based theories of justice are more attractive. They share with utilitarianism the assumption that participants have only the most general end in common, namely, subjective welfare;[85] in contrast to utilitarianism, this general end is seen now to pose important conflicts over its distribution. Individuals prefer more rather than less welfare for themselves, though not necessarily for their social system as a whole. Welfare-based theories can incorporate any of the usual principles of distributive justice; at the same time, they can exhibit greater impartiality by allowing for more variability in preferences for specific outcomes. Reconsider the case of the cooperative. What seems to make both the early and late shopping policies unfair, despite their consistency with common principles of distributive justice, is the fact that each policy disadvantages some participants in terms of providing personal welfare. If welfare is the object of distribution, better policies are suggested: the participants might alternate shopping times, the quality-minded shopping early one day and the economy-minded shopping later the next. Such a solution gives equal consideration to the interests of both, although there remains a problem with welfare-based approaches.

---

[85]Sen (1979).

Assume that the cooperative participants do alternate shopping times so as to equalize personal welfare or bring welfare distribution in line with some other principle of justice (choose any distributive principle). Say that this shopping policy, P_1 yields e units of welfare to the economy-minded participants, the E's, and q units of welfare to the quality-minded participants, the Q's (e and q may or may not be equal, depending on the principle chosen). If the participants have rather ordinary tastes, the means of producing e and q—i.e., P_1 or some variant—are unlikely to be objectionable. According to a pure welfare-based theory, though, any policy that yields e to the E's and q to the Q's must be just as good as P_1. This implication is difficult to accept, should the welfare of some participants derive from very expensive or very modest tastes or prejudicial attitudes.[86]

Imagine, for instance, that, over time, the E's become indifferent to their menu; they eat to live. The Q's, on the other hand, come to crave delicacies; they live to eat. In this event, an alternating shopping policy may yield welfare levels less than e and q. Perhaps, however, the Q's can convince the E's that it would be more efficient to specialize their functions in the organization: the Q's will do all the shopping, while the E's handle clerical duties. The Q's, now, privately decide on a discriminatory shopping policy, P_2—they will shop *really* early, spending most of the food budget on delicacies for themselves and scavenging the previous day's uncollected trash for things to distribute to the E's. Since the E's are satisfied with calories alone and the Q's can satisfy their cravings, such a policy could conceivably yield welfare levels e and q; and, based on the distribution of welfare, P_2 could be just as good or fair as P_1 (possibly even better, if the Q's get more than q because they take perverse pleasure in tricking the E's—a Pareto-efficient move from P_1!). This sort of implication violates widely held notions of fair play.

The cooperative case is deliberately contrived for purposes of argument, but it is not too far removed from reality. In firms, powerful insiders can sometimes waste assets, enrich themselves at others' expense, or otherwise behave irresponsibly, yet still keep shareholders, employees, and customers relatively happy by following a kind of "mushroom theory" (keep them in the dark and cover them with ma-

---

[86]Sen (1979) offers a thorough examination of this issue.

nure). The mushroom metaphor has an element of black humor precisely because we are not indifferent to means of producing human satisfaction. Some means seem better, more impartial, than others. Welfare-based theories tend to miss this point.

The next alternatives in Figure 6-1, resource-based theories of justice, represent a decided improvement over pure welfarism. In such theories, social participants are seen to have similar interests only in very general means to their own diverse ends—just as in functional effectiveness views. Contrary to functional effectiveness views, however, these means or resources are considered objects of conflict; individuals prefer more for themselves. One of the best known resource-based approaches is John Rawls's theory of justice. Rawls assumes that "though men's rational plans do have different final ends, they nevertheless require for their execution certain primary goods, natural and social...whatever one's system of ends, primary goods are necessary means."[87] The primary goods, which are the subjects of social justice, are "rights and liberties, opportunities and powers, income and wealth," as well as grounds for self-respect.[88] In general, Rawls proposes that social systems should be arranged so as to maximize the expectations (for primary goods) of participants who have the least of these goods.[89] In other words, the higher the prospects of the worst-off group, the better the system.

Because Rawls focuses on the distribution of commonly valued resources and not their contribution to personal welfare, his theory avoids the bizarre implications of welfare-based views (e.g., the more one craves caviar, the more one becomes entitled to it). His theory also reflects a greater respect for persons and their individuality than others discussed so far. Compared to single-goal or single-good theories, it allows for a plurality of (nonperverse) personal ends, which may be opposing or incommensurable. Compared to utilitarian and functional theories, it does not permit the sacrifice of individual interests for the sake of some collective consequence that affects participants arbitrarily. Still, Rawls's theory has limitations. By emphasizing re-

---

[87](1971: 93).

[88]Rawls (1971: 92).

[89]As a special case of this general principle, Rawls stresses the priority of basic liberties over other primary goods. A detailed account of the nature of primary goods can be found in Rawls (1982).

sources apart from their contribution to welfare, it not only discounts extreme tastes but, to some extent, special needs or handicaps as well. It is possible that a modified resource-based theory can overcome this difficulty in selected instances.[90] It is less clear that a resource-based principle can be successfully applied to complex organizations (other than as a rough rule of thumb).

Rawls and other advocates of resource-based theories concentrate for the most part on the problem of justice in society as a whole. This is a simpler problem than that of justice within a particular organization, where the identification of commonly valued resources is usually more difficult. Rawls's primary goods, for example, may be reasonable subjects of justice when evaluating the basic structure of society (and Rawls explicitly confines his analysis to this structure).[91] But it is not reasonable to expect each specialized substructure of society to provide this same mix of resources to all participants. Rawlsian primary goods simply imply too much homogeneity of purpose to allow for the variability of ends that participants pursue in specific organizations—like major corporations, in which some shareholders seek profits but not necessarily power, other shareholders seek both, workers seek wages or security or self-fulfillment in varying degrees, customers seek goods or services but not occupational opportunity, and so on. The fact is that different organizations serve different instrumental functions for different participants, even though all the organizations that constitute society or a person's domain of action may together serve a common instrumental function when taken as a whole. This obviously complicates the evaluation of individual organizations.

It seems, then, that the first question a theory of organizational evaluation must answer is not how to distribute or maximize some unproblematic good but, rather, what to adopt as an object of interper-

---

[90]See Sen (1980); Schick (1980); Dworkin (1981).

[91]Rawls (1982: 163) comments:

The same index of primary goods is to be used to compare everyone's social situation, so that this index defines a public basis of interpersonal comparisons for questions of social justice. Primary goods are not, however, to be used in making comparisons in all situations but only in questions of justice which arise in regard to the basic structure. It is another matter entirely whether primary goods are an appropriate basis in other kinds of cases.

sonal value. Empirically, participants in complex organizations do cooperate despite disagreements over the value of goals and the value of resources they expect organizations to provide. Normatively, it is essential to recognize these disagreements, if an impartial respect for persons and their separate interests is to be maintained. It is also worth recognizing that, in order to cooperate fairly or effectively, participants cannot disagree about everything; *some* element of common value is what distinguishes organizations from cases of mere aggregation (e.g., crowds) or exploitation (e.g., slavery). Our earlier analysis (Chapter 2) suggests that resource-based theories are on the right track in proposing that it is agreement on multipurpose means, not ends, that defines this value element and binds many social systems together. The general means these theories specify are just not multipurpose enough. The diversified nature of large-scale organizations calls for a theory further to the right in Figure 6-1—an approach that identifies more fundamental grounds for agreement and accommodates a greater variety of human aims.

A harm-based theory may best fit this requirement. Such a theory would hold that, to cooperate effectively, participants need only have similar interests in the *avoidance* of certain means to whatever ends (or resources) they hope to attain in organizations. In short, our value focus shifts from primary *goods* to primary *bads*. Though harm-based views have been explored by various social philosophers,[92] a completely satisfying view, applicable to the evaluation of organizations, has yet to be developed. I will not pretend to develop one here; but I will try to outline what a harm-based theory of effectiveness might look like, what problems it solves, and what new questions it raises.

Minimizing Harm

Many philosophers have noted that people are very different in what they aim *for* in social life, but very much alike in what they aim to avoid or find harmful.[93] Almost everyone seeks to avoid what is painful, life threatening, disabling, damaging to one's property, prospects,

---

[92]E.g., Mill (1859); Fried (1978); Feinberg (1984).
[93]Baier (1958); Watkins (1963); Popper (1966).

or name. Associated harms generated by organizations could include industrial injuries, diseases from use of products or exposure to by-products, fraud, employment discrimination, and defamation, to name a few. There is considerable societal consensus on the serious-ness of such harms;[94] and, as a matter of justice, everyone is entitled to avoid them. They jeopardize the basic interests of persons, whose equal worth implies that one need not *earn* freedom from harm. There is an important asymmetry between organizational harm production and good production. A major objection to Rawls's resource-based theory was that, from an obligation of society to provide primary goods, we could not logically infer an obligation of each organization to provide this same mix of goods to all participants. The objection does not apply to harms. If society owes members freedom from a par-ticular harm, it does follow that each organization ordinarily has an obligation to avoid inflicting this harm on any participant.

The distributive rule suggested by a harm-based theory—that *no* persons should be subjected to serious harms by organizations—is also less controversial and potentially more impartial than other prin-ciples. Few would wish to maintain that organizations should produce harm or that we should be indifferent to whether they do or not. Even his most conservative colleagues and liberal opponents might agree with George Will that "you can argue about exactly what hospitals should do, but surely they should not spread disease."[95] Like other rules, of course, a no-harm rule entails ambiguities that require clarifi-cation if it is not to mean all things to all people. In the abstract, the principle proposed here specifies that organizations improve—become better, more just, or effective—as they minimize harmful effects on any participants (without inflicting harms on others). The main ambi-guities concern the interpretation of *harm* and *minimization*.

Harms can be broadly defined as impairments of persons' basic interests.[96] Recall that, according to Paul Taylor, basic interests involve "first, whatever is necessary for preserving an individual's autonomy

---

[94]Meier and Short (1982).

[95](1983: 80). The field of medical ethics, incidentally, is one in which a no-harm rule has attracted much serious interest; see Beauchamp and Childress (1983). Some related ethical issues in social research are discussed in Beauchamp et al. (1982).

[96]Kleinig (1978).

as a chooser of his own value system, and second, whatever is necessary for realizing those of a person's ends and goals that are of fundamental importance in his or her self-chosen value system."[97] While this is a very general conception of basic interests, it is possible that some very specific impairments can be identified. We can imagine concrete events that would frustrate virtually anyone's purposes, regardless of what those purposes happen to be: for example, losing one's hand in a punch press. Such impairments will be termed "basic harms" to distinguish them from mere failures to satisfy a personal preference: for example, finding peach ice cream unavailable at the corner grocery (which may not frustrate the next customer). This distinction implies only that some interests are more basic to human well-being, less dependent on subjective tastes, and more deserving of protection than others. It does not imply that harms are limited to active invasions of interests; many failures to benefit another are probable harms—say, malpractice, breach of contract, or "bad samaritan" acts.[98]

In identifying basic harms, it is not necessary, or sensible, to disregard all individual differences, but only differences in subjective preferences. Every harm occurs in a certain situation, and in judging potential harms we must imagine *some* given circumstances: one is crossing the street when hit by a company's truck, one is operating a punch press under terms of employment when losing a hand, etc. A more precise criterion, then, for distinguishing basic harms is whether virtually anyone, *in a particular set of objective circumstances*, but despite any particular set of subjective preferences, would find his or her purposes frustrated by an event.[99] These objective circumstances could include physical characteristics of the person as well as the environment, such as a physical disability requiring the use of a wheelchair. Thus, structural barriers that impair mobility and frustrate the purposes of

---

[97](1978: 49).

[98]Feinberg (1984).

[99]By "virtually" anyone, I mean to exclude only those with extremely unusual motives, e.g., saints who have negligible concern for their own welfare or fanatics who have negligible concern for another's. By "subjective preferences," however, I do mean to exclude a rather wide range of cognitive states, e.g., mental disabilities, beliefs about the material world, religious convictions, etc. Such things are ordinarily not mere matters of taste; they might be better categorized as circumstances of action (i.e., circumstances in which basic harms might occur, as in the case of religious persecution).

virtually anyone in a wheelchair could be basic harms, but not structural barriers around bank vaults that frustrate the purposes of someone who prefers robbery to other sources of income.

The criterion offered above will not settle all disputes concerning
the identification of basic harms. Disputes can still arise about which
circumstances are relevant in describing and categorizing an alleged
harm. In most cases, the more completely the circumstances and history of an event are specified, the more satisfactory the criterion will
prove to be. (It will properly classify as non-harms, for example, most
losses in athletic contests, if the particular competitive context of the
loss is taken into account: many people would be quite happy with a
silver medal in the Olympics, or simply to compete.) But it is clearly
impossible to specify all circumstances surrounding an event, and we
may wish to generalize from specific cases to types of harms, making it
necessary to select *pertinent* circumstances. More theoretical work
needs to be done to isolate factors that make certain circumstances significant; among other things, the inability to avoid circumstances
would seem to increase their relevance, as in matters of race, sex, or
disabilities, which can be bases for harmful discrimination. Such details need not detain us here;[100] for practical purposes, the proposed
harm-criterion is good enough to distinguish a wide variety of basic
harms. (Consider the high utility of associated, but less precise, criteria passed along from generation to generation in ordinary socialization: "How would you like it if someone did that to you?") It could be
used, for instance, to assess the validity of harms recognized, or overlooked, in law. A comprehensive listing of organizationally generated
harms proscribed in legislation, administrative codes, and judicial decisions would require volumes, if not libraries; and law is a logical
starting point in itemizing harms.[101] Some statutes and decisions, however, may just reflect the political influence of dominant groups or historical accident; they may give too much protection to some interests
and too little to others. Even a crude criterion of basic harm could be
helpful in sorting these out. Deciding what to do about basic harms,
once identified, is perhaps the tougher problem.

It is widely accepted that harm minimization (in some sense)

---

[100]See Feinberg (1984) for an informative survey.
[101]Eser (1966); Clinard and Yeager (1980).

should take precedence over other organizational concerns. In many normative systems, including the Anglo-American system of law, it is usually no justification for harmful conduct that an act was performed for the sake of organizational well-being or goal attainment. As systems of law also illustrate, harm minimization can be a practical ideal. People can function, often with a good deal of freedom, under harm-enjoining rules. So can organizations. Although it may be very difficult to satisfy any and all participant preferences (for high profits, job satisfaction, product quality, service, and so on), it is less difficult to respect everyone's rights to avoid basic harms. The harm-minimization principle may become impractical, though, if it is interpreted too narrowly—if minimization is taken to mean that even the most remote risk of harm must be avoided. Such an interpretation would inhibit action to the point of absurdity as well as create theoretical troubles.[102]

There are at least two ways of attempting to minimize harm. One is to try to reduce directly the occurrence of harmful consequences through preventative *interventions*, such as prohibitions or restrictions on conduct that may lead to harm. The other is to try to reduce the personal impact (and maybe, indirectly, the occurrence) of harmful consequences through after-the-fact *liabilities*, such as assignment of compensatory damages for the consequences themselves.[103] Both strategies are sometimes legally imposed on organizations, sometimes voluntarily adopted, but neither strategy is necessarily implied by the harm-minimization principle. One or the other may be logical, depending on the activity. The interventionist approach seems to be more appropriate for dealing with specific activities that are intrinsically harmful. Contamination of food products, for example, or long days of heavy labor for children appear to pose enough risk of harm to warrant preventative restrictions on processing and employment practices. While preventative restrictions and prohibitions may stimulate search for better practices, the interventionist approach has obvious

---

[102]Fried (1978).

[103]The terminology is Stone's (1980); the distinction is common. See also, e.g., Wildavsky (1983), who suggests that liberals tend to favor "anticipation" policies (regulatory interventions), whereas libertarians tend to favor a "resilience" approach (damage corrections). The inherent neutrality of a harm-minimization principle shows up in its lack of bias toward either alternative.

limitations. The only sure way to prevent harm is to prohibit even the most general sorts of activity; to prevent all traffic or industrial injuries, for instance, one would have to prohibit any kind of transportation or industry.

Organizational harm cannot be minimized through extensive prohibitions, because persons' basic interests can be impaired by restrictions on activities as well as engagement in activities. Both activities and their prior restraint must be subjected to the same type of analysis to determine whether they constitute basic harms. If virtually any participant's purposes would be frustrated by prohibition or given restrictions of an activity, despite the risk of harm, it is a basic harm to prohibit or restrict the activity. Almost any participant might choose to avoid the prohibition or certain restrictions of general activities, like transportation or industry, despite the risk that he or she could ultimately be harmed by the activity. What most would not accept, however, and what the principle of harm minimization opposes, is avoidance of liability by organizations that cause harm in the course of an activity. A strict liability approach, which prescribes compensation for harmful consequences, even if unintentionally caused or the result of a reasonable risk,[104] is especially applicable to organizations. From a social-contract perspective, organizations as nonorganic systems of activity cannot themselves literally intend harm, though they may produce harmful consequences; and much of the harm that organizations do produce is probably not intended by the participants. A strict liability standard (such as currently applied to industrial injuries under workers' compensation laws) affirms these points, and it affirms the fundamental point of the harm-minimization principle: basic harms are wrongs that call for some sort of remedial action.

Further research may reveal other ways of dealing with harm and other conditions under which particular strategies are appropriate.[105] Although the harm-minimization principle does not specify exactly *how* to reduce harm (any more than, say, goal-based principles specify how to maximize system goal attainment), it provides at least an orientation for social inquiry and change, and it has some unique implications for organizational evaluation. It suggests, first of all, that harm is a continual prospect in organizational life. This does not

---

[104]Epstein (1980).
[105]See, e.g., Stone (1980, 1982).

mean that organizations are generally evil or "criminogenic,"[106] nor does it mean that organizational policymakers or other participants are normally bent on causing harm. The fact of the matter is simply that synergy in collective action works in more than a benign direction. As Shue illustrates in the case of carcinogens,

> There is no Invisible Hand to guarantee that choices made without regard to health and safety will magically avoid damaging health and safety, especially when the harmful by-products of every individual firm are mixed together...in unconsidered and unintentional and sometimes unkown and unprecedented interacting combinations.[107]

In short, when people act together, they often create harms, along with benefits.[108] Weick has pointed out that organizational participants may initially act together for personal reasons and, later, search for a common goal or good to *justify* their past behavior.[109] Participants, direct and indirect, are also likely to find harms in this enactment process: grounds for *criticizing* past behavior. Of course, one has to look for harm in order to find it.

The harm-minimization principle suggests, secondly, that we *should* look for harm. This implies, for instance, more balanced reporting of organizational goods and bads. Research on organizations has traditionally emphasized goods: profitability, productivity, innovation, motivation, commitment, etc. Bads are no less interesting and, given comparable effort, no less discernible. The vast amount of litigation involving organizations, the frequent reports of investigative journalists, and the growing literature on corporate crime indicate that organizations produce a fair amount of well-defined harm. In the United States, annual deaths resulting from (legally or socially defined) misbehavior by business firms have been estimated in the tens of thousands, serious injuries in the millions, and financial losses in the billions of dollars.[110] The extent of harm caused by governmental, health-care, and other kinds of organizations is more difficult to estimate, but presumably still significant (e.g., unnecessary surgery at a rate of possibly 2 million per year and a cost of $4 billion per year, ac-

---

[106]Cf. Gross (1978).

[107](1981: 596).

[108]Perrow (1984).

[109](1979).

[110]Clinard and Yeager (1980); Schrager and Short (1980).

cording to Meier and Geis[111]). In addition, organizations no doubt produce harms that are not so well-defined in terms of societal or legal expectations. These expectations, and the range of things recognized as harms, increase over time as we learn more about individual capabilities, technological processes, and ways in which human interests can be impaired. (Friedman[112] and White[113] document the expansion of harms in American law.) Research on organizational effectiveness could play a larger role in informing social change by aiding discovery of *potential* as well as clear-cut harms—i.e., by identifying presently accepted practices that have harmful effects and are candidates for legal control in the future. Some obvious examples are employment-at-will[114] and the exportation of hazardous products or processes.[115] With respect to the latter, is there justification for American firms to transfer asbestos production south of the border and impose on Mexican workers a carcinogenic environment that is prohibited in the United States? Organization theorists may prefer to ignore such questions; however, managers, lawmakers, media representatives, and others *will* debate them, resolving them one way or another. It would seem that a theory of organizational effectiveness ought to have something to contribute.

The principle of harm minimization suggests, finally, that organizationally produced harm is worth doing something about. As discussed earlier, appropriate action might involve redirection of activity to prevent some harms, redistribution of resources to compensate for others, but the principle does not advocate *in*action to eliminate harm. And it does not require people to be concerned only with avoiding harm. It is helpful to keep in mind that the minimization of *organizational* harm, indeed any criterion of organizational effectiveness, is hardly the sum and substance of virtue for individual persons.[116] A

---

[111](1979).

[112](1973).

[113](1980).

[114]Blackburn (1980); Werhane (1985).

[115]Shue (1981); Ives (1985).

[116]Once again, it is misleading to think of organizations and persons as analogous entities. We have been dealing here with the evaluation of organizations, not individuals, and there are important differences. For one, conceptions of organizational merit must take into account the potential of organizations to exploit employees and other participants for noble ends.

harm-based theory upholds from the outset the value of individual autonomy. It allows organizational participants to pursue a variety of personal goals and positive ideals of excellence. In contrast to traditional views, it does not impose on participants the oppressive duty of furthering someone else's idea of excellence (as entailed, for instance, in effectiveness criteria derived from abstract organizational goals). The only absolute duty a harm-based theory might place on persons is that of acting without intentionally or directly inflicting basic harms on others.[117] This generally includes the duty of abiding by voluntary contracts and working agreements with other organizational participants, noncontractual duties of forbearance or aid where the autonomy of another human being is on the line, but not duties to the organization itself.

Accountability for direct harm represents a reasonable, minimal standard of interpersonal responsibility, which balances one person's freedom (rights) to pursue private interests against another's. The avoidance of direct, intentional harm in interpersonal transactions, though, may not ensure the goodness of the broader social systems those transactions compose, for systems of action often have indirect and unintended consequences that cause harm. The harm-minimization principle recommends amelioration of these consequences as well, should persons wish to go beyond minimal interpersonal standards and try to better their organizations at large. This prescription is also reasonable because it does not seem fair that some participants must bear the cost of harmful consequences so that others can enjoy beneficial outcomes. How *much* people should care about indirect, unintended system effects—how much they should care whether their organizations, in any overall sense, are fair or effective—is an open question. But most people probably care to some extent, and we expect some people to care quite a lot.

Those whose decisions have little impact on organizations or other participants (e.g., small shareholders, individual customers, or operating employees) may be justified in not worrying a great deal about whether their organizations are any good overall. They are not necessarily irresponsible or immoral if they are concerned mainly about whether an organization is any good *for them* (so long as they ob-

---

[117]Fried (1978).

serve the minimal standard of interpersonal responsibility). On the other hand, we expect those whose decisions have wide impact to show more concern for the organization as a whole and less concern for their own self-interest. Some persons have the power to decide and must decide, on a large scale, who will ultimately benefit from organizations, who will suffer, and to what degree. It is not too much to ask of them to decide impartially. We demand impartiality from those given political power over organizations: judges, legislators, and other officials of the state. In democratic societies, their decisions have in fact displayed a gradual tendency toward minimizing organizational harm.[118] Perhaps it is time that theories of effectiveness encouraged more respect for impartiality by *all* those who play a major role in administering our complex organizations (in particular, top managers).

I have argued that a harm-based theory *is* more impartial because it is easier to specify what no one wants from organizations than what everyone wants. Certainly, administrators ought not disregard profits, wages, services, or other goods; but it is important to recognize these things for what they are—outcomes that satisfy the preferences of *some* participants. If we remain committed to maximizing such outcomes, there may be no logical (unbiased) escape from a relativistic approach to evaluation, which allows us to say only whether an organization is getting better or worse from the viewpoint of an arbitrary constituency.[119] A relativistic approach is not always inappropriate; it is a sensible alternative in cases where a harm-based theory permits us to say nothing else (e.g., where organizations generate not even remote harms). The prevalence of systemic harm, however, means that one's options are not limited to bias or relativism in evaluating organizations. If one is truly concerned with the welfare of all constituents, with the organization as a whole, there is good reason to look beyond positive outcomes in theory and, in practice, to temper one's search for excellence with care for those persons who wind up paying the freight.

---

[118]Stone (1966).
[119]Connolly, Conlon, and Deutsch (1980).

7. Social Reality

In this concluding chapter, I will highlight some of the main points of my analysis and draw further implications for the study of organizations. Above all, I have tried to show that the social-contract metaphor is a powerful one. It is *not* especially powerful if used to depict corporations as personified entities that engage in a mythical social contract with society, as some have recently suggested.[1] Such a depiction, I think, is empirically misleading and normatively problematic. What I have argued is that organizations are not metaphysical or moral persons, but are *themselves* contracts: series of working agreements between natural persons specifying mutual (not necessarily equal or voluntary) rights and obligations. A few final arguments in defense of this view may be helpful—to social scientists who suspect that it denies the essential reality of organizations, and to philosophers who suspect that it denies the moral accountability of organizations.

Organizational Reality

Organization theorists have claimed that their subject matter has "objective reality," that organizations possess "an existence independent of their members and . . . power over peoples' lives."[2] Today such claims are not considered remarkable, but they have provoked controversy in the past.[3] And some theorists still find it worthwhile to address the question, "Are organizations real?" Hall states that "at first glance, this question probably seems inane; . . . organizations sur-

---

[1] E.g., Anshen (1980).
[2] Aldrich (1979: 2).
[3] See Allport (1924).

round us and...we are a part of them most of our lives. But a second look at the question will reveal a very basic issue: whether organizations are anything more than individuals who have come together in an interaction system."[4] Following Warriner[5] and others, Hall mounts a classic attack on the "interactionist" position, the view that organizations are only interaction systems; and he builds a typical case for the popular "realist" position, concluding that, yes, organizations are something more, they are real. This case, however, has some curious aspects.

Perhaps the most curious is why the question is framed in terms of *whether organizations are real* to begin with. Consider the "basic issue" identified by Hall (above); it appears not to concern whether organizations are indeed real, but whether they are one or another kind of reality, one "more than" or not more than a system of interaction. In posing this issue as a question of the reality or unreality of organizations, realists create a diversion that conceals their own assumptions and maligns their opponents. Realists would have us suppose that only a particular (noninteractionist) conception of organizations respects group reality; anyone who disagrees with this conception is cast, fairly or not, as a nonbeliever in the existence of organizations. What realists actually assume is that organizations are not just more than the sum of their parts, not just real, but specific forms of reality having intentional properties we normally attribute to human beings. Hall clearly relies on this conception:

> When we hear statements such as "It is company policy," "Z State University never condones cheating," or "Trans-Rhode Island Airline greets you with a smile," these are recognizable as being about organizations. Organizations do have policies, do and do not condone cheating, and may or may not greet you with a smile. They also manufacture goods, administer policies, and protect the citizenry. These are organizational actions and involve properties of organizations, not individuals. They are carried out by individuals...but the genesis of the actions remains in the organization. The answer to our basic question, then, is: Organizations are real.[6]

---

[4](1977: 23).
[5](1956).
[6](1977: 27).

The attribution of organismic properties to social groups has long been common in realist theories—as advanced by authorities on law,[7] state,[8] society,[9] etc. Such theories usually imply that other views trivialize groups, misrepresenting them as social fictions. Realists have expressed especially sharp opposition to interactionist views that portray organizations as agreements among self-interested individuals. Gierke, for instance, rejects the legal view of organizations as contracts and "treats corporate bodies as real corporate persons...which are not merely *legally* competent...but also really capable of willing and acting."[10] Similarly, Hall rejects the view of organizations as exchange systems and treats them as really willing or goal-seeking entities. Is it necessary, though, to invoke a corporate personality in order to affirm the reality of organizations? Is it necessary in order to explain organizational behavior? Contractual theories propose it is not. These theories, contrary to realists' inferences, do not deny the reality of organizations, but the need for *anthropomorphic images* of organization. Contractualists (like most other interactionists) simply substitute nonorganic realities for organic ones as models of organizational processes.

We can model organizations after all sorts of nonorganic things without falling victim to methodological individualism or some such affliction. Besides contracts, prime examples of interactionist models include games, which have been used as analogs of organization by a number of theorists.[11] I do not wish to argue for the general utility of a game analogy, but games are in some ways better understood than contracts and they serve to illustrate how a contractual model might explain organizational features that realists cite to support their own views.

The Realist Case

Realists frequently remind us that organizations remain virtually unchanged despite replacement of individual participants. Hall takes this fact as evidence that organizations "have an existence of

---

[7]E.g., Gierke (1900).
[8]E.g., Hegel (1821).
[9]E.g., Durkheim (1895).
[10]Hallis (1930: 146).
[11]Goffman (1969); Silverman (1970); Allison (1971).

their own, above and beyond the behavior and performance of individuals."[12] The troublesome word here is *existence*. One can see that organizations, given their continuity, must have existence in the sense of independent qualities, such as structures of their own. But it is not obvious that they must have existence in the sense of organic qualities, that in them, for example, resides the "genesis" of action, as Hall assumes. Imagine that organizations are like games with respect to participant replacement. A game often remains much the same while players change. This suggests that the game has an independent existence. Yet, it does not suggest that the game has a life of its own, above and beyond those of the participants. Games are stable forms of social behavior because some *people* find them worth perpetuating. Just as it is unnecessary to attribute organismic properties to games to account for their stability over time, it is unnecessary to attribute them to organizations.

Another fact about organizations that realists submit in evidence of their position is that organizations have substantial influence over their members: individuals do not have the behavioral flexibility (say, to negotiate rights and duties) that interactionist models imply. Hall remarks, "The organization trains, indoctrinates, and persuades its members to respond on the basis of the requirements of their position. This response becomes quite regularized and routinized and does not involve the interaction frame of reference."[13] What, then, does it involve? Realists have difficulties themselves in explaining response regularity; as we have seen, they have historically had to count on member submission to things like the general will of a social organism, or goals of an organization, which override individual interests and direct group activities. As we have also seen, this solution is questionable on various grounds. It ignores diversity of ends in organizations, underestimates conflict over resources, and takes for granted extraordinarily compliant (if not witless) participants. In contrast, interactionist views are rather straightforward.

Again, compare organizations to common games. Normally, a player cannot change the rules of a game on demand. These rules constrain a player's performance, perhaps even more than the rules of most organizations. The game itself, however, does not will specific

---

[12](1977: 26).
[13](1977: 24–25).

performances; it does not itself train, indoctrinate, or persuade players to behave according to the requirements of their position. People can *agree* with one another to abide by rules, for their own competitive ends, and no special properties need be assigned to games—or organizations—to account for rule-governed behavior. At the same time, people can dispute matters beyond the rules, for example, rewards for participation; they may try to get rules altered or interpreted in their favor. These are also routine events in games and organizations, though one would hardly know it from realist descriptions. All this does not mean that everything is negotiable (as interactionists are charged with believing). Persons currently engaged in a social practice (organizers of a game, employers in an organization) may have power over newcomers in specifying many terms of agreement, the power to forge "contracts of adhesion." Nevertheless, in the game case we do not confuse this power with powers *of the game.* Nor do we confuse expedient rule-following in games with compliance for the sake of *the game's* interests, goals, or requirements. In the case of organizations, avoidance of such confusion is a strength, not a liability, of interactionist models.

There remains a related issue. We sometimes do have reason to attribute *acts* to organizations rather than to their participants. The statement, "Exxon made a profit last quarter," probably makes more sense than, "Some natural persons who associate as Exxon made a profit last quarter." This fact seems to be what realists have in mind in claiming that the group is more than the individual acts of its members, or more than the sum of its parts. Yet, interactionists do not contradict this claim. As discussed in Chapter 2, organizations can have numerous properties that are not simply aggregates of (or reducible to) individual properties. For instance, an organization may produce consequences, like profits, that are true properties of the organization; they come about because of the way people behave *together,* not just as aggregate effects of their separate behaviors. It is proper to say that organizations act in the sense of *producing* these consequences. But it takes a very large leap of faith to say that organizations also act in the sense of *intending* their consequences, that they have goals of their own. Here, interactionists draw the line.

Once more, the game model is useful for purposes of illustration. To say that a game, such as football, produces revenue at many universities is a logical attribution of action to the game; revenue is a synergistic consequence of intercollegiate football. However, to say that the game of football intends to generate revenue is weird. Various persons will have intentions or goals *for* the game: university administrators may intend revenue; players and spectators may intend victory for one team or the other; and of course the game may have consequences that are unintended (e.g., injuries). Still, the game itself intends nothing. As a real but nonliving system of action, it lacks the capacity to prefer revenue over injuries, a win for alma mater, or any of its own outcomes. Likewise, consequences of action may be systemic properties of organizations, while goals of that action may not.

Some theorists have argued that we might differentiate goals *of* an organization from participants' goals *for* an organization by focusing on organizational activities and inferring what "real" or "operative" goals they support.[14] This is not so easy. Two discrete problems tend to be confounded in analyzing organizational activities. The first is to distinguish organizational behavior from nonorganizational behavior. The second is to discover the collective intent of organizational behavior. Inspection of organizational procedures may help us with the first problem but not the second. Suppose that we do study the actions of organizational participants; we may see a wide variety of regular and occasional performances. Some of these performances we wish to call organizational—for example, the preparation and transmission of a report to a supervisor. Some we wish to call nonorganizational or personal—for example, a phone call to a spouse regarding dinner plans. We must have a way of distinguishing the two if we are to mark off the organization as a unit of analysis. In many situations (not all) we can make such a distinction by reference to organizational rules or procedures, as reflected in organizational charts, job descriptions, manufacturing specifications, group customs, and the like. But, while operational procedures may serve to identify organizational behavior, they do not ordinarily establish the organizational *intent* of that behavior, or that it has any real collective intent at all.

Organizational procedures function a lot like rules of a game, a point sometimes made by defenders of organizational intentions, such as Ladd[15] and French.[16] In fact, the game analogy further undermines the case for organizational intent. If we know a game's rules of play (or an organization's procedures), we can often specify which actions

---

[14]Perrow (1961); Hall (1977).
[15](1970).
[16](1979).

count in the game (or count as organizational behaviors). And usually we can infer from these rules how different participants intend the game to turn out (or their goals *for* the organization). But rules of the game do not reveal what the game itself (or an organization) intends. To take another specific example, Ladd[17] assumes that the goal of an organization is inherent in its activities, much the same way as the goal of checkmating the king is inherent in the rules of chess. Certainly, though, checkmating in chess is not something *the game* tries or intends to accomplish. Nor is it a shared goal that the participants work together to achieve. Rather, checkmating the black king is a goal for one participant, checkmating the white king the goal of another, and both work toward their separate purposes within the context of mutually agreeable rules. So too in organizations, operative procedures may only indicate system boundaries, not system intentions.

The Interactionist Case

As mentioned earlier, my own intent is not to push a game analogy but merely to demonstrate how an interactionist model might handle typical claims of social realists (or more precisely, social organicists). A social-contract model would deal with these claims in a similar manner. Why, now, does this whole dispute actually matter? What difference does it make whether we recognize goals *of* an organization or just participants' goals *for* an organization, whether we grant intentionality to organizations or not? What is the harm in accepting the realist proposal to redescribe organizational behavior as the intentional action of a collective being, as French urges,[18] even if this is not quite literally the truth?

Throughout, I have suggested that it is deceptive to call goals *for* an organization, goals *of* an organization. The latter connote a certain degree of unanimity (or at least acceptance) that is rarely evident in complex organizations. In small, cohesive groups with few external dependencies, the same goals *for* an organization may be intended or accepted by all participants. Yet such situations are of limited interest. In larger organizations, like major corporations, goals *for* an organiza-

---

[17](1970).
[18](1984).

tion are diverse and conflicting. And it is generally important to keep track of *whose* goals one is speaking of—goals *for* shareholders, managers, workers, customers, etc. In attempting to isolate goals *of* an organization, realists ultimately fall back on the preferences of some participants: normally, people who hold dominant positions in the organization. Thus, Hall states, "The key to finding out what are the operative goals lies in the actual decisions of the top decision-makers in the organization";[19] French contends that unless such participants have approved decisions concerning the direction of a corporation, "they are not decisions of that corporation."[20] Obviously, people who hold power in organizations have much to say about what goes on. But they very seldom have complete say. And it seems sloppy, at best, to label *their* intentions *organizational* goals. Is it really more enlightening, for instance, to call the decision of a CEO to fight the union for further concessions a goal *of* the organization, versus a goal *for* the organization of top management? Isn't information lost, not added, by the former description?

The descriptive shortcomings of realist theories have been documented in past studies of organizations. Dalton, for example, cites repeated cases of oversimplification by bureaucratic theory, which "assumes that members of an organization are relatively inert and ready to follow the intent of rules." "The theory . . . slights the fact that in the larger organizations, local and personal demands take precedence in most cases."[21] At another level, Allison demonstrates how realist perspectives promote misleading explanations of international affairs.[22] In his seminal account of the Cuban missile crisis, he shows that a game-like model yields a much richer description of events than models which attribute goals and motives to the governments or organizations involved. Strauss[23] and other symbolic interactionists have generated a body of related research,[24] illustrating how social details emerge when groups are viewed as negotiated orders—as bargains over means instead of actors seeking ends. In this tradition, I have

---

[19](1977: 75).
[20](1984: 51).
[21](1959: 265).
[22](1971).
[23](1978).
[24]Fine (1984).

tried to point out the richness of contractual concepts, especially rights. The language of rights (i.e., the expanded Hohfeldian typology outlined in Chapter 3) describes organizational behavior at least as well as realist terms (i.e., goals, roles), and describes more of it.

Perhaps the most controversial aspects of this book, however, are normative. I have argued that general social theories have not only descriptive but prescriptive implications and that realist theories oversimplify with regard to both. I would like to focus on normative issues here and clarify the ethical advantages of the social-contract view.

As Quinton observes,[25] social realism has long been connected with an ethical position that grants intrinsic value to associations; groups are seen to have an irreducible welfare (or "common good") and come to be valued for their own sakes. This ethical connection may not be logically necessary, but it is compelling. It would seem strange to attribute goals, needs, interests, and so forth to social entities without also granting them some claim to satisfaction of these things, some right to our respect as autonomous "beings." Given the supposed higher order of the beast, it is not unusual for this right to overwhelm similar rights of individuals—as in the realist approach of Durkheim:

> The interests of others can have . . . no more intrinsic moral value than our own. In so far, however, as another participates in the life of the group and in so far as he is a member of the collectivity to which we are attached, he tends to take on some of its dignity and he becomes an object of our affection and interest. . . . What binds us morally to others is nothing intrinsic in their empirical individuality; it is the superior end of which they are the servants and instruments.[26]

This end, of course, is the well-being of the group itself.

Few contemporary theorists would express the idea so strongly, but many popular theories incorporate the notion that, as intentional actors, organizations have a good of their own deserving of our esteem. This is evidenced in continued use of *organizational* goal attainment as the standard of system merit or effectiveness. And it is evidenced in continued emphasis on *organizational* goals as ultimate values in the selection of research questions. It is still widely believed

---

[25](1976).
[26](1924: 53).

that organizations should be evaluated on the basis of success in achieving their objectives—and that an administrative science should concentrate on how these objectives are actually attained by organizations. The goal of organizational survival, for instance, remains an implicit value guiding much research, even when attention turns to the environment,[27] corporate social responsibilities,[28] and other external matters. As "ethical givens" for focusing inquiry,[29] organizational goals indicate which facets of reality are significant (those relevant to outcomes like system survival) and which are not. Accordingly, individuals and their interests take on importance only in relation to one's power to affect organizational well-being.[30]

This normative priority is contradicted in everyday affairs, by well-established customs and well-considered moral opinions. Some of our most reputable laws (e.g., the U.S. Bill of Rights and later civil rights laws) have been enacted precisely to defend the intrinsic importance of individual persons against functional requirements for collective goal attainment and welfare. It is not enough to acknowledge that organizations must take antagonistic laws and opinions into account to ensure their survival.[31] The point is that the very existence of these laws and opinions, which acknowledge fundamental rights of individuals, calls into question the rights of organizations to pursue their own goals and, indeed, to survive at all. An interactionist approach also calls into question organizational rights.

Interactionist theories, Quinton notes, have historically been linked with the position of ethical individualism, whereby "social objects, groups or institutions, have no intrinsic value that is not constitutive of the welfare of individual people."[32] In contrast to the implication of social realism, "any value [institutions] possess is purely instrumental." Again, the ethical implication may not be logically necessary, but it is reasonable. In denying that acts of association create social entities with intentional properties of their own, an interactionist is consistent in denying that such acts create entities with in-

---

[27]Aldrich and Pfeffer (1976).
[28]Sethi (1979).
[29]Simon (1957).
[30]Pfeffer and Salancik (1978).
[31]As in Sethi (1979).
[32](1976: 13).

terests, welfares, or worth of their own. Entities lacking the latter features are properly denied rights.[33] Recall the game analogy: Just as association in a game does not create intentional properties of the game, it does not create interests or rights of the game itself; these are all properties of participating individuals. It is no different in organizations.

One might reply that, contrary to the game example, we do attribute legal rights to certain organizations, such as corporations. From an interactionist viewpoint, however, this represents only the adoption of a simplifying bit of fiction—a shorthand way of referring to the rights of some natural persons, which should be (and often is) dropped when it oversimplifies and abridges the rights of other individuals. Hamilton explains that in law,

> most business corporation acts provide that a corporation may sue or be sued in its own name, and it is generally accepted that the power to sue or be sued in its own name is an attribute of an entity. Thus, as a "short and convenient mode" of describing the legal relationships surrounding a corporation, considering the corporation as a separate entity is undoubtedly useful. It should be emphasized, however, that a corporation possesses these attributes, not because it is an entity, but because the business corporation acts so provide. Also, it certainly does not necessarily follow that because a corporation possesses certain entity attributes under the statutes, it possesses other entity attributes as well.[34]

Hamilton concludes that

> whether or not [a corporation] should be deemed a separate "legal entity" or "legal person" should depend on the question to be resolved. A corporation may be an entity for some purposes and not for others. In such circumstances, to argue that a corporation is an entity, and therefore that certain results follow, is to put the cart before the horse.[35]

The central normative weakness of realist theories is that they miss this point. Instead, as French claims, "corporations can be full-

---

[33]Feinberg (1974).
[34](1971: 981).
[35](1971: 1009).

fledged moral persons and have whatever privileges, rights and duties as are in the normal course of affairs granted to moral persons"[36] (like human beings). A concrete case involving corporate rights may help to expose the imprudence of such a view.

Corporate Rights of Speech

In 1978 the United States Supreme Court invalidated a Massachusetts statute restricting corporate spending in public referenda campaigns (specifically prohibited by the statute were corporate expenditures aimed at "influencing or affecting the vote on any question submitted to the voters, other than one materially affecting any of the property, business or assets of the corporation"). In *First National Bank v. Bellotti*[37] the Court held, five to four, that this law violated "the corporation's" rights to free speech. Writing for the majority, Justice Powell said,

> If the speakers here were not corporations, no one would suggest that the State could silence their proposed speech. It is the type of speech indispensable to decisionmaking in a democracy, and this is no less true because the speech comes from a corporation rather than an individual.[38]

Concerned with the implications of the statute for media corporations, Chief Justice Burger added, "The First Amendment does not 'belong' to any definable category of persons or entities: It belongs to all who exercise its freedoms."[39] Realists would no doubt concur, but a more sophisticated position is outlined in Justice White's dissent.

White argues that corporate communication is not on a par with individual expression and thus may be subject to restrictions that do not apply to individual speech. He maintains that the First Amendment values *self*-expression, *self*-realization, and *self*-fulfillment, which are not necessarily furthered by corporate communications: "They do not represent a manifestation of individual freedom or choice."[40] Jus-

---

[36](1979: 207).
[37]435 U.S. 765 (1978).
[38]P. 777.
[39]P. 802.
[40]P. 805.

tice White appreciates that *some* communications of corporations deserve protection as a convenient means of protecting individual First Amendment rights (e.g., in cases of the press or special-interest groups like the NAACP). He finds however, that profit-making corporations generally have no common political or social goals, that communications by corporate managers regarding political or social issues are not ordinarily expressive of the heterogeneous beliefs of shareholders and, therefore, that such communications are not guaranteed full protection as speech *of* the corporation. The speech in question is, in fact, that of managers, and it is proper to disallow the use of corporate funds for the propagation of their political opinions (though, of course, managers may use their own resources for this purpose). In short, measures designed to prevent dominance of political processes by those who control corporate wealth are quite consistent with First Amendment guarantees of a "free marketplace of ideas."[41] An analysis of this sort is consistent with interactionist theories of organization.

O'Kelley[42] mentions a few relevant errors in Justice White's dissent—most important, his failure to conclude that the Massachusetts statute was overbroad. The statute prohibited corporate expenditures for nonbusiness communications even in situations where unanimity of belief is apparent; while these situations may not be the rule, they do arise (e.g., in a corporation sole) and seem wrong to restrict. Nevertheless, in O'Kelley's view, Justice White's mistakes are far less serious than Justice Powell's. The majority opinion confuses corporations with natural persons and overlooks principles established in prior cases. O'Kelley shows that in the past the Court has extended Constitutional rights to corporations only in instances where these organizations are instruments for exercising basic individual rights, that is, where the denial of legal rights to corporations would deny the Constitutional rights of some participants. The Court has repeatedly declined to treat corporations as full-fledged persons with independent rights, but has looked to see *whose* rights are being asserted through the corporate device and what Constitutional protections are available to these individuals. This precedent was ignored by the majority in *Bellotti,* resulting in a decision marked by realist oversimplification.

---

[41]See also Hart and Shore (1979).
[42](1979).

In assuming that corporations have the same rights of speech as natural persons, the Court failed to recognize that the rights being asserted are largely those of top executives, who stand to gain undue protection to channel and enhance their speech through the corporate treasury. More sympathetic reviewers, such as Dan-Cohen,[43] have made much of the *Bellotti* Court's emphasis on the right of individual listeners to *hear* corporate communications—from which the Court derived the right of corporations to speak. It is true that the majority opinion does defend the former more explicitly than the latter, but this is exactly the problem. By taking for granted the source of speech, by treating corporate communications just like those of persons, the Court refused to consider whether there is anything distinctive about modern corporations. For a long time, other courts and legislative bodies have understood that the vast resources concentrated in corporations surely makes them distinctive—and that the power of managers to misuse these resources makes them fit subjects of special regulation.[44]

Corporate contributions to federal election campaigns, for example, have been prohibited by Congress since 1907, the clear intent being to dilute the political influence of corporate wealth, through which business leaders had acquired much control over government offices by the turn of the century.[45] The Supreme Court continues to uphold such restrictions, admitting that corporations pose unique difficulties at least in election campaigns.[46] State referendum and initiative processes also emerged in the early twentieth century to check corporate influence over public officeholders (permitting citizens to circumvent

---

[43](1986).

[44]See Schneider (1986). Justice Renquist remarks in a separate dissent in *Bellotti* (pp. 822–823):

[T]he General Court of the Commonwealth of Massachusetts, the Congress of the United States, and the legislatures of 30 other states of the Republic have considered the matter, and have concluded that restrictions upon the political activity of business corporations are both politically desirable and constitutionally permissible. The judgment of such a broad consensus of governmental bodies expressed over a period of many decades is entitled to considerable deference from this court.

[45]Baldwin and Karpay (1983).
[46]Gray (1984).

corrupt officials and vote directly on legislative propositions); to advance direct democracy, many states enacted restrictions on corporate contributions in ballot-proposition campaigns, similar to federal restrictions in election campaigns. Ironically, by voiding these state restrictions, the *Bellotti* Court invites managers to manipulate political processes that were historically created to deter corporate manipulation of government.

As Schneider points out,[47] the Court apparently believes that corporate money can buy the vote of a politician but not the public's. This may be wishful thinking. Research on mass communication is tricky to interpret, but recent studies suggest that corporate spending can affect voting on referendum-initiative questions. Lydenberg identified sixteen major campaigns in 1978 involving questions of interest to corporate contributors.[48] The side with corporate backing outspent opponents in twelve cases (in eight cases, by margins of 10 to 1 or more), winning eight of these votes. While heavy corporate spending did not ensure victory, all four votes were lost by the corporate-backed side when it spent less than its opponents. Lydenberg found much the same thing in 1980 and 1982.[49] In 1980, seventeen campaigns pitted corporate funding against noncorporate supporters. In fourteen of these, the corporate side outspent opponents (by margins of more than 2 to 1) and won eleven. In three cases, spending was approximately equal on both sides and the corporate side lost two. The 1982 election produced eighteen corporate-noncorporate contests, sixteen of which were dominated by corporate spending. The corporate-backed side won thirteen of these and lost both votes where it was outspent. In a much more careful study of spending effectiveness, Lowenstein examined all California ballot propositions between 1968 and 1980.[50] Twenty-five campaigns exhibited substantial one- sided spending. Overall, the big-spending side won sixteen votes (64%) and lost nine (36%). More significantly, big spenders were almost always successful in defeating propositions they opposed (9 of 10), though they were ineffective in winning passage of propositions they supported (7 of 15).

---

[47](1986).
[48](1979).
[49](1981; 1983).
[50](1982).

Perhaps more disturbing than the probability that money works is how it is spent. Lowenstein documents case after case in which well-financed campaigns were designed not to provide valuable information to listeners, as the *Bellotti* Court supposed, but to deceive and mislead voters. A widely supported 1970 proposition to allow use of gas taxes and vehicle license fees for pollution control and public transportation (Proposition 18) was opposed by trucking, oil, and road construction companies, among others. Opponents spent $333,446, versus supporters' $26,635, and "flooded the state two weeks before the election with billboards that read, "MORE TAXES? NO NO 18."[51] There was no basis in fact to link the proposition to higher taxes, but the message proved decisive: "A poll conducted just prior to the posting of the billboards showed Proposition 18 leading by 64%–22%, with 14% undecided. Yet, on election day, the proposition was defeated by a vote of 46%–54%."[52] Lowenstein concludes that "the content of the messages procured by the one-sided spending has characteristically been deceptive, superficial, irrelevant or otherwise vulnerable to rebuttal, so that the election results may have been less reflective of the will of the voters than would have been the case if spending had been equal. . . . This has occurred in the case of enough ballot propositions that it cannot be regarded as aberrational."[53]

The moral is certainly not that wholesale restrictions on corporate communications are desirable, or that corporate spokespersons are committed liars. It is that "corporate speech" is not just another voice in the marketplace of ideas. Dan-Cohen, defending the logic in *Bellotti* (if not the ruling), argues that institutional pressures shape the official statements of those authorized to speak for corporations, thus making their speech "irreducibly corporate." Since this speech reflects " 'the corporate point of view,' embodying. . .distinctly corporate background. . .values and understandings," it is different from what individuals might say outside of their corporate roles, and it would be "lost to the interested public" were it denied First Amendment protection.[54] On the other hand, it is just as plausible that corporate communications deserve less protection, precisely *because* they are

---

[51]Lowenstein (1982: 534).
[52]Lowenstein (1982: 535).
[53](1982: 517).
[54]Dan-Cohen (1986: 108).

conditioned by institutional forces, which systematically distort them. Sharing Lowenstein's concerns about campaign deception, Schneider maintains that

> [E]ven good people operating in large organizations work under cir-
> cumstances that can be unconducive to seeing and telling the truth.
> To make the point less invidiously, we might remind ourselves how
> readily quite honorable lawyers come to see justice in terms of their
> clients' interests. There are, in short, pressures on the managers of
> large corporations which have nothing to do with the telling of truth,
> and these pressures are institutionalized and strong far beyond those
> on most individuals. And these are pressures which the law may prop-
> erly take into account.[55]

Other than enjoining outright lies, there may be little justification for legal restrictions where managers are actually designated to
speak for a particular group of clients—as in the NAACP cases or, as
specified in the Massachusetts statute, where the property of the corporation is directly affected. But where such a designation is unclear,
as in pronouncements on general governmental questions, some restrictions on corporate expenditures appear reasonable to many students of the law since *Bellotti*.[56] Obviously, any restrictions of this kind
result in messages being lost to the public. So do restrictions on boom-
boxes in subway cars. However, in the corporate case what is lost is not
speech *of* the corporation, but speech *for* the corporation of some person, amplified by company funds. True, it may not be quite the same
as what that person might say in an unofficial capacity; yet it is probably not what someone in another position might say *for* the corporation either. Union employees, in their roles, might well prefer to
communicate a different message than senior executives. Indeed, their
message could be as sound, from "the corporate point of view," as top
management's (e.g., recent public proposals to reorganize Allegis
Corporation by the Air Line Pilots, who gained sufficient investor support to force the resignation of Chairman Richard Ferris).[57] It seems

---

[55](1986: 1261).

[56]Including Dan-Cohen (1986). Concrete regulatory recommendations are
outlined by Mastro et al. (1980); Lowenstein (1982); and Ross (1985).

[57]Chicago *Tribune*, June 11, 1987.

rather arbitrary to call the utterances of powerful people "corporate speech" (which conveys an illusion of unity), while dissenting participants can speak only for themselves. And it seems careless to give the former a blank check to commit corporate resources to any issue that strikes their interest.

In Sum

Empirically, realist-organismic models obscure numerous things that go on behind the corporate veil. Normatively, they dress up individual rights as organizational rights, a disguise that can disadvantage nonpowerful participants. Interactionist alternatives, such as a social-contract model, shed more light on internal dealings in organizations and reduce the risk that any basic interests of individuals will be sacrificed for some alleged collective good. The normative implications of a contractual view can be summarized as follows.

Natural persons, as intentional individuals, are capable of organizing to further their own interests and well-being. The well-being of persons has intrinsic value and this is expressed in the recognition of individual rights. Organizations, in contrast, have no intentions, interests, or well-being of their own, nothing of intrinsic value that warrants respect as a matter of right. They cannot have moral rights (any rights independent of legal rules) and they cannot have legal rights for their own sakes, since they have no "sakes." Still, organizations—governments, corporations, unions, etc.—can acquire legal rights on behalf of natural persons. It is useful to extend a legal right to organizations when this facilitates the enjoyment of a prior moral or legal right by all participating individuals. Realists are less particular about accepting organizational rights. A common mistake is to assume that an activity which benefits individuals and deserves protection when performed by them likewise benefits the members of an organization and deserves protection when "performed by" the organization. The trouble is that, unlike individual action, action attributed to an organization may be intended by and benefit only some influential members of the social body. In this event, organizational rights to the act may not protect individual claim-rights, but individual power. An important virtue of social-contract theory is that it reminds us of the difference.

A contractual model provides a helpful framework for addressing other normative issues, such as corporate social performance questions. It deals with the complaint that the concept of "social responsibility" does not make clear sense when applied to organizations.[58] Viewing organizations as nonorganic systems of interaction suggests that they can have neither moral rights *nor* moral duties, i.e., social responsibilities. This does not mean that organizations are therefore exempt from public evaluation and regulation, as some have inferred.[59] Quite the contrary. While it may be illogical to expect organizations to behave responsibly, like natural persons, it is not illogical to expect organizations to display those moral or social qualities we find desirable in similar systems, like games. It is certainly odd to ask whether a game is itself behaving responsibly, but it is perfectly reasonable to ask whether the game is fair, right, harmful, or something of this sort. I think most would agree that a potentially violent game, to the extent that it entails penalties for injurious acts, is socially preferable to a comparable game that entails no penalties, but allows the participants to inflict unlimited injury on one another to advance their own cause. So also in the case of organizations: those that minimize harmful consequences to participants are preferable from a contractual perspective (as discussed in Chapter 6).

In all probability, such a perspective will justify *stronger* public policies toward organizationally produced harms than an organismic-realist view. A contractual view is more likely, for example, to encourage a strict liability policy, since it denies organizations the kinds of intention-related excuses for their acts that we often accept from natural persons. From the idea that organizations are moral persons, Ozar derives the implication that corporations may be absolved from moral responsibility under conditions where human beings might be excused:[60] where decision makers cannot anticipate the injurious consequences of organizational behavior, where loss of control over organizational processes creates damage, and so forth. Some neighbors of Union Carbide, employees of Johns-Manville, customers of A. H. Robins, and others could properly object that very significant cor-

---

[58]As charged by Letwin (1978).
[59]E.g., Hessen (1979a).
[60](1979).

porate liabilities are trivialized by granting organizations the privilege of such personalized defenses. Contractualists would object as well.

In the end, advocates of a moral-person, realist, or organismic model of organization give away too much in the way of corporate rights and gain too little in the way of corporate accountability. Philosophers may try to tack corporate social responsibilities onto this model, but the project is self-defeating. Social responsibilities have small cash value, because the value of the organization itself is inflated in accounting for them. A social-contract theory fixes our attention on more practical concerns. It treats social performance questions as part of the larger problem of fairly allocating benefits and burdens, rights and duties, among those who participate (in any way) in organized activities. To paraphrase Lessnoff,[61] if this contractual focus is not one of near universal applicability, perhaps it ought to be.

---

[61](1986).

References

Agassi, Joseph
"Methodological individualism." British Journal of Sociology, 1960, 11: 244–270.
Albrow, Martin
"The study of organizations — Objectivity or bias?" In J. Gould (Ed.), Penguin Social Sciences Survey, 1968: 146–167. Harmondsworth, England: Penguin, 1968.
Aldrich, Howard E.
Organizations and Environments. Englewood Cliffs, N.J.: Prentice-Hall, 1979.
Aldrich, Howard E., and Jeffrey Pfeffer
"Environments of organizations." In Alex Inkeles, James Coleman, and Neil Smelser (Eds.), Annual Review of Sociology, 2: 79–105. Palo Alto, Calif.: Annual Reviews, 1976.
Aldridge, Alan
Power, Authority and Restrictive Practices. Oxford: Basil Blackwell, 1976.
Alexander, Lawrence A.
"Zimmerman on coercive wage offers." Philosophy & Public Affairs, 1983, 12: 160–164.
Allen, Robert W., and Lyman W. Porter (Eds.)
Organizational Influence Processes. Glenview, Ill.: Scott, Foresman, 1983.
Allison, Graham
Essence of Decision. New York: Little, Brown, 1971.
Allport, Floyd H.
"The group fallacy in relation to social science." American Journal of Sociology, 1924, 29: 668–703.
Anshen, Melvin
Corporate Strategies for Social Performance. New York: Macmillan, 1980.
Arrow, Kenneth J.
"Why people go hungry." New York Review of Books, 1982, 29 (July 15): 24–26.
Ashford, Nicholas A.
Crisis in the Workplace: Occupational Disease and Injury. Cambridge, Mass.: MIT Press, 1976.

246

Asplund, Christer
   Some Aspects of Workers' Participation. Brussels: International Confedera-
   tion of Free Trade Unions, 1972.
Bacow, Lawrence S.
   Bargaining for Job Safety and Health. Cambridge, Mass.: MIT Press, 1980.
Baier, Kurt
   The Moral Point of View. Ithaca, N.Y.: Cornell University Press, 1958.
Baldridge, J. Victor, David V. Curtis, George P. Ecker, and Gary L. Riley
   "Alternative models of governance in higher education." In Gary L. Riley
   and J. Victor Baldridge (Eds.), Governing Academic Organizations: 2-25.
   Berkeley, Calif.: McCutchan, 1977.
Baldwin, Fletcher N., Jr., and Kenneth D. Karpay
   "Corporate political free speech: 2 U.S.C. section 441b and the superior
   rights of natural persons." Pacific Law Journal, 1983, 14: 209-241.
Barbour, Ian G.
   Myths, Models and Paradigms. New York: Harper & Row, 1974.
Barker, Ernest
   Principles of Social and Political Theory. London: Oxford University Press,
   1951.
Barker, Ernest
   Greek Political Theory, 5th ed. London: Methuen, 1960.
Barnard, Chester I.
   The Functions of the Executive. Cambridge, Mass.: Harvard University
   Press, 1938.
Barnes, Barry
   Scientific Knowledge and Sociological Theory. London: Routledge & Kegan
   Paul, 1974.
Batstone, Eric, Ian Boraston, and Stephen Frenkel
   Shop Stewards in Action. Oxford: Basil Blackwell, 1977.
Batstone, Eric, Ian Boraston, and Stephen Frenkel
   The Social Organization of Strikes. Oxford: Basil Blackwell, 1978.
Baxandall, Rosalyn, Linda Gordon, and Susan Reverby (Eds.)
   America's Working Women. New York: Random House, 1976.
Beauchamp, Tom L., and James F. Childress
   Principles of Biomedical Ethics, 2d ed. New York: Oxford University Press,
   1983.
Beauchamp, Tom L., Ruth R. Faden, R. Jay Wallace, Jr., and LeRoy Walters (Eds.)
   Ethical Issues in Social Science Research. Baltimore, Md.: Johns Hopkins
   University Press, 1982.
Becker, Brian E.
   "Concession bargaining: The impact on shareholders' equity." Industrial
   and Labor Relations Review, 1987, 40: 268-279.
Benn, Stanley I.
   "Egalitarianism and the equal consideration of interests." In J. Roland Pen-

nock and John W. Chapman (Eds.), Equality: Nomos IX: 61–78. New York: Atherton, 1967.

Benn, S.I., and R.S. Peters
The Principles of Political Thought. London: George Allen & Unwin, 1959.

Benson, J. Kenneth
"Innovation and crisis in organizational analysis." Sociological Quarterly, 1977, 18: 3–16.

Bentham, Jeremy
An Introduction to the Principles of Morals and Legislation. New York: Hafner, 1948. (Original, 1789)

Bentham, Jeremy
Anarchical Fallacies. In John Bowring (Ed.), The Works of Jeremy Bentham, Volume II: 489–534. New York: Russell & Russell, 1962. (Original, 1838–43)

Berlin, Isaiah
"Two concepts of liberty." Reprinted in Isaiah Berlin, Four Essays on Liberty: 118–172. London: Oxford University Press, 1969. (Original, 1958)

Berlin, Isaiah
"Introduction." In Isaiah Berlin, Four Essays on Liberty: ix–lxiii. London: Oxford University Press, 1969.

Betton, John, and Gregory G. Dess
"The application of population ecology models to the study of organizations." Academy of Management Review, 1985, 10: 750–757.

Black, Max
Models and Metaphors. Ithaca, N.Y.: Cornell University Press, 1962.

Blackburn, John D.
"Restricted employer discharge rights: A changing concept of employment at will." American Business Law Journal, 1980, 17: 467–492.

Blakely, Edward J., and Philip Shapira
"Industrial restructuring: Public policies for investment in advanced industrial society." Annals of the American Academy of Political and Social Science, 1984, 475: 96–109.

Bluestone, Barry, and Bennett Harrison
The Deindustrialization of America. New York: Basic Books, 1982.

Blumer, Herbert
"Sociological implications of the thought of George Herbert Mead." American Journal of Sociology, 1966, 71: 535–548.

Boulding, Kenneth E.
"General systems theory—The skeleton of science." Management Science, 1956, 2: 197–208.

Bourgeois, L. J., III
"Strategic management and determinism." Academy of Management Review, 1984, 9: 586–596.

Bradshaw, Thornton, and David Vogel
Corporations and Their Critics. New York: McGraw-Hill, 1981.

Braverman, Harry
Labor and Monopoly Capital. New York: Monthly Review Press, 1974.

Brickman, Philip, and Donald T. Campbell

"Hedonic relativism and planning the good society." In M. H. Appley (Ed.), Adaptation-Level Theory: A Symposium: 287–302. New York: Academic Press, 1971.

Brown, Richard H.

"Social theory as metaphor." Theory and Society, 1976, 3: 169–197.

Brown, William

"A consideration of 'custom and practice.'" British Journal of Industrial Relations, 1972, 10: 42–61.

Buchanan, James M.

Cost and Choice. Chicago: Markham, 1969.

Buckland, W. W., and Arnold D. McNair

Roman Law and Common Law, 2d ed. Revised by F. H. Lawson. London: Cambridge University Press, 1965.

Burke, Edmund

Reflections on the Revolution in France. London: Dent, 1910. (Original, 1790)

Burns, James MacGregor

The Deadlock of Democracy. Englewood Cliffs, N.J.: Prentice-Hall, 1963.

Burns, Tom, and G.M. Stalker

The Management of Innovation. London: Tavistock, 1961.

Burrell, Gibson, and Gareth Morgan

Sociological Paradigms and Organizational Analysis. London: Heinemann, 1979.

Cameron, Kim S., and David A. Whetten

"Organizational effectiveness: One model or several?" In Kim S. Cameron and David A. Whetten (Eds.), Organizational Effectiveness: A Comparison of Multiple Models: 1–24. New York: Academic Press, 1983.

Campbell, John P.

"On the nature of organizational effectiveness." In Paul S. Goodman and Johannes M. Pennings (Eds.), New Perspectives on Organizational Effectiveness: 13–55. San Francisco: Jossey-Bass, 1977.

Cappelli, Peter

"Plant-level concession bargaining." Industrial and Labor Relations Review, 1985, 39: 90–104.

Cappelli, Peter, and Robert B. McKersie

"Labor and the crisis in collective bargaining." In Thomas A. Kochan (Ed.), Challenges and Choices Facing American Labor: 227–245. Cambridge, Mass.: MIT Press, 1985.

Carey, George W.

"Separation of powers and the Madisonian model: A reply to the critics." American Political Science Review, 1978, 72: 151–164.

Carrell, Michael R., and Christina Heavrin

Collective Bargaining and Labor Relations. Columbus, Ohio: Merrill, 1985.

Cartwright, Dorwin, and Alvin Zander (Eds.)

Group Dynamics, 2d. ed. Evanston, Ill.: Row, Peterson, 1960.

Chamberlain, Neil W.
The Union Challenge to Management Control. New York: Harper, 1948.

Claude, Richard P.
"The classical model of human rights development." In Richard P. Claude (Ed.), Comparative Human Rights: 6–50. Baltimore, Md.: Johns Hopkins University Press, 1976.

Clinard, Marshall B., and Peter C. Yeager
Corporate Crime. New York: Free Press, 1980.

Cohen, G.A.
"Capitalism, freedom and the proletariat." In Alan Ryan (Ed.), The Idea of Freedom: 9–25. Oxford: Oxford University Press, 1979.

Cohen, Michael D., and James G. March
Leadership and Ambiguity. New York: McGraw-Hill, 1974.

Coker, F. W.
Organismic Theories of the State. New York: Columbia University Press, 1910.

Coleman, James S.
Power and the Structure of Society. New York: Norton, 1974.

Coleman, James S.
The Asymmetric Society. Syracuse, N.Y.: Syracuse University Press, 1982.

Commons, John R.
Legal Foundations of Capitalism. New York: Macmillan, 1924.

Comte, Auguste
Positive Philosophy. Translated by Harriet Martineau. In Gertrud Lenzer (Ed.), Auguste Comte and Positivism: 69–306. New York: Harper & Row, 1975. (Original, 1830–42)

Comte, Auguste
System of Positive Polity. Translated by J. H. Bridges. In Gertrud Lenzer (Ed.), Auguste Comte and Positivism: 307–476. New York: Harper & Row, 1975. (Original, 1851–54)

Conard, Alfred F.
Corporations in Perspective. Mineola, N.Y.: Foundation Press, 1976.

Congressional Record
"National Employment Priorities Act." May 2, 1983: 328–329.

Connolly, Terry, Edward J. Conlon, and Stuart Jay Deutsch
"Organizational effectiveness: A multiple-constituency approach." Academy of Management Review, 1980, 5: 211–217.

Connolly, William E.
The Terms of Political Discourse, 2d ed. Princeton, N.J.: Princeton University Press, 1983.

Cook, Karen S.
"Exchange and power in networks of interorganizational relations." Sociological Quarterly, 1977, 18: 62–82.

Cooke, William N.
Union Organizing and Public Policy. Kalamazoo, Mich.: W.E. Upjohn Institute for Employment Research, 1985.

Corbin, Arthur L.
"Legal analysis and terminology." Yale Law Journal, 1919, 29: 163–173.

Coser, Lewis A.
"Durkheim's conservatism and its implications for his sociological theory." In Kurt H. Wolff (Ed.), Emile Durkheim, 1858–1917: 211–232. Columbus, Ohio: Ohio State University Press, 1960.

Coulson, Margaret A.
"Role: A redundant concept in sociology? Some educational considerations." In J.A. Jackson (Ed.), Role: 107–128. Cambridge: Cambridge University Press, 1972.

Cranston, Maurice
Freedom. New York: Basic Books, 1953.

Crozier, Michael
The Bureaucratic Phenomenon. Chicago: University of Chicago Press, 1964.

Cummings, Larry L.
"Emergence of the instrumental organization." In Paul S. Goodman and Johannes M. Pennings (Eds.), New Perspectives on Organizational Effectiveness: 56–62. San Francisco: Jossey-Bass, 1977.

Cyert, Richard M., and James G. March
A Behavioral Theory of the Firm. Englewood Cliffs, N.J.: Prentice-Hall, 1963.

Daft, Richard L.
Organizational Theory and Design, 2d ed. St. Paul, Minn.: West, 1986.

Daft, Richard L., and Richard M. Steers
Organizations. Glenview, Ill.: Scott, Foresman, 1986.

Dahl, Robert A.
A Preface to Democratic Theory. Chicago: University of Chicago Press, 1956.

Dahrendorf, Ralf
Life Chances. Chicago: University of Chicago Press, 1979.

Dalton, Melville
Men Who Manage. New York: Wiley, 1959.

Dan-Cohen, Meir
Rights, Persons, and Organizations. Berkeley, Calif.: University of California Press, 1986.

Davidson, Eugene
The Trial of the Germans. New York: Macmillan, 1966.

Davis, S. Rufus
The Federal Principle. Berkeley, Calif.: University of California Press, 1978.

Day, Robert, and JoAnne V. Day
"A review of the current state of negotiated order theory: An appreciation and a critique." Sociological Quarterly, 1977, 18: 126–142.

Defoe, Daniel
A General History of the Pyrates. Edited by Manuel Schonhorn. Columbia, S.C.: University of South Carolina Press, 1972. (Original, 1724)

Derber, Milton

    The American Idea of Industrial Democracy, 1865–1965. Urbana, Ill.: University of Illinois Press, 1970.

Dewey, Richard

    "The theatrical analogy reconsidered." American Sociologist, 1969, 4: 307–311.

Dickens, William T., and Jonathan S. Leonard

    "Accounting for the decline in union membership, 1950–1980." Industrial and Labor Relations Review, 1985, 38: 323–334.

Donaldson, Lex

    In Defence of Organization Theory. Cambridge: Cambridge University Press, 1985.

Donaldson, Thomas

    Corporations and Morality. Englewood Cliffs, N.J.: Prentice-Hall, 1982.

Dorn, James A.

    "Introduction: Economic liberties and the judiciary." Cato Journal, 1985, 4: 661–687.

Dunbar, Tony, and Linda Kravitz

    Hard Traveling. Cambridge, Mass.: Ballinger, 1976.

Durkheim, Emile

    The Division of Labor in Society. Translated by George Simpson. New York: Macmillan, 1933. (Original, 1893)

Durkheim, Emile

    Montesquieu and Rousseau. Translated by Ralph Manheim. Ann Arbor, Mich.: University of Michigan Press, 1960.

Durkheim, Emile

    The Rules of Sociological Method. Translated by Sarah A. Solovay and John H. Mueller. New York: Free Press, 1938. (Original, 1895)

Durkheim, Emile

    Sociology and Philosophy. Translated by D.F. Pocock. New York: Free Press, 1974. (Original, 1924)

Dworkin, Gerald B.

    "Compulsion and moral concepts." Ethics, 1968, 78: 227–233.

Dworkin, Ronald

    Taking Rights Seriously. Cambridge, Mass.: Harvard University Press, 1978.

Dworkin, Ronald

    "What is equality?" Philosophy & Public Affairs, 1981, 10: 185–246, 283–345.

Edwards, Richard, and Michael Podgursky

    "The unraveling accord: American unions in crisis." In Richard Edwards, Paolo Garonna, and Franz Todtling (Eds.), Unions in Crisis and Beyond: 14–60. Dover, Mass.: Auburn House, 1986.

Eisenberg, Melvin A.

    The Structure of the Corporation. Boston: Little, Brown, 1976.

Elazar, Daniel J.

    "Is federalism compatible with prefectorial administration?" Publius, 1981, 11: 3–22.

Ellis, Desmond P.
"The Hobbesian problem of order: A critical appraisal of the normative solution." American Sociological Review, 1971, 36: 692–703.

Epstein, Richard A.
A Theory of Strict Liability. San Francisco: Cato Institute, 1980.

Eser, Albin
"The principle of 'harm' in the concept of crime: A comparative analysis of the criminally protected legal interests." Duquesne University Law Review, 1966, 4: 345–417.

Etzioni, Amitai
A Comparative Analysis of Complex Organizations, rev. ed. New York: Free Press, 1975.

Ewing, David W.
Freedom Inside the Organization. New York: McGraw-Hill, 1977.

Farber, Henry S.
"The extent of unionization in the United States." In Thomas A. Kochan (Ed.), Challenges and Choices Facing American Labor: 15–43. Cambridge, Mass.: MIT Press, 1985.

Farberman, Harvey A.
"A criminogenic market structure: The automobile industry." Sociological Quarterly, 1975, 16: 438–457.

Fayol, Henri
General and Industrial Management. Translated by Constance Storrs. London: Pitman, 1949.

Feinberg, Joel
Social Philosophy. Englewood Cliffs, N.J.: Prentice-Hall, 1973.

Feinberg, Joel
"The rights of animals and unborn generations." In W. T. Blackstone (Ed.), Philosophy and Environmental Crisis: 43–68. Athens, Ga.: University of Georgia Press, 1974.

Feinberg, Joel
Harm to Others. New York: Oxford University Press, 1984.

Ferman, Louis A., and Jeanne P. Gordus
Mental Health and the Economy. Kalamazoo, Mich.: W. E. Upjohn Institute for Employment Research, 1979.

Fine, Gary Alan
"Negotiated orders and organizational cultures." Annual Review of Sociology, 10: 239–262. Palo Alto, Calif.: Annual Reviews, 1984.

Finlay, William
"Industrial relations and firm behavior: Informal labor practices in the West Coast longshore industry." Administrative Science Quarterly, 1987, 32: 49–67.

Fischer, Frank, and Carmen Sirianni (Eds.)
Critical Studies in Organization and Bureaucracy. Philadelphia: Temple University Press, 1984.

Flathman, Richard E.
The Practice of Rights. Cambridge: Cambridge University Press, 1976.

Flathman, Richard E.
    "Moderating rights." In Ellen Frankel Paul, Jeffrey Paul, and Fred D. Miller, Jr. (Eds.), Human Rights: 149–171. Oxford: Basil Blackwell, 1984.
Fox, Alan
    "Managerial ideology and labour relations." British Journal of Industrial Relations, 1966, 4: 366–378.
Francis, Mark
    "Herbert Spencer and the myth of laissez-faire." Journal of the History of Ideas, 1978, 39: 317–328.
Frankena, William K.
    "Natural and inalienable rights." Philosophical Review, 1955, 64: 212–232.
Frankfurt, Harry G.
    "Coercion and moral responsibility." In Ted Honderich (Ed.), Essays on Freedom of Action: 65–86. London: Routledge & Kegan Paul, 1973.
Freeman, John H.
    "The unit of analysis in organizational research." In Marshall W. Meyer (Ed.), Environments and Organizations: 335–351. San Francisco: Jossey-Bass, 1978.
Freeman, Richard B.
    "Individual mobility and union voice in the labor market." American Economic Review, 1976, 66: 361–391.
Freeman, Richard B., and James L. Medoff
    What Do Unions Do? New York: Basic Books, 1984.
French, Peter A.
    "The corporation as a moral person." American Philosophical Quarterly, 1979, 16: 207–215.
French, Peter A.
    Collective and Corporate Responsibility. New York: Columbia University Press, 1984.
French, Wendell L.
    The Personnel Management Process, 5th ed. Boston: Houghton Mifflin, 1982.
Fried, Charles
    Right and Wrong. Cambridge, Mass.: Harvard University Press, 1978.
Fried, Charles
    Contract as Promise. Cambridge, Mass.: Harvard University Press, 1981.
Friedland, William H., and Dorothy Nelkin
    Migrant: Agricultural Workers in America's Northeast. New York: Holt, Rinehart and Winston, 1971.
Friedman, Kathi V.
    Legitimation of Social Rights and the Western Welfare State. Chapel Hill, N.C.: University of North Carolina Press, 1981.
Friedman, Lawrence M.
    A History of American Law. New York: Simon & Schuster, 1973.
Friedman, Lawrence M.
    Total Justice. New York: Russell Sage Foundation, 1985.

Friedman, Milton, and Rose Friedman
  Free to Choose. New York: Harcourt Brace Jovanovich, 1980.
Frost, Peter
  "Toward a radical framework for practicing organizational science." Academy
  of Management Review, 1980, 5: 501–507.
Galbraith, Jay R.
  Organization Design. Reading, Mass.: Addison-Wesley, 1977.
Gallie, W. B.
  "Essentially contested concepts." Proceedings of the Aristotelian Society,
  1956, 56: 167–198.
Garfinkel, Harold
  Studies in Ethnomethodology. Englewood Cliffs, N.J.: Prentice-Hall, 1967.
Garson, G. David, and Michael P. Smith
  "On public policy for self-management: Toward a bill of rights for working
  people." In G. David Garson and Michael P. Smith (Eds.), Organizational
  Democracy: 115–136. Beverly Hills, Calif.: Sage, 1976.
Georgiou, Petro
  "The goal paradigm and notes towards a counter paradigm." Administrative
  Science Quarterly, 1973, 18: 291–310.
Gerhardt, Uta
  "Toward a critical analysis of role." Social Problems, 1980, 27: 556–569.
Gewirth, Alan
  Reason and Morality. Chicago: University of Chicago Press, 1978.
Giddens, Anthony
  "Positivism and its critics." In Tom Bottomore and Robert Nisbet (Eds.), A
  History of Sociological Analysis: 237–286. New York: Basic Books, 1978.
Gierke, Otto
  Political Theories of the Middle Age. Translated by Frederic William
  Maitland. Cambridge: Cambridge University Press, 1900.
Gilmore, Grant
  The Death of Contract. Columbus, Ohio: Ohio State University Press, 1974.
Gluckman, Max
  Politics, Law and Ritual in Tribal Society. Chicago: Aldine, 1965.
Goffman, Erving
  Strategic Interaction. Philadelphia: University of Pennsylvania Press, 1969.
Goldthorpe, John H.
  "The development of social policy in England, 1800–1914." Transactions of
  the Fifth World Congress of Sociology: 41–56. Louvain, Belgium: Interna-
  tional Sociological Association, 1964.
Gordus, Jeanne Prial, Paul Jarley, and Louis A. Ferman
  Plant Closings and Economic Dislocation. Kalamazoo, Mich.: W. E. Upjohn
  Institute for Employment Research, 1981.
Gough, J. W.
  The Social Contract, 2d ed. London: Oxford University Press, 1957.
Gouldner, Alvin W.
  Patterns of Industrial Bureaucracy. Glencoe, Ill.: Free Press, 1954.

Gray, John A.
"Corporate identity and corporate political activities." American Business Law Journal, 1984, 21: 439–461.

Gross, Edward
"Universities as organizations: A research approach." American Sociological Review, 1968, 33: 518–544.

Gross, Edward
"The definition of organizational goals." British Journal of Sociology, 1969, 20: 277–294.

Gross, Edward
"Organizations as criminal actors." In Paul R. Wilson and John Braithwaite (Eds.), Two Faces of Deviance: 199–213. St. Lucia, Queensland: University of Queensland Press, 1978.

Gutman, Herbert G.
Work, Culture, and Society in Industrializing America. New York: Knopf, 1976.

Gwyn, W. B.
The Meaning of the Separation of Powers. (Tulane Studies in Political Science, Volume IX.) The Hague, Netherlands: Martinus Nijhoff, 1965.

Hacker, Andrew
"Introduction: Corporate America." In Andrew Hacker (Ed.), The Corporation Take-Over: 1–14. Garden City, N.Y.: Doubleday, 1965.

Hall, Richard H.
Organizations: Structure and Process, 2d ed. Englewood Cliffs, N.J.: Prentice-Hall, 1977.

Hall, Richard H.
"Effectiveness theory and organizational effectiveness." Journal of Applied Behavioral Science, 1980, 16: 536–545.

Hall, Richard H.
Organizations: Structure and Process, 3d ed. Englewood Cliffs, N.J.: Prentice-Hall, 1982.

Hallis, Frederick
Corporate Personality. London: Oxford University Press, 1930.

Hamilton, Robert W.
"The corporate entity." Texas Law Review, 1971, 49: 979–1009.

Hamilton, Robert W.
"Response [to Hessen]." Hastings Law Journal, 1979, 30: 1351–1352.

Hammer, Tove Helland, and Robert N. Stern
"Employee ownership: Implications for the organizational distribution of power." Academy of Management Journal, 1980, 23: 78–100.

Hannan, Michael T., and John Freeman
"Obstacles to comparative studies." In Paul S. Goodman and Johannes M. Pennings (Eds.), New Perspectives on Organizational Effectiveness: 106–131. San Francisco: Jossey-Bass, 1977.

Harre, R.
The Philosophies of Science. London: Oxford University Press, 1972.

Harris, Candee S.
    "The magnitude of job loss from plant closings and the generation of replace-
    ment jobs: Some recent evidence." Annals of the American Academy of Polit-
    ical and Social Science, 1984, 475: 15–27.
Harrison, Bennett
    "The international movement for prenotification of plant closures." Indus-
    trial Relations, 1984, 23: 387–409.
Hart, Gary, and William Shore
    "Corporate spending on state and local referendums: First National Bank of
    Boston v. Bellotti." Case Western Reserve Law Review, 1979, 29: 808–829.
Hart, H. L. A.
    "Between utility and rights." Columbia Law Review, 1979, 79: 828–846.
Hatch, Elvin
    Culture and Morality. New York: Columbia University Press, 1983.
Havighurst, Harold C.
    "Limitations upon freedom of contract." Arizona State Law Journal, 1979:
    167–187.
Hayek, F. A.
    The Counter-Revolution of Science. New York: Free Press, 1955.
Hayek, F. A.
    The Constitution of Liberty. Chicago: University of Chicago Press, 1960.
Hayek, Friedrich A.
    The Mirage of Social Justice. (Law, Legislation and Liberty, Volume 2). Chi-
    cago: University of Chicago Press, 1976.
Hegel, G. W. F.
    Philosophy of Right. Translated by T. M. Knox. London: Oxford University
    Press, 1952. (Original, 1821)
Hesse, Mary B.
    Models and Analogies in Science. Notre Dame, Ind.: University of Notre
    Dame Press, 1966.
Hesse, Mary B.
    "Models versus paradigms in the natural sciences." In Lyndhurst Collins
    (Ed.), The Use of Models in the Social Sciences: 1–15. London: Tavistock,
    1976.
Hesse, Mary B.
    "Theory and value in the social sciences." In Christopher Hookway and
    Philip Pettit (Eds.), Action and Interpretation: 1–16. Cambridge: Cambridge
    University Press, 1978.
Hessen, Robert
    In Defense of the Corporation. Stanford, Calif.: Hoover Institution, 1979(a).
Hessen, Robert
    "A new concept of corporations: A contractual and private property model."
    Hastings Law Journal, 1979(b), 30: 1327–1350.
Higginson, Stephen A.
    "A short history of the right to petition government for the redress of griev-
    ances." Yale Law Journal, 1986, 96: 142–166.

Hirschman, Albert O.
Exit, Voice, and Loyalty. Cambridge, Mass.: Harvard University Press, 1970.

Hochner, Arthur, and Daniel M. Zibman
"Capital flight and job loss: A statistical analysis." In John C. Raines, Lenora E. Berson, and David McI. Gracie (Eds.), Community and Capital in Conflict: 198–210. Philadelphia: Temple University Press, 1982.

Hoebel, E. Adamson
The Law of Primitive Man. Cambridge, Mass.: Harvard University Press, 1954.

Hohfeld, Wesley Newcomb
Fundamental Legal Conceptions. New Haven, Conn.: Yale University Press, 1923.

Holen, Arlene, Christopher Jehn, and Robert P. Trost
Earnings Losses of Workers Displaced by Plant Closings. Alexandria, Va.: Center for Naval Analyses, 1981.

Homze, Edward L.
Foreign Labor in Nazi Germany. Princeton, N.J.: Princeton University Press, 1967.

Horwitz, Morton J.
The Transformation of American Law, 1780–1860. Cambridge, Mass.: Harvard University Press, 1977.

Horwitz, Robert H. (Ed.)
The Moral Foundations of the American Republic, 3d ed. Charlottesville, Va.: University Press of Virginia, 1986.

House, Ernest R.
Evaluating with Validity. Beverly Hills, Calif.: Sage, 1980.

Huntington, Samuel P.
"The Founding Fathers and the division of powers." In Arthur Maass (Ed.), Area and Power: 150–205. Glencoe, Ill.: Free Press, 1959.

Ives, Jane H. (Ed.)
The Export of Hazard. Boston: Routledge & Kegan Paul, 1985.

Jensen, Michael C., and William H. Meckling
"Theory of the firm: Managerial behavior, agency costs and ownership structure." Journal of Financial Economics, 1976, 3: 305–360.

Johnson, M. Bruce (Ed.)
The Attack on Corporate America. New York: McGraw-Hill, 1978.

Jones, J. Walter
The Law and Legal Theory of the Greeks. London: Oxford University Press, 1956.

Kahn, Robert L., Donald M. Wolfe, Robert P. Quinn, and J. Diedrick Snoek
Organizational Stress. New York: Wiley, 1964.

Kanter, Rosabeth Moss
Men and Women of the Corporation. New York: Basic Books, 1977.

Kanter, Rosabeth Moss, and Derick Brinkerhoff
"Organizational performance: Recent developments in measurement." Annual Review of Sociology, 1981, 7: 321–349.

Kast, Fremont E., and James E. Rosenzweig (Eds.)
Contingency Views of Organization and Management. Chicago: Science Research Associates, 1973.

Kast, Fremont E., and James E. Rosenzweig
Organization and Management, 4th ed. New York: McGraw-Hill, 1985.

Katz, Daniel, and Robert L. Kahn
The Social Psychology of Organizations, 2d ed. New York: Wiley, 1978.

Keeley, Michael
"A social-justice approach to organizational evaluation." Administrative Science Quarterly, 1978, 23: 272–292.

Keim, Gerald D.
"Corporate social responsibility: An assessment of the enlightened self-interest model." Academy of Management Review, 1978, 3: 32–39.

Kessler, Friedrich
"Contracts of adhesion—Some thoughts about freedom of contract." Columbia Law Review, 1943, 43: 629–642.

Klein, Benjamin, Robert G. Crawford, and Armen A. Alchian
"Vertical integration, appropriable rents, and the competitive contracting process." Journal of Law and Economics, 1978, 21: 297–326.

Kleinig, John
"Crime and the concept of harm." American Philosophical Quarterly, 1978, 15: 27–36.

Knight, Frank H.
"Freedom as fact and criterion." International Journal of Ethics, 1929, 39: 129–147. Reprinted in Frank H. Knight, Freedom and Reform: 1–18. New York: Harper & Row, 1947.

Knight, Frank H.
Freedom and Reform. New York: Harper & Row, 1947.

Kochan, Thomas A., Harry C. Katz, and Robert B. McKersie
The Transformation of American Industrial Relations. New York: Basic Books, 1986.

Konvitz, Milton R. (Ed.)
Judaism and Human Rights. New York: Norton, 1972.

Kronman, Anthony T.
"Contract law and distributive justice." Yale Law Journal, 1980, 89: 472–511.

Krupp, Sherman
Pattern in Organizational Analysis. Philadelphia: Chilton, 1961.

Kuhn, Thomas S.
The Structure of Scientific Revolutions, 2d ed. Chicago: University of Chicago Press, 1970.

Ladd, John
"Morality and the ideal of rationality in formal organizations." The Monist, 1970, 54: 488–516.

Lakatos, Imre, and Alan Musgrave (Eds.)
Criticism and the Growth of Knowledge. London: Cambridge University Press, 1970.

Lauterpacht, H.
    International Law and Human Rights. New York: Praeger, 1950.
Lawrence, Paul R., and Jay W. Lorsch
    Organization and Environment. Homewood, Ill.: Irwin, 1969.
Lawrence, Robert Z.
    "The myth of U.S. deindustrialization." Challenge, 1983, 26 (November-December): 12–21.
Leblebici, Huseyin
    "Transactions and organizational forms: A re-analysis." Organization Studies, 1985, 6: 97–115.
Lessnoff, Michael
    Social Contract. Atlantic Highlands, N.J.: Humanities Press, 1986.
Letwin, William
    "Social responsibility of business in an insurance state." In Edwin M. Epstein and Dow Votaw (Eds.), Rationality, Legitimacy, Responsibility: 131–155. Santa Monica, Calif.: Goodyear, 1978.
Leventhal, Gerald S.
    "What should be done with equity theory?" In Kenneth J. Gergen, Martin S. Greenberg, and Richard H. Willis (Eds.), Social Exchange: 27–55. New York: Plenum, 1980.
Licht, Walter
    Working for the Railroad. Princeton, N.J.: Princeton University Press, 1983.
Lilienfeld, Robert
    The Rise of Systems Theory. New York: Wiley, 1978.
Lincoln, Yvonna S. (Ed.)
    Organizational Theory and Inquiry. Beverly Hills, Calif.: Sage, 1985.
Lindblom, Charles E.
    "The science of muddling through." Public Administration Review, 1959, 19: 79–88.
Lindblom, Charles E.
    The Intelligence of Democracy. New York: Free Press, 1965.
Lindblom, Charles E.
    Politics and Markets. New York: Basic Books, 1977.
Linton, Ralph
    The Study of Man. New York: Appleton-Century, 1936.
Lipset, Seymour Martin, and William Schneider
    The Confidence Gap. New York: Free Press, 1983.
Little, I. M. D.
    A Critique of Welfare Economics. Oxford: Oxford University Press, 1950.
Llewellyn, Karl N.
    "What price contract?—An essay in perspective." Yale Law Journal, 1931, 40: 704–751.
Locke, Edwin A.
    Book review: In Defense of the Corporation. Academy of Management Review, 1979, 4: 475–477.

Locke, John
  Two Treatises of Government. Edited by Peter Laslett, 2d ed. London: Cambridge University Press, 1967. (Original, 1690)
Lowenstein, Daniel H.
  "Campaign spending and ballot propositions: Recent experience, public choice theory and the First Amendment." UCLA Law Review, 1982, 29: 505–641.
Lukes, Steven
  Individualism. New York: Harper & Row, 1973.
Lustig, R. Jeffrey
  "The politics of shutdown: Community, property, corporatism." Journal of Economic Issues, 1985, 19: 123–152.
Lydenberg, Steven D.
  Bankrolling Ballots. New York: Council on Economic Priorities, 1979.
Lydenberg, Steven D.
  Bankrolling Ballots Update 1980. New York: Council on Economic Priorities, 1981.
Lydenberg, Steven D.
  "Business big-spenders hit the referenda votes." Business and Society Review, 1983, No. 47 (Fall): 53–55.
Lyons, Daniel
  "Welcome threats and coercive offers." Philosophy, 1975, 50: 425–436.
Lyons, Daniel
  "The last word on coercive offers—(?)" Philosophy Research Archives, 1981.
Lyons, David
  Rights. Belmont, Calif.: Wadsworth, 1979.
MacCallum, G. C.
  "Negative and positive freedom." Philosophical Review, 1967, 76: 312–334.
Macfarlane, Alan
  The Origins of English Individualism. Oxford: Basil Blackwell, 1978.
Machan, Tibor R.
  "The petty tyranny of government regulation." In Tibor R. Machan and M. Bruce Johnson (Eds.), Rights and Regulation: 259–288. San Francisco: Pacific Institute for Public Policy Research, 1983.
Machlup, Fritz
  "Theories of the firm: Marginalist, behavioral, managerial." American Economic Review, 1967, 57: 1–33.
Macpherson, C. B.
  The Political Theory of Possessive Individualism. Oxford: Oxford University Press, 1962.
Madison, James
  Federalist No. 10. In Clinton Rossiter (Ed.), The Federalist Papers: 77–84. New York: Mentor, 1961.
Madison, James
  Federalist No. 51. In Clinton Rossiter (Ed.), The Federalist Papers: 320–325. New York: Mentor, 1961.

Maitland, Ian
    The Causes of Industrial Disorder. London: Routledge & Kegan Paul, 1983.
Mandelbaum, Maurice
    History, Man, and Reason. Baltimore, Md.: Johns Hopkins Press, 1971.
Manuel, Frank
    The New World of Henri Saint-Simon. Cambridge, Mass.: Harvard University Press, 1956.
Manuel, Frank
    The Prophets of Paris. Cambridge, Mass: Harvard University Press, 1962.
March, James G.
    "The business firm as a political coalition." Journal of Politics, 1962, 24: 662–678.
March, James G., and Herbert A. Simon
    Organizations. New York: Wiley, 1958.
Martin, Donald L.
    "Is an employee bill of rights needed?" In M. Bruce Johnson (Ed.), The Attack on Corporate America: 39–43. New York: McGraw-Hill, 1978.
Martin, Philip L.
    Labor Displacement and Public Policy. Lexington, Mass.: Lexington Books, 1983.
Martindale, Don
    The Nature and Types of Sociological Theory. Boston: Houghton Mifflin, 1960.
Marx, Karl
    On the Jewish Question. In Saul K. Padover (Ed.), The Karl Marx Library, Volume 5: 169–192. New York: McGraw-Hill, 1974. (Original, 1843)
Marx, Karl
    Critique of the Gotha Program. In Saul K. Padover (Ed.), The Karl Marx Library, Volume 1: 488–506. New York: McGraw-Hill, 1971. (Original, 1875)
Marx, Karl, and Frederick Engels
    Manifesto of the Communist Party. In Saul K. Padover (Ed.), The Karl Marx Library, Volume 1: 79–107. New York: McGraw-Hill, 1971. (Original, 1848)
Masterman, Margaret
    "The nature of a paradigm." In Imre Lakatos and Alan Musgrave (Eds.), Criticism and the Growth of Knowledge: 59–89. London: Cambridge University Press, 1970.
Mastro, Randy M., Deborah C. Costlow, and Heidi P. Sanchez
    "Taking the initiative: Corporate control of the referendum process through media spending and what to do about it." Federal Communications Law Journal, 1980, 32: 315–369.
McCarthy, W. E. J.
    The Role of Shop Stewards in British Industrial Relations. London: HM Stationery Office, 1966.
McCloskey, H. J.
    "Liberalism." Philosophy, 1974, 49: 13–32.

McCloskey, H. J.
"Respect for human moral rights versus maximizing the good." In R. G. Frey (Ed.), Utility and Rights: 121–136. Minneapolis, Minn.: University of Minnesota Press, 1984.

McConnell, Grant
Private Power and American Democracy. New York: Knopf, 1967.

McConnell, T. R.
"Faculty government." In Harold L. Hodgkinson and Richard L. Meeth (Eds.), Power and Authority: 98–125. San Francisco: Jossey-Bass, 1971.

McIlwain, Charles Howard
The Growth of Political Thought in the West. New York: Macmillan, 1932.

McMullen, Ernan
"History and philosophy of science: A marriage of convenience?" In Robert S. Cohen and Marx W. Wartofsky (Eds.), Boston Studies in the Philosophy of Science, vol. 32: 585–601. Boston: D. Reidel, 1976.

McTaggart, J. McT. Ellis
Philosophical Studies. New York: Longmans, Green, 1934.

Meier, Robert F., and Gilbert Geis
"The white-collar offender." In Hans Toch (Ed.), Psychology of Crime and Criminal Justice: 427–443. New York: Holt, Rinehart & Winston, 1979.

Meier, Robert F., and James F. Short, Jr.
"The consequences of white-collar crime." In Herbert Edelhertz and Thomas D. Overcast (Eds.), White-Collar Crime: An Agenda for Research: 23–49. Lexington, Mass.: Lexington Books, 1982.

Melden, A. I.
Rights and Persons. Berkeley, Calif.: University of California Press, 1977.

Meltz, Noah M.
"Labor movements in Canada and the United States." In Thomas A. Kochan (Ed.), Challenges and Choices Facing American Labor: 315–334. Cambridge, Mass.: MIT Press, 1985.

Meyer, Marshall W.
Theory of Organizational Structure. Indianapolis, Ind.: Bobbs-Merrill, 1977.

Mill, John Stuart
On Liberty. Edited by Currin V. Shields. Indianapolis, Ind.: Liberal Arts Press/Bobbs-Merrill, 1956. (Original, 1859)

Miller, Arthur Selwyn
The Modern Corporate State. Westport, Conn.: Greenwood, 1976.

Miller, David
"Constraints on Freedom." Ethics, 1983, 94: 66–86.

Minogue, K. R.
"Natural rights, ideology and the game of life." In Eugene Kamenka and Alice Erh-Soon Tay (Eds.), Human Rights: 13–35. New York: St. Martin's, 1978.

Mintzberg, Henry
The Nature of Managerial Work. New York: Harper & Row, 1973.

Mintzberg, Henry
"Mintzberg's final paradigm." Administrative Science Quarterly, 1978, 23 (letter): 635–636.

Mintzberg, Henry
The Structuring of Organizations. Englewood Cliffs, N.J.: Prentice-Hall, 1979.

Mintzberg, Henry
Power In and Around Organizations. Englewood Cliffs, N.J.: Prentice-Hall, 1983.

Mohr, Lawrence B.
"The concept of organizational goal." American Political Science Review, 1973, 67: 470–481.

Mooney, James D., and Alan C. Reiley
The Principles of Organization. New York: Harper & Brothers, 1939.

Morgan, Gareth
Images of Organization. Beverly Hills, Calif.: Sage, 1986.

Mueller, Addison
"Contracts of frustration." Yale Law Journal, 1969, 78: 576–597.

National Council on Employment Policy
"The displaced worker in American society: An overdue policy issue." Washington, D.C., 1983. Included in Industrial Policy: Hearings before the Subcommittee on Economic Stabilization of the Committee on Banking, Finance and Urban Affairs; United States House of Representatives, Ninety-eighth Congress; June 9–30, 1983. Washington, D. C. : U. S. Government Printing Office, 1983.

Naylor, James C., Robert D. Pritchard, and Daniel R. Ilgen
A Theory of Behavior in Organizations. New York: Academic Press, 1980.

Nisbet, Robert A.
Social Change and History. London: Oxford University Press, 1969.

Nord, Walter R.
"Dreams of humanization and the realities of power." Academy of Management Review, 1978, 3: 674–678.

Nozick, Robert
"Coercion." In Sidney Morgenbesser, Patrick Suppes, and Morton White (Eds.), Philosophy, Science, and Method: 440–472. New York: St. Martin's, 1969.

Nozick, Robert
Anarchy, State, and Utopia. New York: Basic Books, 1974.

O'Kelley, Charles R., Jr.
"The Constitutional rights of corporations revisited: Social and political expression and the corporation after First National Bank v. Bellotti." Georgetown Law Journal, 1979, 67: 1347–1383.

Olson, Mancur, Jr.
The Logic of Collective Action. Cambridge, Mass.: Harvard University Press, 1965.

Oppenheim, Felix
 " 'Constraints on freedom' as a descriptive concept." Ethics, 1985, 95: 305–309.
Ortony, Andrew (Ed.)
 Metaphor and Thought. Cambridge: Cambridge University Press, 1979.
Ozar, David T.
 "The moral responsibility of corporations." In Thomas Donaldson and Patricia H. Werhane (Eds.), Ethical Issues in Business: 294–300. Englewood Cliffs, N.J.: Prentice-Hall, 1979.
Padover, Saul K. (Ed.)
 The Complete Madison. New York: Harper & Brothers, 1953.
Paine, Thomas
 Rights of Man. Edited by Henry Collins. Harmondsworth, England: Penguin, 1969. (Original, 1791–92)
Painter, Sidney
 Mediaeval Society. Ithaca, N.Y.: Cornell University Press, 1951.
Painter, Sidney
 A History of the Middle Ages. New York: Knopf, 1953.
Palmer, Gill
 British Industrial Relations. London: George Allen & Unwin, 1983.
Parsons, Talcott
 The Structure of Social Action. New York: Free Press, 1949.
Parsons, Talcott
 "Suggestions for a sociological approach to the theory of organizations—I." Administrative Science Quarterly, 1956, 1: 63–85.
Pennings, Johannes M., and Paul S. Goodman
 "Toward a workable framework." In Paul S. Goodman and Johannes M. Pennings (Eds.), New Perspectives on Organizational Effectiveness: 146–184. San Francisco: Jossey-Bass, 1977.
Perkin, Harold
 "Individualism versus collectivism in nineteenth-century Britain: A false antithesis." Journal of British Studies, 1977, 17: 105–118.
Perrow, Charles
 "The analysis of goals in complex organizations." American Sociological Review, 1961, 26: 854–866.
Perrow, Charles
 Normal Accidents. New York: Basic Books, 1984.
Perrow, Charles
 Complex Organizations, 3d ed. New York: Random House, 1986.
Perry, Nick
 "A comparative analysis of 'paradigm' proliferation." British Journal of Sociology, 1977, 28: 38–50.
Perry, Thomas D.
 "A paradigm of philosophy: Hohfeld on legal rights." American Philosophical Quarterly, 1977, 14: 41–50.

Pfeffer, Jeffrey
   Power in Organizations. Marshfield, Mass.: Pitman, 1981.
Pfeffer, Jeffrey, and Gerald R. Salancik
   The External Control of Organizations. New York: Harper & Row, 1978.
Phillips, D. C.
   "Organicism in the late nineteenth and early twentieth centuries." Journal of
   the History of Ideas, 1970, 31: 413–432.
Phillips, D. C.
   Holistic Thought in Social Science. Stanford, Calif.: Stanford University
   Press, 1976.
Pickle, Hal, and Frank Friedlander
   "Seven societal criteria of organizational success." Personnel Psychology,
   1967, 20: 165–178.
Pilon, Roger
   "Corporations and rights: On treating corporate people justly." Georgia Law
   Review, 1979, 13: 1245–1370.
Pinder, Craig C., and V. Warren Bourgeois
   "Controlling tropes in administrative science." Administrative Science Quar-
   terly, 1982, 27: 641–652.
Plato
   The Republic. Translated by Desmond Lee, 2d ed. Harmondsworth, En-
   gland: Penguin, 1974.
Pondy, Louis R., Peter J. Frost, Gareth Morgan, and Thomas C. Dandridge (Eds.)
   Organizational Symbolism. Greenwich, Conn.: JAI Press, 1983.
Pondy, Louis R., and Ian I. Mitroff
   "Beyond open system models of organization." In Barry M. Staw (Ed.), Re-
   search in Organizational Behavior, Volume 1: 3–39. Greenwich, Conn.: JAI
   Press, 1979.
Popper, Karl R.
   The Poverty of Historicism, 3d ed. London: Routledge & Kegan Paul, 1961.
Popper, Karl R.
   Conjectures and Refutations, 2d ed. London: Routledge & Kegan Paul,
   1965.
Popper, Karl R.
   The Open Society and Its Enemies, 5th ed. Princeton, N.J.: Princeton Uni-
   versity Press, 1966.
Preston, Larry M.
   "Freedom, markets, and voluntary exchange." American Political Science
   Review, 1984, 78: 959–970.
Price, James L.
   "The study of organizational effectiveness." Sociological Quarterly, 1972, 13:
   3–15.
Quinton, Anthony
   "Social objects." Proceedings of the Aristotelian Society, 1976, 76: 1–27.
Rakoff, Todd D.
   "Contracts of adhesion: An essay in reconstruction." Harvard Law Review,
   1983, 96: 1173–1284.

Raphael, D. D.
　　Moral Philosophy. Oxford: Oxford University Press, 1981.
Rapoport, Anatol
　　"Foreword." In Walter Buckley (Ed.), Modern Systems Research for the Be-
　　havorial Scientist: xiii–xxii. Chicago: Aldine, 1968.
Rawls, John
　　A Theory of Justice. Cambridge, Mass.: Harvard University Press, 1971.
Rawls, John
　　"Social unity and primary goods." In Amartya Sen and Bernard Williams
　　(Eds.), Utilitarianism and Beyond: 159–185. Cambridge: Cambridge Uni-
　　versity Press, 1982.
Reich, Robert B.
　　The Next American Frontier. New York: Times Books, 1983.
Reiman, Jeffrey H.
　　"The fallacy of libertarian capitalism." Ethics, 1981, 92: 85–95.
Reynolds, Morgan
　　"The case for ending the legal privileges and immunities of trade unions." In
　　Seymour Martin Lipset (Ed.), Unions in Transition: 221–238. San Fran-
　　cisco: Institute for Contemporary Studies, 1986.
Rhenman, Eric
　　Industrial Democracy and Industrial Management. London: Tavistock,
　　1968.
Riley, Patrick
　　Will and Political Legitimacy. Cambridge, Mass.: Harvard University Press,
　　1982.
Robbins, Stephen P.
　　Organization Theory, 2d ed. Englewood Cliffs, N.J.: Prentice-Hall, 1987.
Robertson, A. H.
　　Human Rights in the World, 2d ed. New York: St. Martin's, 1982.
Robinson, Donald L.
　　Slavery in the Structure of American Politics, 1765–1820. New York: Har-
　　court Brace Jovanovich, 1971.
Rose, Joseph B., and Gary N. Chaison
　　"The state of the unions: United States and Canada." Journal of Labor Re-
　　search, 1985, 6: 97–109.
Ross, Susan L.
　　"Corporate speech on political issues: The First Amendment in conflict with
　　democratic ideals?" University of Illinois Law Review, 1985, No. 2: 445–472.
Rousseau, Jean-Jacques
　　The Social Contract. In Ernest Barker (Ed.), Social Contract: 167–307. Lon-
　　don: Oxford University Press, 1947. (Original, 1762)
Royal Commission on Trade Unions and Employers' Associations, 1965–1968
　　(Donovan Commission) Report. London: HM Stationery Office, 1968.
Rutland, Robert Allen
　　The Birth of the Bill of Rights. Boston: Northeastern University Press, 1983.
Ryan, Cheyney C.
　　"The normative concept of coercion." Mind, 1980, 89: 481–498.

Sabine, George H.
A History of Political Theory, 3d ed. New York: Holt, Rinehart and Winston, 1961.

Saint-Simon, Claude-Henri de
On the Industrial System. In Ghita Ionescu (Ed.), The Political Thought of Saint-Simon: 153–181. London: Oxford University Press, 1976. (Original, 1821)

Scanlon, Thomas
"Nozick on rights, liberty, and property." Philosophy & Public Affairs, 1976, 6: 3–25.

Schelling, Thomas C.
"On the ecology of micromotives." The Public Interest, 1971, 13 (Fall): 61–98.

Schick, Frederick
"Toward a logic of liberalism." Journal of Philosophy, 1980, 77: 80–98.

Schneider, Carl E.
"Free speech and corporate freedom: A comment on First National Bank of Boston v. Bellotti." Southern California Law Review, 1986, 59: 1227–1291.

Schonhorn, Manuel
Introduction to Daniel Defoe, A General History of the Pyrates. Columbia, S.C.: University of South Carolina Press, 1972.

Schrager, Laura Shill, and James F. Short
"How serious a crime? Perceptions of organizational and common crimes." In Gilbert Geis and Ezra Stotland (Eds.), White-Collar Crime: Theory and Research: 14–31. Beverly Hills, Calif.: Sage, 1980.

Scott, W. Richard
Organizations: Rational, Natural, and Open Systems. Englewood Cliffs, N.J.: Prentice-Hall, 1981.

Scott, William G.
Organicism: The moral anesthetic of management." Academy of Management Review, 1979, 4: 21–28.

Selznick, Philip
TVA and the Grass Roots. Berkeley, Calif.: University of California Press, 1949.

Selznick, Philip
Leadership in Administration. Evanston, Ill.: Row, Peterson, 1957.

Sen, Amartya
"Utilitarianism and welfare." Journal of Philosophy, 1979, 76: 463–489.

Sen, Amartya
"Equality of what?" In Sterling M. McMurtin (Ed.), The Tanner Lectures on Human Values, 1: 195–220. Salt Lake City, Utah: University of Utah Press, 1980.

Sen, Amartya
Poverty and Famines. Oxford: Oxford University Press, 1981.

Sen, Amartya
"The food problem: Theory and policy." Third World Quarterly, 1982, 4: 447–459.

Sen, Amartya
    Resources, Values and Development. Cambridge, Mass.: Harvard University Press, 1984.
Sethi, S. Prakash
    "A conceptual framework for environmental analysis of social issues and evaluation of business response patterns." Academy of Management Review, 1979, 4: 63-74.
Shapere, Dudley
    "The paradigm concept." Science, 1971, 172: 706-709.
Shue, Henry
    "Exporting hazards." Ethics, 1981, 91: 579-606.
Sieghart, Paul
    The International Law of Human Rights. Oxford: Oxford University Press, 1983.
Silverman, David
    The Theory of Organizations. London: Heinemann, 1970.
Simon, Herbert A.
    Administrative Behavior, 2d ed. New York: Free Press, 1957.
Simon, Walter M.
    "Herbert Spencer and the social organism." Journal of the History of Ideas, 1960, 21: 294-299.
Singer, Ethan A., and Leland M. Wooten
    "The triumph and failure of Albert Speer's administrative genius: Implications for current management theory and practice." Journal of Applied Behavioral Science, 1976, 12: 79-103.
Smith, Adam
    The Wealth of Nations. Edited by Edward Cannan. New York: Modern Library, 1937. (Original, 1776)
Speer, Albert
    Inside the Third Reich. Translated by Richard and Clara Winston. New York: Macmillan, 1970.
Squires, Gregory D.
    " 'Runaway plants,' capital mobility, and black economic rights." In John C. Raines, Lenora E. Berson, and David McI. Gracie (Eds.), Community and Capital in Conflict: 62-97. Philadelphia: Temple University Press, 1982.
Starbuck, William H., and Paul C. Nystrom
    "Designing and understanding organizations." In Paul C. Nystrom and William H. Starbuck (Eds.), Handbook of Organizational Design, Volume 1: ix-xxii. Oxford: Oxford University Press, 1981.
Steers, Richard M.
    Organizational Effectiveness. Santa Monica, Calif.: Goodyear, 1977.
Stephens, Jerone
    "The Kuhnian paradigm and political inquiry: An appraisal." American Journal of Political Science, 1973, 17: 467-488.
Stone, Christopher D.
    Where the Law Ends. New York: Harper & Row, 1975.

Stone, Christopher D.

"The place of enterprise liability in the control of corporate conduct." Yale Law Journal, 1980, 90: 1–77.

Stone, Christopher D.

"Corporate vices and corporate virtues: Do public/private distinctions matter?" University of Pennsylvania Law Review, 1982, 130: 1441–1509.

Stone, Julius

Social Dimensions of Law and Justice. London: Stevens, 1966.

Stone, Katherine Van Wezel

"The post-war paradigm in American labor law." Yale Law Journal, 1981, 90: 1509–1580.

Storey, John

The Challenge to Management Control. London: Kogan Page, 1980.

Strauss, Anselm

Negotiations. San Francisco: Jossey-Bass, 1978.

Strauss, Anselm, Leonard Schatzman, Danuta Ehrlich, Rue Bucher, and Melvin Sabshin

"The hospital and its negotiated order." In Eliot Freidson (Ed.), The Hospital in Modern Society: 147–169. New York: Free Press, 1963.

Strauss, Anselm, Leonard Schatzman, Rue Bucher, Danuta Ehrlich, and Melvin Sabshin

Psychiatric Ideologies and Institutions. Glencoe, Ill.: Free Press, 1964.

Strike, Kenneth A.

"The role of theories of justice in evaluation: Why a house is not a home." Educational Theory, 1979, 29: 1–9.

Summers, Clyde W.

Individual protection against unjust dismissal: Time for a statute." Virginia Law Review, 1976, 62: 481–532.

Sundquist, James L.

Constitutional Reform and Effective Government. Washington, D.C.: Brookings Institution, 1986.

Taylor, Charles

"Neutrality in political science." In Peter Laslett and Walter Runciman (Eds.), Philosophy, Politics and Society, 3d Series: 25–57. Oxford: Blackwell, 1967.

Taylor, Frederick Winslow

The Principles of Scientific Management. New York: Harper, 1911.

Taylor, Frederick Winslow

"The principles of scientific management." In Jay M. Shafritz and Philip H. Whitbeck (Eds.), Classics of Organization Theory: 9–23. Oak Park, Ill.: Moore, 1978. (Originally published in Bulletin of the Taylor Society, Dec. 1916)

Taylor, Paul W.

"On taking the moral point of view." In Peter A. French, Theodore E. Uehling, Jr., and Howard K. Wettstein (Eds.), Midwest Studies in Philosophy, 3: 35–61. Morris, Minn.: University of Minnesota, Morris, 1978.

Thayer, Frederick
"General system(s) theory: The promise that could not be kept." Academy of Management Journal, 1972, 15: 481–493.

Thompson, James D.
Organizations in Action. New York: McGraw-Hill, 1967.

Thompson, Kenneth
"Organizations as constructors of social reality (I)." In Graeme Salaman and Kenneth Thompson (Eds.), Control and Ideology in Organizations: 216–236. Cambridge, Mass.: MIT Press, 1980.

Thompson, Victor A.
Bureaucracy and the Modern World. Morristown, N.J.: General Learning Press, 1976.

Thurow, Lester C.
The Zero-Sum Society. New York: Penguin, 1981.

Tilly, Louise A.
"Food entitlement, famine, and conflict." In Robert I. Rotberg and Theodore K. Rabb (Eds.), Hunger and History: 135–151. Cambridge: Cambridge University Press, 1985.

Toulmin, Stephen
Human Understanding. Princeton, N.J.: Princeton University Press, 1972.

Ullmann, Walter
The Individual and Society in the Middle Ages. Baltimore, Md.: Johns Hopkins Press, 1966.

U.S. Chief of Counsel for Prosecution of Axis Criminality
Nazi Conspiracy and Aggression. Washington, D.C.: U.S. Government Printing Office, 1946.

U.S. Commission on Civil Rights, Rocky Mountain Regional Office
People Who Follow the Crops. Washington, D.C.: U.S. Government Printing Office, 1978.

U.S. Congress, House of Representatives; Subcommittee on Labor-Management Relations of the Committee on Education and Labor
Worker Dislocation, Capital Flight, and Plant Closings. Hearings held on May 18, 1983. Washington, D. C.: U.S. Government Printing Office, 1984.

U.S. Congress, House of Representatives; Subcommittee on Labor-Management Relations of the Committee on Education and Labor
Report: The Failure of Labor Law—A Betrayal of American Workers. Washington, D. C.: U.S. Government Printing Office, 1984.

U.S. Congress, Office of Technology Assessment
Technology and Steel Industry Competitiveness. Washington, D.C.: U.S. Government Printing Office, 1980.

U.S. Department of Labor, Task Force on Economic Adjustment and Worker Dislocation
Economic Adjustment and Worker Dislocation in a Competitive Society. Washington, D.C.: U.S. Department of Labor, 1986.

VandeVeer, Don
"Coercion, seduction, and rights." The Personalist, 1977, 58: 374–381.

Van de Ven, Andrew H.
    "A process for organizational assessment." In Edward E. Lawler III, David A. Nadler, and Cortlandt Cammann (Eds.), Organizational Assessment: 548–568. New York: Wiley, 1980.
Vile, M. J. C.
    Constitutionalism and the Separation of Powers. London: Oxford University Press, 1967.
Vlastos, Gregory
    "Justice and equality." In Richard B. Brandt (Ed.), Social Justice: 31–72. Englewood Cliffs, N.J.: Prentice-Hall, 1962.
von Bertalanffy, Ludwig
    General System Theory. New York: Braziller, 1968.
Warriner, Charles K.
    "Groups are real: A reaffirmation." American Sociological Review, 1956, 21: 549–554.
Watkins, J. W. N.
    "Negative utilitarianism." Proceedings of the Aristotelian Society, 1963, supp. vol. 37: 95–114.
Weber, Max
    Economy and Society. Edited by Guenther Roth and Claus Wittich. New York: Bedminster Press, 1968. (Original, 1925)
Weick, Karl E.
    The Social Psychology of Organizing, 2d ed. Reading, Mass.: Addison-Wesley, 1979.
Weiler, Paul
    "Promises to keep: Securing workers' rights to self-organization under the NLRA." Harvard Law Review, 1983, 96: 1769–1827.
Weiler, Paul
    "Striking a new balance: Freedom of contract and the prospects for union representation." Harvard Law Review, 1984, 98: 351–420.
Wellman, Carl
    A Theory of Rights. Totowa, N.J.: Rowman & Allanheld, 1985.
Werhane, Patricia H.
    Persons, Rights, and Corporations. Englewood Cliffs, N.J.: Prentice-Hall, 1985.
Wertheimer, Alan
    "Freedom, morality, plea bargaining, and the Supreme Court." Philosophy & Public Affairs, 1979, 8: 203–234.
White, G. Edward
    Tort Law in America. New York: Oxford University Press, 1980.
Whyte, William Foote, Tove Helland Hammer, Christopher B. Meek, Reed Nelson, and Robert N. Stern
    Worker Participation and Ownership. Ithaca, N.Y.: Cornell University, ILR Press, 1983.

Wildavsky, Aaron
"Foreword: If regulation is right, is it also safe?" In Tibor R. Machan and M. Bruce Johnson (Eds.), Rights and Regulation: xv–xxv. San Francisco: Pacific Institute for Public Policy Research, 1983.

Will, George F.
"Our feckless universities." Newsweek, 1983, March 28: 80.

Williams, Bernard
Morality. New York: Harper & Row, 1972.

Wing, Charles
Evils of the Factory System. London: Saunders & Otley, 1837.

Wolin, Sheldon S.
Politics and Vision. Boston: Little, Brown, 1960.

Yago, Glenn, Hyman Korman, Sen-Yuan Wu, and Michael Schwartz
"Investment and disinvestment in New York, 1960–80." Annals of the American Academy of Political and Social Science, 1984, 475: 28–38.

Young, Oran R.
Resource Regimes. Berkeley, Calif.: University of California Press, 1982.

Yuchtman, Ephraim, and Stanley E. Seashore
"A system resource approach to organizational effectiveness." American Sociological Review, 1967, 32: 891–903.

Zammuto, Raymond F.
Assessing Organizational Effectiveness. Albany, N.Y.: State University of New York Press, Albany, 1982.

Zey-Ferrell, Mary, and Michael Aiken (Eds.)
Complex Organizations: Critical Perspectives. Glenview, Ill.: Scott, Foresman, 1981.

Zimmerman, David
"Coercive wage offers." Philosophy & Public Affairs, 1981, 10: 121–145.

Zimmerman, David
"More on coercive wage offers: A reply to Alexander." Philosophy & Public Affairs, 1983, 12: 165–171.

Index